MW01014228

PERILS
OF THE
SOUL

PERILS OF THE SOUL

ANCIENT WISDOM
and the
New Age

JOHN RYAN HAULE

SAMUEL WEISER, INC.

York Beach, Maine

For *Lukas Adam Haule*

First published in 1999 by
Samuel Weiser, Inc.
P.O. Box 612
York Beach, ME 03910-0612
www.weiserbooks.com

Copyright @ 1999 John Ryan Haule

All rights reserved. No part of this publication may be reproduced or transmitted in any form or by any means, electronic or mechanical, including photocopying, recording, or by any information storage and retrieval system, without permission in writing from Samuel Weiser, Inc. Reviewers may quote brief passages.

Library of Congress Cataloging-in-Publication Data

Haule, John R.
  Perils of the soul : ancient wisdom and the new age / John Haule.
    p.   cm.
  Includes bibliographical references and index.
  ISBN 1-57863-107-6 (pbk. : alk. paper)
  1. New Age movement.   I. Title.
BP605.N48H38   1999
299'. 93—dc21   98-50576
                                                        CIP

EB

Typeset in 10.5 pt. Aldine401 BT

"Luminous egg" art on cover and in book is personal logo designed by John Ryan Haule.

Printed in the United States of America

08 07 06 05 04 03 02 01 00 99
10 9   8   7   6   5   4   3   2   1

The paper used in this publication meets the minimum requirements of the American National Standard for Permanence of Paper for Printed Library Materials Z39.48–1984.

TABLE OF CONTENTS

ACKNOWLEDGMENTS

Thanks to my literary agent, Katherine Boyle, who first had the idea that my interests are specially suited to a sympathetic, yet critical, review of New Age phenomena to a book that falls outside the usual categories by standing in the middle. As early responses from publishers showed little enthusiasm for this middle position, I am grateful, not only to Katie for her persistence, but also to Larry Dossey for reading the entire manuscript and writing an endorsement, and to my friend C. Michael Smith, for introducing my work to Dr. Dossey. The book would not have been published without the support of Betty Lundsted at Samuel Weiser.

In addition, thanks to my partner, Ann, for being eager to hear every new subchapter and for suggesting supportive material, to my son Lukas for several of the analogies from the popular media, and to my brother James who offered stylistic improvements.

Chapter

1

MYSTICISM AND BUNK IN THE NEW AGE

All forms, be they human, animal, plant, or even apparently inert mineral, radiate a surrounding field of energy into the environment. This field or aura expresses the quality and nature of the form which it interpenetrates and surrounds.

(TANSLEY, 1984, P. 2)

What we call "consciousness" consists of waves of information that move from spirit into matter and then back again into spirit.

(WOLF, 1991, P. 43)

I believe there is a system around us that transcends time as it transcends space.

(VALLEE, 1988, P. 253)

[Dr. John E.] Mack says, "The furthest you can go at this point is to say there's an authentic mystery here. And that is, I think, as far as anyone ought to go. But that's a powerful, powerful place to come to at this point."

(BRYAN, 1995, P. 269)

*B*ack in the 1970s, when I could still find Earth Shoe stores, I pretty much memorized Carlos Castaneda's books about his apprenticeship with Yaqui shaman, Don Juan Matus. No matter that they more closely resembled novels than anthropological field work. They had a ring of truth to them. The "impossible" events they described had parallels with Buddhism and Sufism (Islamic mysticism) as well as with mythic themes from all over the world. Furthermore, I could vouch for a few of the incidents as being close to my own experience.

I had had a minute or two of religious ecstasy myself in the early 60s that had convinced me of the truth of theology and led me to enter a kind of monastery. There, my dreams told me I had no business pronouncing monastic vows. A close friend introduced me to the writings of C. G. Jung. But instead of working on my dreams, I dived into a psychological account of the depth, significance, and universality of mystical experience—a breath of fresh air that freed me from the dogmatic constraints of Christianity. I earned a Ph.D. in psychology and religion, and wore my Earth Shoes into the college classroom, where I generally included books by Castaneda on the reading lists for my courses.

I found that my students' narrow attitudes about the nature of religion needed a dose of Castaneda's "mind-blowing" experience to open them up to a feel for the life-changing potential of a religious worldview. I emphasized the subjective nature of an encounter with the Wholly Other and the effects it could have upon one's everyday existence. The only students who objected to Castaneda's central position on the reading list were a few from the Third World. They told me that nobody believed this stuff any more, only the old people—the same reaction most of my Christian students had to Christianity. But they also whispered, "This stuff is dangerous, you ought to stay away from it."

Castaneda was the bridge between the tie-dyed, psychedelic 60s and the human consciousness movement that, in its proliferation of psychic techniques for healing, life-management, and general amazement, has come to be called the "New Age." The view taught in New Age workshops shares a common perspective with Castaneda's novels: the conviction, based on personal experience, that the world is not as it appears. As a people, we have limited our thinking, accepting a narrow, materialistic view of ourselves as flesh-and-blood bodies, but the evidence is all around us that we are much more.

According to Don Juan, Carlos' mentor, when we really *see* another human being—that is with shamanic eyes—we do not contemplate the limbs, trunk, and head of a fleshly body, but rather apprehend an egg-shaped bundle of luminous fibers. This vision seems impossible, even fantastic, because our everyday consciousness has been confined by a public "agreement" into which we have all been socialized as children. We *learn* to see the world in material terms by attending to only one of those luminous fibers and ignoring the rest. If we can learn to pay attention to the "gaps" in our everyday stream of consciousness, we are in for a "monumental shock." We will find ourselves in a world of "unimaginable power." This view is not so different from that of New Age aura readers. They, too, view the human body as an egg-shaped luminosity with powerful implications unheard of in biology or mainstream medicine.

I was introduced to Castaneda's books by a friend in the editorial department of Encyclopaedia Britannica—my first "real job" after leaving the religious order. I was famous at Britannica for having been lucky enough to prepare the prospectus for an article on psychedelic experience. This prompted Brad to leave a copy of *The Teachings of Don Juan* (1968) on my desk as his parting gift. He had decided to "drop out" of the "Establishment" and join the "Movement." I never heard from him again. In fact, most people who served as major landmarks in my life have similarly disappeared. Had I not seen them eating lunch in the company cafeteria or buying Earth Shoes downtown, I might think they themselves represented "gaps" in my own stream of consciousness.

Castaneda's second volume was given to me as a 30th-birthday present from a friend in graduate school. She too has disappeared—although her prize-winning book on Haitian Voodoo has turned up on bookstore shelves in recent years. Once I had read Castaneda's second novel, *A Separate Reality* (1971), I was hooked and began buying hardcover editions as soon as they were published. A passage in the third volume, *Journey to Ixtlan* (1972, pp. 125–126), provided me with a useful perspective on the so-called New Age. Don Juan tells Carlos that "power" takes on different shapes, depending on our relationship to it. At first, we merely hear about power. We find the reports interesting, but we cannot see that it has anything to do with us. Then, at the second stage, power begins to manifest itself "uncontrollably" in our lives, so that we have to take it seriously, even though we do not understand what it is all about. Finally, we find that power lives within us and controls our actions, although it also obeys our command.

I found an identity somewhere between the first and second of these stages. I thought of myself as a bemused onlooker of New Age phenomena, but evidently I underestimated. At a recent meeting of professors and alumni of my graduate school, I discovered that I am one of the "disappeared." Although I have not ceased to produce academic papers and books, or even to teach, I did "drop out" of my university position. In the eyes of some of them, I have compromised my academic neutrality by getting too involved. Apparently my biggest mistake is that, in the late 70s, I went to Zurich and trained to be a Jungian analyst, so I could spend my life paying attention to the gaps in people's awareness. I am not sufficiently "mainstream" anymore.

I find myself occupying a kind of "middle position": taking "power" seriously, but not so enthusiastically as to set sail for Haiti or Australia in hopes of myself becoming an initiate. This makes me an "armchair philosopher" in the view of those who have done these things. Because I have not dived into some non-Western river of alternative experience, I seem to have set up my desk and file cabinets beside the "mainstream" after all. Do I lack the requisite courage, or sufficient foolishness? From where I sit, my position seems quite reasonable. I figure that, if the gaps are right here in my consciousness, I already have everything I need to expand my awareness. I do not have to become a Native American wannabe. My potential to expand into the world of "monumental shock" will manifest itself as I need it. I expect to "evolve" in my own manner, so that I do not become a stranger to either the ordinary world or to the world of power.

Don Juan has an encouraging word to say about this, too. He reports that most individuals who learn shamanism forsake the world of public reality to live exclusively in the other world. In doing so, they gain nothing. They just give up one world for another and become as much trapped and limited in the world of power as they formerly were in the material world. This, too, has been a guiding notion for me. I like to think of myself as one who is learning from and yet critical of the New Age, intrigued by its mystical potential, yet put off by all the bunk that has become associated with it.

One "magnificent (albeit flaky) being" who has not disappeared from my life, has the dubious distinction of being the last manager of my favorite Earth Shoe store in Boston. The Earth Shoe fad was already waning when I stopped in to buy several pairs of "negative-heel" foot apparel to sustain me over the four years I planned to spend in Zurich. The store was empty of customers as I swung open the door. Kathy, with her red curly hair and form-fitting pink-and-purple garb, stepped out from behind the counter and held up both hands imperiously: "Stop right where you are! Don't move! I want to read your aura." This was my introduction to a New Ager of the first water.

Complying, perhaps as much out of astonishment as curiosity, I watched her glazed, impenetrable face as she scanned me for a few moments and then returned to consensus reality. She announced that I had a good healthy aura, rather clearer than most, but one disturbed by an area of smokiness that she guessed was due to my indulging in too much bacon. She immediately withdrew the comment about the bacon, however, saying she might well be wrong about anything so specific. The flamboyance of her self-presentation surely merited the greatest skepticism, and I cannot vouch for the reported clarity of the aura, as no one else has ventured to read it. But she was right about the bacon. I have a great love of bacon and avocado sandwiches. For me, the comment about bacon was the most salient remark she made, although I have found her to be right again and again in other matters as well.

That remark has caused me a good deal of thought. How could she *see* bacon in my aura? Is this something that belongs to my "luminous egg"? Should I imagine that one of its bright fibers corresponds to a man standing at a kitchen counter slathering toast with mayonnaise and ripe, mushy avocado before carefully laying in crisp slices of freshly fried bacon and ravenously biting into it? A man with a bacon addiction? What gaps in my awareness could account for this? Especially since I *know* I like bacon. There is nothing "monumentally shocking" about it. The information is trivial, but the fact that she came up with it on our first meeting is rather intriguing. A small-scale, but classic, problem was posed for me: Where is the dividing line between mysticism and bunk?

Eventually, I asked Kathy how she did it, whether she *saw* auras all the time or "switched on" some latent skill most of us do not know we have. She said she normally has to "shift her consciousness" from the view of the ordinary physical world to that of the aura. But, at other times, she may catch a glimpse of an aura out of the corner of her eye. She mentioned an incident in which she visited a friend at his house and glimpsed, at the periphery of her vision, his infant son crawling into the hallway from the kitchen. What she saw was not a distinct image of the infant, but the gigantic golden flare of his aura. She said she had never seen so huge an aura and concluded the boy was destined for great things.

Excluding the unverifiable (but possibly accurate) conclusion that the boy was possessed of extraordinary powers, I find that this kind of report makes a good deal of sense. Kathy apprehends auras, not with the ordinary sense capabilities of her eyes—reflected light particles (photons) impinging on her retina—but by attending to something that cannot be "seen" in any ordinary sensory manner. In fact, she has to shut out the ordinary world by "shifting her consciousness" or catching a glimpse out of the corner of her eye. This corresponds very well to the teachings of Don Juan, who calls twilight a "time of power." It is precisely when our eyes are hindered in their everyday work by faint lighting (dusk) or by a failure to focus (corner of the eye), that we are best able to attend to the "gaps" in our visual field. In such moments, the visual field may be filled with something other, something not available to our retinas. The English language has only one word for "seeing" things that are not "there" according to the rods and cones of our retinas: imagination. Although Kathy *imagined* the bacon in my aura, it was nevertheless really there. *Imagination* has given her visionary access to an invisible reality.

This begins to sound like bunk. We have a terminology problem. The word, *imagination*, has come to mean that which is private, arbitrary, and supremely "unreal." This is why aura readers generally go out of their way to insist they are not "imagining" what they claim to see. Don Juan and Kathy are in agreement that there is nothing arbitrary or unreal about the luminous egg. Yet they also insist they have to go into an altered state of consciousness in order to *see* it. Thus, we are presented with two meanings of the word *see* and two meanings for *imagination*.

Castaneda solves this problem for his readers by calling the ordinary sensory function of the eyes "seeing" (spelled in ordinary type). To this he contrasts the shamanic (altered state) visionary capacity, which he calls *"seeing"* (spelled in italics). I shall use his simple convention throughout this book in order to make clear the distinction between sensory seeing and visionary *seeing*.

The French scholar of Islamic mysticism, Henry Corbin (1969, 1978), has run into an analogous difficulty with the words *imagination, imaginal*, and the like. The Sufis claim to enter an "Imaginal Realm," a *seen* world not available to the physical senses, although there is nothing arbitrary or private about it. It is an objective reality, they say, verifiable by anyone who is able to enter it. They thus claim that *imagination* possesses a reality function unknown to ordinary consciousness. What they *imagine* is what Don Juan and Kathy *see*. Corbin solved his terminology problem by distinguishing between "imagination" (not capitalized), referring to the everyday meaning of the word, and "Imagination" (capitalized) to refer to objective, reliable access to invisible realities. I am making the same distinction, but will italicize *imagination* to refer to the objective reality of what is *seen* and leave "imagination" in ordinary type when the word refers to what is subjective and arbitrary.

Having clarified terminology, we can now restate the problem. Kathy claims to *see* an aura with her *imagination*, not to see it with the retinas of her eyes. Our problem arises insofar as her *sight* has access to what really exists, although invisibly. What could be filling the space between Kathy and the bacon in my aura? Years ago, when I asked her, she told me it was "energy." She *sees* energy. I was fairly sure this explanation was bunk, having learned in high school physics that "energy" is not a thing at all, but a hypothetical construct invented to describe changes in movement. A white cue ball manifests energy by moving in a straight line across green felt until it collides with a striped ball. It moves more slowly after the collision, because it has transferred some of its energy to the striped ball. The latter, no longer at rest, now has sufficient energy to roll into the corner pocket. There is no "energy," either to be seen with the eyes or to be *seen* with the *imagination*. There are only balls rolling with greater or lesser speed.

The energy theory took me nowhere. I thought I had surely uncovered one of the most common manifestations of bunk in New Age thinking. But it hardly denied the truth of what Kathy had *seen*. So, for some months, off and on, I tried to pay attention when people entered the periphery of my vision. I also attempted, when I found myself in dimly lit rooms or subway stations, to see if I could detect any luminosity above the head or around the shoulders of the people in my vicinity. All to no avail. It was some years later—long after having traded in my Earth Shoes for Birkenstocks—that some experiences of *imaginative sight* led me to think that perhaps I have a latent and fragmentary ability to *see* auras after all.

In the first incident, a patient came in for her weekly session, seemingly aglow with a silvery light. I asked what had happened in the past week. She spoke of a telephone encounter with her intrusive mother in which she, for the first time, managed to assert her need to have a life of her own. Such a victory ought to make anyone glow. But the glow I *saw* was not the pink rosiness of healthy cheeks. What I *saw* was impossible. Human skin does not glow with a silvery light. I looked more closely, trying to determine how this silvery illusion might have been created. I could find nothing in her flesh-and-blood face to justify my vision. She seemed silvery only when I did not look too closely. I had to conclude that this must be an *imaginal* perception—something that did not present itself to the sensory field of my bodily eyes. *Imagination* must have taken over to fill me in on the state of her psychological being, for what I *saw* was accurate to her experience of herself.

In the second instance, I was giving a lecture on the spiritual implications of the AIDS crisis in the basement of a large hotel in San Francisco. It was a dreadful location—pillars everywhere and bad lighting. The audience was surprisingly large, probably two or three hundred people, who had moved their chairs into a chaotic configuration to avoid having pillars obstruct their view of me. As a result, I could not see the whole audience in a single glance and had to turn widely from right to left to make eye contact. As I focused on my message, I noticed, out of the corner of my eye, that five or six people scattered throughout the audience seemed to have large bronze flares above their heads. When I tried to locate the individuals that seemed to be generating this effect, I could not find them. The flares only appeared when I was facing away from them. Furthermore, the bronze color gave me a shock of recognition. I realized I had been *seeing* it in my brother for the last couple of years, although I had not consciously noticed it before. At the time of the lecture, my brother was lying in his bed in another part of the city, ill with AIDS. I concluded that the bronze auras I thought I was *seeing* might have been showing me the people in the audience who were also afflicted with the disease I was talking about.

What was going on here? A man who does not claim to *see* auras suddenly thinks he can after beginning to take accounts of aura reading seriously. Does this represent a sensible growth from Don Juan's stage one to stage two? Is it some kind of self-delusion? Narcissistic self-aggrandizement? The patient with the silvery glow seemed to justify the illusion with her account of the telephone conversation with her mother, but there was no way to verify what I had *seen* at the lecture. Still, the fact that I *recognized* the bronze color as a perception that had lain below the threshold of consciousness when I visited my brother brought with it a note of conviction. This surely pointed to a gap in my consciousness; if there was any truth to what I had *seen* at the lecture, I must have been *seeing* my brother's aura for some time without noticing it.

Because the AIDS crisis has affected me very deeply, another factor may be involved. Perhaps I could *see* auras as a kind of latent potential that only appeared when I was emotionally involved, although focusing on something else. Does this also apply to my first encounter with Kathy? Does the fact that we became friends and have stayed in touch over the years imply an emotional connection that made an accurate reading possible? Surely I have an emotional connection with my patient who manifested the silvery glow. It is not possible to work with a patient in the absence of such a connection. Psychoanalysis calls it "transference" and "countertransference." Freud called transference "the main thing."

Nonsensory *seeing* and reality-accessing *imagination* imply some kind of invisible *connection* between the reader and the read. Perhaps emotional involvement is the key. If I accurately *saw* bronze flares in the hotel basement, it would not be unrealistic to suppose that I had an emotional connection with the men who seemed to produce them. I was speaking on a topic that is tragically meaningful to anyone who has AIDS or is losing a loved one to the disease. Kathy's *seeing* the golden flare of the infant probably also presupposed an emotional connection. After all, the boy's father was her friend.

The emotion hypothesis alerted me to another analogy. In my therapeutic work as a Jungian analyst, gaps in my patients' accounts of their experience very frequently have a direct effect upon me. If they are telling me a sad story, I do not just think how miserable those events must have been for them or identify with their role in the drama and feel their sadness along with them. I also notice things they are *not* telling me—the gaps. A note of panic, for instance, or triumph may be heard in the account. Sometimes this can be attributed to tone of voice, choice of imagery, or body language. If so, it makes little sense to speak of *seeing* and *imagination*. I have simply seen and heard.

But often I cannot identify *how* I picked up that note of panic. I cannot point to anything that was said or to how it was said. I merely notice that a panic has begun vaguely to gnaw at *me*. If intuition comes to my aid, I may even *see* something. Perhaps I will suddenly reexperience my own panic at age 11, when I was alone and lost in the woods at night on a Boy Scout camping trip. Or, in the case of the patient mentioned earlier, maybe I will be transported back to a scene in her life, one that she drew me into weeks or months earlier when she told me the tragic story of her mother's death in an automobile accident when she was 9. In this case, I found it useful to interrupt her story to tell her what I was feeling: "Boy, that must have made you feel like a kid who's lost in the woods at night, wondering if you will ever be found!"

The patient may discard my observation as irrelevant to her experience. But frequently she reacts with a shock of recognition and begins to tell her story with a greater depth of emotion. When this happens, the validity of my own gnawing panic is demonstrated as a *mutual* fact. I feel what she has *not* been feeling on account of a gap in her consciousness. But how did *I* know it, since it was *her* (unconscious) feeling? By some mystical process, *imagination* supplies the link. Silent, invisible, emotional connections like this are perhaps not so hard to imagine as the *seeing* of auras. For it is at least not foreign to our everyday way of thinking to speak of a room as being "filled with emotion" that can be felt by anyone who enters.

Kathy thought the emotion theory made a good deal of sense. Energy, she said, expresses itself emotionally. When she *sees* something in a person's aura, she also *feels* it. It is the *feeling*, in fact, that tells her how to identify what she has *seen*. She said she *feels* an aura much the way I feel the note of panic in my patient's story. It somehow produces an image. Years ago it produced the image of bacon. Just the other day, she saw watermelons in someone's "arms." The watermelons were so unexpected that they ruptured the stream of my consciousness. In the gap, I glimpsed a man dashing to the kitchen during a television comercial to cut himself a thick slice of the pink, dripping fruit. He flicks a few stray black seeds into the sink before returning to his favorite program. Surely not as compelling as bacon, but then bacon was *my* addiction.

Bacon, watermelons, scary nights: if this is "energy," then energy must have something to do with the way we live. Something like Freud's "libido" and Jung's "psychic energy." It is always directed at something, interested in something. The energy of rolling billiard balls expresses no intention, interest, addiction, or panic. Presumably, billiard balls also have no auras.

Suppose what aura readers are claiming to *see* is the energy described in the so-called "new physics," the "unimaginable world" of quantum mechanics. Einstein showed that matter and energy are interchangeable, and a series of other investigators has found that the components of the atom only *sometimes* act like matter. The electron, for example, exists as an unspecified "cloud" of merely "probable" locations, unless we try to "see" it with our scientific instruments. When we succeed in "seeing" it this way, it is as though the cloud collapses and the electron becomes a material object at a certain specific location.

The investigations of the "new physics" thus bear a certain resemblance to those of aura reading. What we "see" depends on how we look. When we look directly at another person, we see arms, legs, head, facial expression, characteristic gestures—in short, a living human body. When we look away, we may perhaps *see* an apparently impossible cloud of luminous "probabilities"—a bronze flare may indicate the presence of AIDS or a great golden glow the promise of spiritual excellence. As soon as we whirl around and directly face the body that seems to have generated this luminous display, the aura collapses and we again observe an ordinary human body.

Science has been getting more and more abstruse and fantastic over the course of the last century. We have barely accustomed ourselves to remember that the solid-looking table in front of us is actually comprised more of space than of matter, with subatomic particles arranged like countless little solar systems. Now we are asked to imagine that those tiny planets and suns that comprise the wood of the table are actually not "there" at all. They are only clouds of probabilities, invisible little packets of energy vibrating in multiple dimensions.

When we apply this vision of reality to our bodily selves, we conceive of a unity comprised of organs which are in turn constituted of tissues. These latter are compounded of cells which are made up of molecules, the molecules of atoms, and the atoms of energy packets. Thus in the last analysis, our bodies are composed of an unimaginable number of energy "quanta," all vibrating in several dimensions and all in sufficient harmony with one another that the highly complicated physical and psychological organism we call a human being can maintain its stability and continuity through perhaps eighty years of life.

What we see as the limbs and trunk, hair, eyes, and fingernails of this body are little more than fragmentary abstractions to which we have access through our sense organs. Because our sense organs respond merely to tiny segments of the electromagnetic spectrum over which energy quanta "broadcast," we must conclude there is a great deal more to our body than we can see, hear, touch, smell, and taste. Furthermore, as we know from observing ripples on ponds and hearing distortions in radio reception, waves from different sources interfere with one another, causing complicated patterns. It is surely reasonable to think that the countless bundles-upon-bundles of wave-generators that are our bodies impinge upon the bodies of other people in ways that lie well outside the scope of our sense organs.

Consequently, aura readers may be picking up something "vibratory." As they scan someone's aura, they may be "witnessing" the intersection of their own vibrating bundles of energy with those of the subject. The subject's energy pattern disturbs the reader's in the same way my patient's panic disturbed my peacefulness. The energy of her panic interfaced in a nonsensory manner with my calm energy and somehow produced a leap of *imagination,* so that a memory of being lost in the woods appeared in a gap in my awareness. It is not unlikely that *imagination* fills the gaps in our daily wakefulness in much the same way that our dreams represent life's issues for us every night in our sleep.

In the end, therefore, I am left with a series of analogies, each a reasonable guess, but hardly constituting an overwhelmingly convincing proof. Still, the bunk factor seems to have been reduced. Each step along the way is "thinkable," even if the aura reader's claim to *see* energy seems naive on first hearing. When an aura reader tells you have eaten too much bacon, presumably the bacon has contributed some rather heavy or smoky energy bundles to the midsection of your luminous egg. It is intriguing to think, too, that we humans may be in constant communication with one another in a wholly nonsensory manner and that we may gain access to this by a kind of *dreaming*. *Dreaming* (in italics) is another of Castaneda's conventions. Like *"seeing"* and *"imagination,"* it refers to the human ability to gain objective information while in an altered state of consciousness.

Ultimately this seems to be the central claim in all New Age literature, that human consciousness is far more than we have hitherto imagined. Those of us who stand on the fringes of the New Age bemused and intrigued have, in Don Juan's language, merely "heard about power." We may even have had one or two instances in which "power" events happened to us. But we have not yet reached the point at which power lives in us, controlling our actions, but obeying our command.

We fail to *see* an aura because we have not learned to attend to the salient luminous fiber that generates it. We probably each have pretty nearly a full complement of fibers and are latently capable of unimaginable feats of extrasensory skill. But we are too interested in our bacon sandwich to notice these other dimensions. It may even be a good thing that we are, for those other dimensions might well be too fascinating for us. We might fail to notice traffic lights if we had unhindered access to them.

For real New Agers, the individuals who know power lives within them, our hesitations sound like weak excuses motivated by a neurotic fear of the unknown. For them the choice is clear. Either we open the eyes of our *imaginations* and *see*, or we stumble in the darkness of a sensory night. Aura reading is no novelty. It represents an evolutionary leap in human consciousness. Those who are using alternate strands of their luminous eggs constitute a vanguard, an elite corps of the human race somehow chosen to show the rest of us the way forward into the New Age. We bemused onlookers wonder why we should follow. What in the last analysis would we gain by learning to read auras?

In my therapeutic work, paying attention to the gaps in awareness is essential. This places me on the fringe of the New Age. I sport just this side of the "monumental shock" of the truly unthinkable, as I stay on the lookout for the emotional realities that appear in the gaps—that note of panic or triumph and the image *dreamed* up to accompany it. It seems I am in touch with the good old-fashioned facts of everyday life. I know it is effective to say, "You sound like a child who is lost in the woods at night." I doubt the effectiveness of, "When you talk like that, your aura shrinks."

My son, Lukas, who barely stands on the fringe of the New Age, long ago relegated Kathy to the outer darkness of raving lunacy. But while I was working on this chapter (a fact he had no sensory way of knowing), he phoned me from his university dormitory in Chicago to say he had decided he had been "too hard on Kathy." He proceeded to give an account of the events of the preceding night. While waiting with two friends in the lobby of a university building, they all had remarked that a "dark spirit" seemed to be brooding over the campus. They spoke of an uncanny feeling they had. Lukas elaborated on his visionary field, comparing it with scenes from the movie, *Jacob's Ladder*, in which an un-real light seemed to give everything a demonic hallucinatory quality.

The next day he found that quite a few others were talking about what a weird night it had been. As the day went on, he learned that several fights between students had broken out during the wee hours. He seemed to be finding confirmations everywhere of the dark intimations he had earlier shared with his friends. Evidently, there really had been some sort of "dark spirit" hovering over the campus. While he was fortunate enough to have *seen* it, as it were, out of the corners of his eyes and was forewarned, other individuals were caught up in it. His concluding words were: "I still don't believe in reading auras. That's clearly impossible. But there's no doubt there are things out there that we can't see. They make things happen."

Chapter

2

FOUR AGES OF HUMAN EVOLUTION

At one time human nature was split in two, an executive part called a god, and a follower part called a man. Neither part was conscious.

(JAYNES, 1976, P. 84)

Who in the outside world has worked wonders, raised the dead, expelled demons? No one. Such deeds are done by monks. It is their reward. People in secular life cannot do these things, for, if they could, what then would be the point of ascetic practice and the solitary life?

(CLIMACUS, 1982, P. 83)

Cosmic Consciousness is. . . a consciousness of the cosmos, that is, of the life and order of the universe. . . . There occurs . . . an indescribable feeling of elevation, elation and joyousness, . . . a sense of immortality, a consciousness of eternal life . . .

(BUCKE, 1977, P. 2)

The Age of Pisces dawned with the story of a man who rose from the dead, but was no ghost. He could eat bread and drink wine, and still had the marks of the nails in his hands. Yet there was something startling about him. Sometimes he shone whiter than snow and could walk through walls. His disciples found they could speak in their own rude tongue and be understood by Persians and Medes. They had the same powers as the risen man. They gave the blind sight, made the lame walk, and they could even cast out devils. Whole towns emptied, as the god-struck followers retired to caves and stone huts in the deserts of Egypt, Syria, and Palestine.

Now, with Aquarius on the horizon, we hear some of the same themes. People who have been declared dead have returned to tell us of the brightly shining beings they have seen and the transcendent feelings and convictions that have turned their values upside down. Others are able to see us all as shining egg-shaped auras of light, and by manipulating them heal our solid bodies of flesh. A white buffalo was recently born in Wisconsin—possibly in fulfillment of a Lakota millennial prophecy. People are experimenting with lucid dreaming, out-of-body journeys, and shamanism. Others claim to be "downloading" wisdom from aliens, intergalactic beings of light, who beam love and exotic knowledge onto this planet from distant stars or "mother ships." Their message—despite its techno-jargon—is structurally almost identical with Gnostic mythologies that flourished two thousand years ago.

What is going on here? Is New Age enthusiasm a throw-back to earlier ages we thought had passed? Does the prospect of a new century, a new millennium, a New Age, bring out the most harebrained concoctions of the human mind? Does an impending series of zeroes in our reckoning of the years remind us of death and put us on the lookout for the evidence of something eternal?

A century ago, when the impressive figure of 1900 loomed in the immediate future, Europe and America witnessed a spiritualism craze. People gathered around tables in Victorian parlors to hold "séances" in which the spiritually gifted contacted the souls of the dead and relayed their messages to the living. One of the most extraordinary of these mediums, Mlle. Hélène Smith of Geneva, claimed to have discovered former lives in fifteenth-century India and on the planet Mars. She brought back marvelous stories from the red planet about its advanced technology at a time when astronomers had discovered what appeared to be "canals" in its surface—possible evidence of an intelligent civilization.

The Swiss psychologist Theodore Flournoy studied Mlle. Smith intensively for five years and in 1900 published a book on his findings, *From India to the Planet Mars* (1963). Although only three years earlier he had confessed that the Martian language the medium spoke had a strangeness and consistency that inclined him to accept its extraterrestrial origins, by the conclusion of his work he had determined that the seemingly extra-planetary tongue was a syllable-for-syllable encoded version of French. Once the system for transforming the sounds of "Martian" into those of Mlle. Smith's own language were uncovered, all the idioms and slang of contemporary French speech were clearly revealed.

Flournoy showed, too, that every one of Hélène's amazing factual references to 15th-century India could be found in her father's library. Everything was due to "cryptomnesia," "hidden forgetting." Facts she had long forgotten reappeared when she "shifted her consciousness" into séance mode. Information she thought she derived from extraterrestrials and journeys through time turned out to be nothing more than what she could have told us herself a few years earlier—before she forgot. *From India to the Planet Mars*, therefore, became a classic in 20th-century psychology, showing that events experienced as taking place "outside" the observer can be fruitfully shown to arise from "within."

It also raised a fire-storm of criticism from offended believers in the factual reality of spiritualist claims. Flournoy only *seemed* to have debunked their favorite medium. Actually, he was a narrow-minded and benighted rationalist. Was the New Age about to explode into action 100 years ago, until it was smothered by the scientific obsessions of the dying Old Age? Were the Martians speaking only to be muzzled by the psychologists?

Now that the New Age mentality has gained some real strength, perhaps we will finally hear what they have to tell us. Or are we indeed inclined to fool ourselves at the end of centuries and millennia? For we are faced again today with claims resembling those of Hélène Smith: astral journeys to distant stars, channeling the wisdom of aliens, and the like. New Agers speak of angels, totem animals, and aliens who perform gruesome experiments upon humans by the tens of thousands. And if we try to speak of psychodynamics, archetypes, psychic energy, and the self, they hear us denying the reality of their experience. "Your angels are *nothing but* unconscious projections," they hear us say. They want none of it.

A patient of mine was taken on a guided imagery journey to a planet in the system Sirius, where she was told that this foreign orb was her home planet. She is not really an Earthling; she is a Sirian sent here to instruct the rest of us. When I pointed out that she could view this intergalactic journey as a dream that describes how painfully alienated she feels everyday in her dealings with her associates, she smiled indulgently. "You can look at it that way if you wish," she said; "but you only have part of the story."

I have no doubt my attempted interpretation had merit, and it is also true that an alienated person needs to find a new identity. But from Sirius? As a Jungian analyst, I want to see this story *symbolically*. But my patient insists on its literal truth. Am I muzzling her as Flournoy did his Hélène? Would not someone who had *really* traveled to Sirius have been "monumentally shocked"? Would it not have rearranged her lifeworld? Surely it should have become the central issue in our meetings for months thereafter. In fact, however, it has not. I have heard nothing more about it. Although muzzling cannot be excluded, the Sirian visit must have played some other role in my patient's life.

Evidently, the visit functioned as a declaration of this patient's belief in the New Age. She wants to believe she is part of a revolution in human consciousness, one of a new breed already living in the new Aquarian world. Her trip to Sirius proves to her that she has the psychic powers that identify her as part of that elite. New Agers speak of a giant leap forward in human evolution that has barely begun. We will all be changed in the twinkling of an eye, perhaps in the year A.D. 2000 or perhaps when the stars show that the Age of Pisces has yielded to that of Aquarius.

The New Age embraces a mythic form of history, in which the order of the cosmos directs our destiny and may be read in the sky. They say that Pisces has been a narrow-minded and contentious age. They point to its logo, a pair of fish swimming in opposite directions, symbolizing duality, contradiction, war, and the rationality of right versus wrong. They hope that Aquarius, the Water-Bearer, is about to wash us clean of our contentions and open the way to a new harmony—a Global Village on Spaceship Earth; a new paradigm of wholeness and ecology furthered by decentralized networks of communication; the fall of jealous, controlling governments; and, especially, transpersonal "psychic" powers that will so far transcend our old consciousness that we will have no more interest in our petty disagreements.

They are certainly right about one thing. Our relationship to the zodiac is changing. Astronomy verifies the starry facts involved. Somewhere around A.D. 2200,[1] the rising Sun on the first day of Spring will find itself in the sign of Aquarius. For the last 2000 years, the sign of Pisces has stood at the horizon on the first day of Spring. These are observable facts having to do with the movement of sun and stars and the wobble of the Earth's axis. But the New Age interprets them in a mythic

---

[1] According to the precession of the equinoxes, an astrological age lasts about 2160 years. I have rounded these numbers to simplify the argument and assumed the traditional year of Christ's birth as the beginning of the Age of Pisces.

manner. Just as an individual born in the sign of Aquarius may be expected to have a different conscious attitude from one born in Pisces, so now the entire planet is expected to change its outlook.

HIƧTᵒRICAL OVERVIEW

The mentalities of Pisces and Aquarius are only two astrological steps in the evolution of human consciousness. If we wish to make sense of expected New Age changes, it will help to move back a couple of steps to the Age of Taurus (4400 B.C. to 2200 B.C.) and follow human consciousness as it changed from the Taurean to the Arian age and then to that of Pisces. This will give us a context in which to understand the nature of New Age claims.

Put briefly, human consciousness in the Age of Taurus and before was characterized by a dreamy sort of "cosmic consciousness," an awareness of the cosmos as a whole and one's own participation in it. Six thousand years ago and more, our ancestors were unaware of the clear distinction we make between knowledge gained from the five senses and that derived from *dreaming, seeing,* and *imagination.* Although unable to think conceptually as we do, the ancients had certain advantages that we have lost. They could find game animals, water, friends, and enemies, not only by close sensory observation as we would, but also *imaginally.* They just "knew" where to dig for water or in which direction the deer were grazing.

In the Age of Aries (2200 B.C. to A.D. 1), this ability was largely lost. Aries was a chaotic age, full of war and displacement, in which people had to be cunning to survive. They had to develop a more thought-oriented approach to life, which they gained only by suppressing cosmic consciousness.

This suppression has continued through the Age of Pisces (A.D. 1 TO A.D. 2200). As logic and analysis have been raised to a high art, cosmic consciousness has not only been forgotten, but its occasional manifestations have fallen into distrust and ridicule. Imagination has become for us the touchstone of irreality. Only scientific verification can be trusted. Our experimental precision has given us technological advances, but has also snuffed out the flame of spirituality.

The Age of Aquarius (A.D. 2200 to A.D. 4400) is expected to see new developments in the use of cosmic consciousness. Many of its enthusiasts, having little acquaintance with history, believe this to be the first large-scale manifestation of the mystic talent ever to have appeared in the history of the human race. Clearly they are mistaken, and it surely remains to be seen whether cosmic consciousness in the New Age will be used for new purposes.

The phrase, "cosmic consciousness," was made famous by Canadian physician, Richard Maurice Bucke, who had a monumental experience of great spiritual power in the late nineteenth century. He found himself suddenly and without warning taken up from the ground in a ball of light, where his mind was opened to the vastness of the cosmos and his own kinship with it. I have known people who have had such experiences and been scared half to death. They feared they might be going insane and treated the experience as a great secret to be hidden at all cost. As a result, they felt themselves isolated from the rest of the human race, alienated, cast out, unworthy to pretend to normality.

Bucke took the opposite course. He began a lengthy study to find others, living and dead, who had had similar experiences. By interviewing his contemporaries and digging other testimonies out of libraries, he found about a hundred of them. In 1901, he published *Cosmic Consciousness: A Study in the Evolution of the Human Mind,* a book that deserves to be called the first New Age argument for the evolution of consciousness. Darwin's *Origin of Species*, he said, confined itself to changes in anatomical, bodily form. It needed to be expanded to show how the human species itself is evolving from "simple consciousness," the mere registration of the world, through "self-consciousness," the awareness of personal identity, to "cosmic consciousness."

> Cosmic consciousness is a third form which is as far above Self Consciousness as is that above Simple Consciousness. . . . The prime characteristic of cosmic consciousness is . . . a consciousness of the cosmos, that is, of the life and order of the universe. . . . There occurs . . . an illumination which alone would place the individual on a new plane of existence, . . . a state of moral exaltation, an indescribable feeling of elevation, elation and joyousness, . . . a sense of immortality, a consciousness of eternal life, . . . a conviction . . . that he has it already. . . . Our descendants will sooner or later reach, as a race, the condition of cosmic consciousness, just as, long ago, our ancestors passed from simple to self consciousness" (Bucke, 1977, pp. 2–3).

"Cosmic consciousness" is a wonderfully descriptive term, but the evolutionary hypothesis is clearly bunk. For the fact is that cosmic consciousness is not a new talent appearing in some specially-favored individuals in the last few centuries of the Age of Pisces. Evidence from the Age of Taurus and before demonstrates that cosmic consciousness is very likely as old as humanity, older for sure than self-consciousness.

THE AGE OF TAURUS

The Age of Taurus marked the end of the time when, according to Julian Jaynes, "human nature was split in two, an executive part called a god, and a follower part called a man. Neither part was conscious" (Jaynes, 1976, p. 84). Jaynes' argument (*The Origin of Consciousness in the Breakdown of the Bicameral Mind*, 1976) is based on our two-sided brain. Studies on individuals who have lost the connection between the two hemispheres show that the right side[2] is intuitive and comes up with images of a holistic nature and strong emotional charge. It is the source of cosmic consciousness. The left brain is logical and conceptual; it is the source of language and reason.

Jaynes presents a mass of compelling data showing that cosmic consciousness was gradually—and with great regret—lost during the Age of Aries. He calls this the "breakdown of the bicameral mind." When the "bicameral" or "two-roomed" mind was operating naturally, in the Age of Taurus and before, people had *imaginal* access to a greater cosmos through the right side of their brain. At that time, the left side had barely begun to develop. Writing had not been invented. People "thought," perhaps, mostly in images.

We get a taste for the difference in function between the two sides of our brain whenever we drive on a heavily trafficked interstate while carrying on a discussion with our passenger. The ideas we consider, as well as the rhetorical devices we use to get our point across, are handled by the rational left half of our brain. This is what our pre-Taurean ancestors had not developed. Simultaneous with the discussion, we are driving. We maintain an ever-changing picture of the traffic flow—the steady progress of the mass of dependable drivers, sticking to their lanes, maintaining a constant speed. Speckled throughout are the wanderers, the laggards, and the ambitious. We see the whole picture at once—ahead, behind, and alongside—with ourselves in the middle, moving with and through this dynamic whole. We make decisions without thinking, right foot moving between accelerator and brake, hands on the wheel, eyes

---

[2] For some people, especially the left-handed, the employment of the two hemispheres is reversed.

swinging between windshield and mirrors. This complicated work is being done by the right side of the brain, as though in complete ignorance of the discussion going on between the inhabitants of the front seat.

Six thousand years and more ago, people lived exclusively in that right-brained driving mentality. They saw themselves moving with and through the flow of nature: landscape, weather patterns, the movement of animals and people. This was already a cosmic consciousness of a sort. People were immersed in the world and nature and felt themselves kin to it all. They surely were part of the oneness of the natural world. But there is more. The smaller cosmos of the natural world was riddled with gaps through which the "voice of the goddess" spoke the wisdom and painted the images of a greater cosmos.

Jaynes insists on the auditory nature of that voice. In an age when people were not "conscious" in any modern sense, they could not contrive narrative descriptions of themselves and "had no analog selves to 'see' themselves in relation to others. They were what we would call signal-bound, that is, responding each minute to cues in a stimulus-response manner and controlled by those cues" (Jaynes, 1976, p. 140). Jaynes finds compelling evidence in cuneiform inscriptions from the earliest centuries of Aries that those "cues" were experienced as the voice of a goddess.

> "The goddesses . . . who are the seven children of the brood of Bau that were begotten by the lord Ningirsu, to *utter* favorable decisions by the side of the lord Ningirsu" . . .

> The goddess Ninegal is praised as "*counselor*, exceeding wise *commander*, princess of all the great gods, exalted *speaker*, whose *utterance* is unrivaled" (Jaynes, 1976, p. 180–181).

A powerful dramatization of what it must have been like to live in this pre-Taurean world emerges from the diary of American photographer, Loren McIntyre, who, in 1969, was lost in the upper Amazon region of Brazil and captured by a band of Mayoruna Indians. Living in a nearly inaccessible jungle near the headwaters of the Amazon River, the Mayoruna were untouched by civilized developments which characterized the Age of Aries. McIntyre found himself in a world very close to cosmic consciousness. His story was published twenty-one years later by his Rumanian explorer friend, Petru Popescu (1991). McIntyre furnished the foreword.

Although not mistreated, apart from having his artifacts of civilization destroyed (camera, watch, sneakers), McIntyre knew the Mayoruna would not let him escape. At the same time, he was not sure he wanted to flee, as survival seemed more likely in the company of these naked denizens of an ancestral world. He was worried, however, because there was a tension in the group he could not comprehend. The Mayoruna seemed up to something that made no sense. Every morning they rose, burned their village, moved a few miles into the wilderness, and built a new village.

McIntyre's linguistic ability was limited to several European languages, while the Mayoruna knew no tongue but their own. Consequently, spoken exchanges of information were out of the question. Feeling the need to establish some kind of friendly, nonverbal contact, McIntyre noticed the headman sitting cross-legged, crafting an arrow. He sat down beside him in an identical posture and began his own handiwork. Once he was thoroughly immersed in the rhythmic motions of braiding a belt from strips of palm twine, he distinctly, although inaudibly, *heard* a message from the headman: *Some of us are friends* (Popescu, 1991, p. 80).

Could it be that he had actually *heard* this unspoken communication? It seems to be a minor instance of what Jaynes calls the "voice," only this time emanating from another human, not a god. For McIntyre, this was an unimaginable event, and it caused a "monumental shock." He struggled within himself for a while, trying to assimilate the experience, and eventually pulled himself together enough to attempt a reply. But, as the message he had received was not exactly verbal or auditory, he rejected the idea of simply speaking words within his mind: *I'm also a friend; you can trust me.* Instead, he tried to *feel* the sentiments of that thought, to fill himself up with friendliness. He held that feeling a few moments and then waited to see what would happen. In his mind, the thought formed: *I know* or "[m]aybe just the feeling of that answer, with words in English hurrying in to illustrate it" (Popescu, 1991, p. 81). In a short time, the headman rose and offered the white man his nearly finished arrow. McIntyre accepted it as a gift, a tangible statement that communication had been achieved.

As the days passed, he began to pick up more and more of this silent "beaming," primarily from the headman, but sometimes also fragmentary thoughts from the tribespeople as a whole, emerging blurrily out of a kind of crowd murmur. "I felt I couldn't tell exactly when a communication started, but it probably built to a point when I 'found it' at the surface of my mind and was forced to apply my own words to it" (Popescu, 1991, p. 91).

At times he wondered if he were going crazy. The ability to communicate by "beaming" delivered a disorienting shock, but his rational attempts to explain it away were opposed by two undeniable facts. The messages were consistent, and he had no alternative but to trust them.

Events eventually revealed that the community was dealing with an attempted political *coup*. The hostile and enigmatic man McIntyre had been calling "Red Cheeks" intended to seize control of the community. He realized this the day Red Cheeks and his three followers were found dead with poisoned arrows protruding from their chests. But the Mayoruna continued on with their aimless journeying as though nothing had happened. The "beaming" told him the headman was orchestrating some kind of return. The Mayoruna were *traveling back to the beginning.* But what "beginning"? It obviously had something to do with death, otherwise why the apparently aimless wandering from day to day after burning the village each morning? McIntyre gathered also that this was some kind of *magical* journey and that the headman himself was uncertain of success, but had no alternative (Popescu, 1991, p. 116).

The journey culminated in a ritual enhanced by the ingestion of hallucinogenic plants. McIntyre's own hallucinatory experience is the only evidence we have for what it must have been like for the Mayoruna.

> What I see in front of me changes. Though I keep watching a three-dimensional landscape of trees, secondary roots, and hanging parasites so dense that my eyes can't conquer more than a hundred yards of it, a re-arrangement happens. Nothing disappears from the picture, and nothing is added, except an extra depth. The hundred yards of distance suddenly look as extended and spacious as a few hundred miles (Popescu, 1991, p. 153).

He concludes that, despite his life's work of exploring nature beyond the reaches of civilization, he had never really been "part of nature" as he had imagined. Not even the Indians in their daily life were merely "part of nature." All humans have "always belonged to a vaster space."

Although the language barrier prevented any ordinary sort of verification of McIntyre's observations, it seems clear that the attempted *coup* had posed a threat to the static, harmonious world of the tribe, and that, to restore themselves, they had to reconnect with their origins in cosmic consciousness. They had to kill off their former, *coup*-tainted existence in a series of deaths (the burning of one village after another) until they had moved back to a mythic beginning, the time before time began, which was opened to them through the ingestion of their hallucinogenic drugs.

In the language of Julian Jaynes, they had to open their inner ears to the voice. Evidently, even these children of nature, untouched by civilization, who had not lost the capacity for telepathic "beaming," had to follow a strenuous and uncertain regimen in order to open a gap between the small cosmos of the natural world and the greater eternal cosmos. It is reasonable to conclude that, even in the rather placid and static world of our pre-Taurean ancestors, it was the headmen, the shamans, and the kings who had the most reliable access to cosmic consciousness.

THE AGE OF ARIES

The monumental event that inaugurated the Age of Aries in 2200 B.C. was an agricultural revolution in the Middle East. Before this event, people lived by "subsistence." Each family and village produced just what it needed to survive from year to year, with perhaps a little left over to trade with neighbors. People in the Age of Taurus lived in harmony with the seasons of the year and the life-cycles of the plants and animals who shared the world with them.

Around the dawning of Aries, changes in climate and advances in social organization made it possible for food to be grown in far greater abundance than a village could consume. This development set large portions of the populace free to pursue other occupations. Most of them migrated to the larger towns and trading centers, which grew haphazardly at alarming rates. The Age of Aries was therefore dominated by some of the earliest cities in human history, great urban collections of the rich, the skilled, and the poverty-stricken. Kings and professional soldiers held the civil power; priests and religious specialists worked at aligning the visible world with the world of the gods; merchants and traders amassed riches that enabled massive building projects; and the preponderant majority performed slave labor or became outlaws and predators. The world was organized from the top down as a hierarchy maintained by brute force. Royal ambitions led to wars between the city-states, which in turn resulted in large-scale displacements, migrations, and slavery.

All of this was unknown in the thoroughly rural life of the Taurean age. Six millennia back in the prehistory of our species, the world was suffused with life and power, and the gods were very near. A Sumerian proverb from the Age of Aries suggests the quality of consciousness those people had: "Act promptly, make your gods happy!" (Jaynes, 1976, p. 204), which seems to mean: "Don't *think*, maintain the spontaneity of your cosmic consciousness." Such advice would only be given to people who still had some memory for cosmic consciousness, but tended in their everyday lives to rely on the left half of their brains. According to the maxim, left-brain thinking was dangerous business because it silenced the voices of the gods and made them "unhappy."

If the Age of Taurus is symbolized by the heavy, slow-moving, earth-bound bull, Aries represents a bursting out of ambition and aggression that races up mountain peaks like a ram. Cosmic consciousness weakened as people had to struggle with lawlessness and insecurity inside the new cities, as well as with frequent brutal wars between them. They had to depend more and more on the calculations of the left side of their brains. The world of the gods lost its naive immediacy and was, for the first time, formulated in left-brain language.

Because the gods no longer spoke through the voice that had been available to every individual, the truths of cosmic consciousness had to be expressed in a new form. Great narrative epics were elaborated and written down for generations yet unguessed, saying, in effect, that the gods have spoken to our ancestors and this is their message. In the Bible, for example, God walked in the garden with Adam and Eve. He also walked with Abraham and bargained with him over the destruction he intended to inflict on Sodom. He spoke with Isaac, Noah, and Moses and laid down the laws which his people had to follow if they expected their God to protect them.

The Bible, the Zoroastrian *Yashts*, the writings of Confucius and Lao Tse in China, the Vedanta scriptures of India—all of these implied a tragic "fall" had occurred in the distant past. The sin of Adam and Eve excluded them from the garden and their intimacy with God. In China, the Tao, the cosmic order of the universe, had been forgotten and had to be remembered through meditation. According to Hinduism, the vast majority of us live in ignorance (*avidya*). The scriptures were written to awaken us to the truth that *Thou art That*. Our true identity is the *atman*, no bigger than a thumb, that dwells within us all. Furthermore, the *atman* inside each of us is no different from *brahman*, the energy that pervades all that is. What we see in the natural world is nothing but the veil of *Maya*, an illusion that hides an invisible, greater reality. Each of these scriptures elaborates codes of conduct, designed to restore order in a chaotic world and to open our eyes and ears to timeless cosmic truths.

Jaynes sees the change in consciousness during the Age of Aries reflected in the art work of the ancient Middle East. We can see the figures of kings and their counselor-gods carved on ancient steles, great monoliths recording successful wars and outlining codes of conduct. In the beginning, the kings were the associates of the gods, gaining wisdom effortlessly, directly from a divine voice. They are depicted standing side-by-side with their divine counselors, listening for the inspiration needed to give moral and political direction to the people. But by the end of the age, when the fall had become an undeniable fact, the kings are shown on their knees, begging for guidance (Jaynes, 1976, pp. 223–235). Uncertainty regarding cosmic consciousness had become the rule, whereas it had been the exception only two millennia earlier.

After the fall from cosmic consciousness, people had to become devious to survive. A new attitude was celebrated in the wily hero Odysseus, who tricked and out-witted his way from thralldom to the goddess Calypso (very likely an image for the static realm of the cosmic goddess who brooked no opposition to her voice), through multiple life-threatening adventures, until he could reach the safety of home (Jaynes, 1976, pp. 272–277). Consciousness of an "I," separate from the world and the gods, emerged from these chaotic conditions. Cosmic consciousness belonged, now, to a mythic past. In the waning years of Aries, history and philosophy emerged as the first indications of a new, critically conscious way of being. The "rational animal" was born.

THE AGE OF PISCES

By the beginning of our own time, the Age of Pisces, even the great mythic narratives had fallen into question. The rational bureaucracies of the Greek and Roman empires organized cities and towns under the religion of the emperor. Local gods lost prestige, and the imperial divinities took on a distant and political meaning. This caused a massive crisis of identity, and people began to seek out elements of the old cosmic consciousness that had survived in the countryside. They devised "mystery religions," some of which used drugs, dance, and music to attain oneness with the universe. Even the conquerors invited holy men from the vanquished territories of the East to teach them the old religions.

In the transition between Aries and Pisces, a great enthusiasm for cosmic consciousness emerged between 200 B.C. and A.D. 200 called Gnosticism. Christianity has spoken disparagingly of Gnosticism as though it were merely one of many doctrinal heresies belonging exclusively to its own history. This is a narrow, erroneous view, for there were Jewish and pagan Gnostics before there were Christian Gnostics, who were in fact late-comers and decidedly a minority.

The central idea of Gnosticism was *gnosis*, a kind of emotionally charged knowledge of the heart, a direct experience of the divine, and indeed of the greater, eternal cosmos. *Gnosis* was a natural capacity of every human being. We have it before we are born and will have it again after we die. During our earthly sojourn and exile, however, we tend to forget our origins and destiny and remain ignorant of *gnosis*. We forget because of the heavy stupidity of our bodies, with their unruly instincts that seduce us into believing no more than we can see, hear, smell, taste, and touch. The huge underclass of the world is content with this sensory knowledge and very likely slaves to its instincts. Gnosticism called this underclass the *sarkikoi*, the "flesh people," benighted, sorry wretches who had not the slightest inkling of spiritual realities.

The mid-level component of human nature was the soul (*psyche*) with its capacity for the visionary knowledge of *seeing, dreaming,* and *imagination*. The rather small middle class who had discovered their souls were called the *psychikoi*, the "soul people." They lived a higher form of life than the flesh people and had a genuinely spiritual form of consciousness.

The elite, the Gnostics who had mastered *gnosis*, had gone beyond the soul and gained access to the spirit (*pneuma*). They were the *pneumatikoi* or "spirit people." In addition to visionary knowledge, they had *gnosis*, direct knowledge of the One. They had seen through to the source of the two worlds—the natural world and the eternal cosmos. For them, *gnosis* was the complete form of cosmic consciousness, and they did their best to disseminate its mysteries.

Although scholars have discovered a great variety of Gnostic maps of the greater cosmos, most of these grand images share a common structure. Generally, the Earth is seen as the kernel of a series of concentric spheres, each becoming more purely spiritual as we move outward. The ultimate source of the cosmos is the ineffable One, who is pure light. The One "emanates" the cosmos like rays of light from a sun, each ray and fragment of ray becoming an individual being of light. Humans, too, have been emanated and are beings of light. We are the most material of ensouled beings, but inside each of us is a genuine spark of eternal light. Beings in the spheres furthest from the One are comprised of increasing impurity (matter)—so much so, that, even above the human realm, beings of light can forget their origin and destiny. Some of these, called Archons, have set up little fiefdoms for themselves, wielding absolute power over spheres occupied by lesser beings for their own power and glory. In at least one Gnostic sect, the Yahweh of the Jews is identified as the Archon, demiurge of the Earth.

Based on the story of Jesus, a man who demonstrated monumental powers over life and death because of his close kinship with the highest divinity, early Christianity was filled with cosmic consciousness. The Christ who rose from the dead, passed through walls, and appeared transfigured on Mount Tabor, where he shone whiter than snow and conversed as an intimate with Elijah and Moses, could even be seen as the prototype for the spirit people of Gnosticism. He was co-eternal with the One, "emptied himself of his divinity" in order to become the light of the world and reveal to us our spiritual origin and destiny. His most eloquent Apostle said, "I live now, no longer I, but Christ lives in me."

No wonder Christianity's struggle for self-definition found its first opponent in Gnosticism. According to Christianity, the Gnostics over-emphasized the indwelling God, the Holy Spirit, to such an extent that individuals were encouraged to draw their own cosmic maps, derived entirely from their own personal visions. *Gnosis* could be abused and so many variant doctrines elaborated, that the truth itself could become as diffuse and unmappable as a patch of fog. Christianity fought Gnosticism by insisting on a single map of the cosmos, revealed through a linear historical process that began with Adam and led through Noah, Abraham, Moses, David, and the prophets of Israel, culminating in Jesus of Nazareth. Only the Church that succeeded him, the Body of Christ on Earth, had the authority to distinguish truth and illusion; and it employed the new disciplines of history and philosophy to accomplish this.

Even by the end of the second century, when it had won its struggle for self-definition against the diffuse pressures of Gnosticism, there still remained a tension in Christianity between mystical experience (*gnosis*) and the officially defined dogmas articulated by those rational, but mystically-inclined, scholars we now call the Fathers of the Church. By the end of the third century, Christianity knew itself. For the world at large, however, living within the political structure of the Roman Empire, it was just another minority group, a "mystery religion" with its roots in the rebellious land of Israel.

It rose from its status as a mystery religion to the religion of the empire through Emperor Constantine's vision in A.D. 313—a vision right out of cosmic consciousness: a cross-like image accompanied by a voice that promised, "In this sign shall you conquer." Two streams of Christianity resulted from this event: a mystical form that kept cosmic consciousness alive among the very few, and a legalistic and philosophical form that tied its wagon to political power and sought to translate cosmic consciousness into left-brain language for the purpose of creating a theocracy to control the majority.

After that momentous visionary event in A.D. 313, Christianity was established as the dominant religio-cultural form of Western civilization. Rational elaboration of its doctrines was left in the hands of theologians for at least a thousand years. The vast majority still deserved to be called "flesh people," as they carried on a dreary daily struggle for existence, tempered only by theological promises of a more blessed and rewarding life to come after death. Earthly life was an exile from heaven, a sojourn in the realm of matter, in which God was testing their mettle— to see if they could act *as though* the eternal cosmos were more real than the material hardships apprehended by the senses.

Gnostic aspirations persisted, however, among an elite, men and women who left the cities to gather in and around monasteries where they hoped to live an unfettered spiritual existence. One of the most significant of these was a certain John "Climacus," John the "Ladder Man," who lived some fifty years in the Sinai desert and who, at the end of his life in about A.D. 700, summarized what he had learned in one of the most influential books of Christian mysticism, *The Ladder of Divine Ascent* (1982). For the past 1300 years, this book has been read aloud during Lent in all Orthodox Christian monasteries. It thus not only provides a window into the spirituality of the Dark Ages, but reveals one of the most important sources of modern Christian mysticism.

John Climacus lived most of his life at the foot of Mount Sinai, where legend locates the encounter between Yahweh and Moses and the carving of the Ten Commandments. I climbed that mountain in my Earth Shoes in March of 1977, while on a tour led by Israel's Archaeological Society. Mount Sinai is little more than a very large, round-topped hill with a fairly gradual slope, but it impresses its visitors profoundly. It is absolutely silent up there on the summit, with tawny brown rock and sand stretching in all directions and a sparkling blue sky overhead. I thought as I stood there that God had never left this spot.

At the foot of the mountain stands the Monastery of St. Catherine, possibly little changed from the days of the Ladder Man. As far as I was concerned, however, it was just another building. The week I was there, the Jews were eating matzo in honor of the Passover and their own forty years in this desert, and the monks of St. Catherine were celebrating Holy Week—the one week of the year visitors are not allowed inside to view the magnificent mural of Christ's transfiguration at the top of

Mount Tabor. I was not sorry. I had no interest in entering the building. I wanted to be outside in the desert. The stone huts which the anchorites had inhabited centuries before were still standing, scattered about on the sides of the low hills, clustered around tiny stone chapels, and looking for all the world as though the holy men and women would return at any moment.

I knew this is where I would have lived, had I been born thirteen centuries earlier, on the *outskirts* of monastic life, communing with the God who seemed palpable in the very air that filled this sacred land. I wanted no roof and no walls to stand between me and that eternal Being. Above all, I wanted no intermediaries and no organized community life to moderate and temper God's presence. I would have lived outside that monastery the way I live outside the New Age, savoring its presence, but keeping my own counsel, following my own path.

John Climacus must have felt somewhat the same. He spent his first three years rather near the monastery in a small community under the direction of a man he himself selected for his holiness. After the completion of this "novitiate," he retired to a place called Tholas, seven miles from the monastery walls, where he lived in relative isolation for the next forty years. Near the end of that period, he spent two years inside the walls of St. Catherine's, as a guest of the Abbot. Finally, he was elected, against his own protests, Abbot of the monastery, where he lived his last few years and where, at the request of the Abbot of a monastery located at the southern tip of the Sinai peninsula, he wrote *The Ladder*.

Based on the biblical image of Jacob's vision of angels ascending and descending between Heaven and Earth, *The Ladder of Divine Ascent* is a thirty-step catalog of the virtues a monk must attain and the vices he must overcome. It reveals John Climacus as a consummate Director of Souls, whose central concern is the personal obstacle each individual has to surmount in order to climb that ladder and gain union with the One. He begins with, and returns constantly to, the virtue of obedience—an emphasis that may perplex a modern reader inclined to pre-judge "perfect obedience" as a kind of infantilization. But John's notion of obedience can only be understood when we remember that a monastery is an entirely voluntary institution.

Why did people join? John gives three reasons: some have hit bottom in their sinfulness and are searching for a higher principle on which to ground their lives, others are convinced of the reality of the Kingdom of God and enter a monastery to devote themselves to it, and a few are after oneness with God in love. All of these people are convinced of the reality of *soul*, but find that they are soul-people only intermittently.

They wish to live in and through their souls more consistently. They want their gaps opened so they can *see* the eternal cosmos every day and every moment of their lives.

Obedience is more than following rules. It is a spiritual and emotional attachment to one's director, somewhat in the manner that Carlos Castaneda was bound to Don Juan. In the early books, Carlos is frequently ready to give up his work out of conscious fear or disgust, but he always returns because something within him is gripped by this irrational process and will not rest until it is satisfied. Carlos is "obedient" to Don Juan, but "obedience" seems a paltry word to describe his fascination and unconscious conviction that a monumental transformative process is involved. In much the same way, Climacus recommends an obedient attachment to a director uniquely suited to free us from the flesh world and open our eyes to the world of the soul.

Clearly, the Ladder Man began directing souls long before his election as Abbot. His forty years of anchorite isolation had to have been interrupted daily by monks seeking his guidance. In the course of those decades, transforming himself and directing others, he became the Don Juan Matus of his day, a master of the spiritual life, possessed of such vision and cunning that he could accurately *see* the people whose souls he directed. He looked right through their gaps and glimpsed the lifeworld in which they were living, knowing it thoroughly, grasping how it could be "stopped," so that they could step out of it and enter the greater cosmos.

He helped them accomplish this "stoppage" by assigning paradoxical tasks. We might think of how Carlos was directed to find his "spot" in Don Juan's ramada. He spent an entire night moving from place to place within that open-air porch, questioning, doubting, and searching until he finally fell asleep in the precise location where he felt most at peace. On another occasion, he was asked to gaze at a bush until he could see, not the foreground of its leaves and stems, but the background of its shadows and gaps.

Similarly, Climacus tells the story of a certain Isidore (Climacus, 1982, pp. 97–99), a monk who had belonged to the ruling class of Alexandria and proved to be "a troublemaker, cruel, sly, and haughty." He was ordered[3] to stand at the gate of the monastery and bend his knee to everyone who passed in or out and say, "Pray for me, Father, because I

---

[3] Climacus tells this story in praise of the wisdom of the Abbot who preceded him. It might well be a story illustrating his own wisdom, but humbly disguised. In any event, it surely illustrates the style of his own directorship of souls.

am an epileptic." This was his only occupation for seven years and, when at the end of that time he was invited to rejoin the community, he begged to be allowed to continue at the gate, for he knew that death was very near. His request was granted, and he died ten days later, "humbly and gloriously passing on to the Lord."

> While he was still alive, I asked this great Isidore how he had occu-
> pied his mind while he was at the gate, and this memorable man
> did not conceal anything from me, for he wished to be of help. "At
> first I judged that I had been sold into slavery for my sins," he said.
> "So I did penance with bitterness, great effort, and blood. After a
> year my heart was no longer full of grief, and I began to think of a
> reward for my obedience from God Himself. Another year passed
> and in the depths of my heart I began to see how unworthy I was to
> live in a monastery, to encounter the fathers, to share in the divine
> Mysteries. I lost the courage to look anyone in the face, but lower-
> ing my eyes and lowering my thoughts even further, I asked with
> true sincerity for the prayers of those going in and out" (Climacus,
> 1982, p. 98).

We might read this story as a description of the effects of a living *koan*, in the tradition of a Zen master who assigns an irrational problem to be meditated upon for weeks and years ("What is the sound of one hand clapping"), until the aspirant's habits of thought have been thoroughly frustrated and a transforming intuition emerges through the gap. The world of Isidore's Alexandrian arrogance had to be "stopped," as Don Juan would say, before he could encounter the monumental shock that the soul's cosmos lurked humbly at the inauspicious gate.

Modern readers of *The Ladder* will be struck by the primitivity and ignorance of most of those seventh-century monks. Isidore's learning and familiarity with giving orders would surely have justified his arro-gance. As long as he lived among them, he could not have helped but be reminded of his own excellence. From the viewpoint of the natural world, his arrogance was justified. If his old world had not been "stopped," the monastery would have served only to reinforce his com-placency. He would have gained nothing by leaving his position of power in the city. But, because his director had seen through the arro-gant veil of his Maya, he was given a task that opened the eyes of his soul.

The Ladder was written for flesh people who had not merely "heard about" soul, but who had intermittently glimpsed its reality intruding into their daily lives, who wanted to experience it as something that lives within them, controlling their lives and yet responding to their will. They entered the monastery in a spirit of impotence, realizing that they could not accomplish this transformation on their own, but looking for guidance from more accomplished soul people.

For flesh people, sin is a breaking of the rules that incurs the wrath of God; they flee sin out of fear. Soul people see things differently. For them, sin is a distraction that makes us overlook the gaps in our consciousness and hides the life of the soul. What soul people call "sin" is too subtle for flesh people even to notice. What flesh people call gluttony is an overeating that is dangerous for the body. Soul people, by contrast, convict themselves of gluttony even in the midst of their fasting, for any interest in food that distracts us from the experience of God's presence may lead to further forgetting.

> I once was sitting in my cell having become slack. Indeed I was thinking of leaving it. But some visitors came, and when they began to praise me for leading the life of a hesychast [a practitioner of "stillness"], my slackness gave way to vainglorious thoughts and I was amazed by the manner in which this three-horned demon stood up against all the others (Climacus, 1982, pp. 267–268).

In this personal confession, Climacus reveals his own continuing struggle with the ego-centered demands of the flesh world. For the monk of some attainment, "flesh" is a much subtler thing than the gross temptations of gluttony, lust, or avarice. It has to do with what stands in the way of recognizing the nearness of God. "Stillness of soul is the accurate knowledge of one's thoughts and is an unassailable mind" (Climacus, 1982, p. 262). One who knows one's thoughts, *sees* through the gaps and encounters God. "If it happens that, as you pray, some word evokes delight or remorse within you, linger over it; for at that moment your guardian angel is praying with you" (Climacus, 1982, p. 275).

The most disturbing images from *The Ladder* occur in Step Five, where Climacus takes us into the "Prison," a building located about a mile from the main monastery to which monks retired in obedience to fight the grimmest battles with their flesh (Climacus, 1982, pp. 121–131). Very likely, some of these men had been frankly insane before their consignment. After a few days or weeks in that place, however, it is hard to imagine any would have been judged "sane" by modern standards. The Ladder Man spent thirty days there, and his descriptions imply that these were the men whose only hope for trailing along in the humblest ranks of the soul people was to act as though their bodies did not exist. If many of them were not insane when they chose to enter that place, we must conclude that it had to have been some monumental glimpse of soul that kept them there.

> With knees like wood, as a result of all the prostrations, with eyes dimmed and sunken, with hair gone and cheeks wasted and scalded by many hot tears, with faces pale and worn, they were no different from corpses. Their breasts were livid from all the [self-inflicted] beatings, which had even made them spit blood. There was no rest for them in beds, no clean and laundered clothing. They were bedraggled, dirty, and verminous. . . .
>
> Believe me, brothers, I am not making all this up.
>
> Often they came to the great judge, to that angel among men—I mean the shepherd [the Abbot]—and they would plead with him to put irons and chains on their hands and necks, to bind their legs in the stocks and not to release them until death—or even afterward (Climacus, 1982, p. 125).

In the context of the seventh century, these men were pursuing their souls at the most basic and literal level. Thirteen centuries later, now that our eyes are on the dawning of Aquarius, an institution like this "Prison" would not even qualify as a psychiatric hospital for the hopelessly insane. During the course of the Age of Pisces, human consciousness has undergone an immense change. In the early centuries of our present age, human beings struggled with their instincts in a manner that leaves us confused and horrified. Surely we have not risen above our addictions to drugs and sex; we witness drive-by shootings and ethnic cleansings. But we can no longer countenance the literal denial of our bodies and our instincts. Something very important has transpired.

In a word, that "something" was the Renaissance, the rebirth of Western civilization, the rediscovery of the world and our bodies, the resurgence of interest in the pre-Christian scholars of Greece and Rome. A foremost figure of the Renaissance, the Italian poet Petrarch, tells a very important story about climbing a mountain. In 1336, at the age of 32, he ascended Mount Ventoux with his brother Gherardo and had a monumental experience that caused him to give up his self-described "dissolute" life in Avignon. Jacob Burckhardt describes that moment:

His whole past life, with all its follies, rose before his mind; he remembered that ten years ago that day he had quitted Bologna a
young man, and turned a longing gaze towards his native country; he
opened a book which was then his constant companion, the *Confessions* of St. Augustine, and his eye fell on the passage in the tenth
chapter: "and men go forth, and admire lofty mountains and broad
seas, and roaring torrents, and the ocean, and the course of the stars,
and turn away from themselves while doing so." His brother, to
whom he read these words, could not understand why he closed the
book and said no more (Burckhardt, 1944, pp 180-181).

What a double difference we have here. Seven centuries before,
Climacus would never have climbed that mountain. He would have
seen it as an idle distraction from the life of the soul. Seven centuries after Petrarch, we—with or without Earth Shoes—would take the majestic
view from the summit as a lovely reward for the labors of climbing.
Petrarch devoted his life to demonstrating that Christianity had nothing
to fear from the natural world or the great classics of Greece and Rome.
He did this bravely and with the most sincere conviction, even though
his soul was torn by the temptations that world stirred up in him. He
stood on the cusp between the first half of Pisces and the second, where
the beauties of the natural world constituted a soul-shattering challenge.
He led us into this world, but had to remain silent about what he saw.

The natural world was the LSD of the early Renaissance, the great
"mind-blower." It is as if Western civilization woke up one morning and
said, "My God, just *look* at this world we've been living in—how could
we have been so blind?" From this point on, it was no longer possible to
treat our bodies as corpses. Physical beauty became an ideal to be
sought. The arts burst out of their mystical fixation and began to explore
the bodily realities—first of biblical and mythological themes and then
of the natural world for its own sake.

Gnosis did not die, however. Indeed, it could be mentioned again by
name. For, although the Ladder Man devoted his life and his book to the
pursuit of that mystical knowledge, he dared not use a word reeking of
heresy and paganism. *Gnosis* remained, but in the second half of Pisces,
it has gained a connection with matter. Alchemy was one of the most
long-lasting and significant manifestations of this tendency. Every alchemist worked in two rooms: one for experiments (*laboratorium*) and one
for prayer and study (*oratorio*). They sought to produce a material object
that would not only transmute lead into gold, but that would transmute
the alchemists as well, and open their eyes to the greater cosmos. In the

following anonymous text, the author describes what he saw when he dropped consecrated red wine into a vessel of alchemically prepared rain water:

> Then put in two drops, and you will see the light coming forth from the darkness; whereupon little by little put in every half of each quarter hour first three, then four, then five, then six drops, and then no more, and you will see with your own eyes one thing after another appearing by and by on the top of the water, how God created all things in six days, and how it all came to pass, and such secrets as are not to be spoken aloud and I also have not the power to reveal. Fall on your knees before you undertake this operation. Let your eyes judge of it; for thus was the world created. Let all stand as it is, and in half an hour after it began it will disappear.
>
> By this you will see clearly the secrets of God, that are at present hidden from you as from a child. You will understand what Moses has written concerning the creation; you will see what manner of body Adam and Eve had before and after the Fall, what the serpent was, what the tree, and what manner of fruits they ate: where and what Paradise is, and in what bodies the righteous shall be resurrected; not in this body that we have received from Adam, but in that which we attain through the Holy Ghost, namely in such a body as our Saviour brought from heaven (cited in Jung, 1944, p. 246).

The alchemists were aspiring soul people and, in their cosmic consciousness, many of them *saw* a biblically correct map of the cosmos. For others, fragments of the biblical map were jumbled together with stranger visions. A new Gnostic plethora of cosmic structures lying uneasily side by side. The *gnosis* of the alchemists was inspired by the physical wonders they produced in their laboratories: the marvelous fact, for example, that the elusive liquid metal, quicksilver, would boil away violently and form a red powder (oxide of mercury) that could then be converted back into shiny rolling spheres of seeming silver when heated gently.

In their view, the substances the alchemists manipulated were the *souls* of the metals and salts. They wrote not of "common mercury," but of "our Mercurius," and they treated him as a helpful but dangerous trickster. In the end, though, their laboratories caused the downfall of alchemy. For they made real physical discoveries, isolated elements, determined some of the properties of what we call chemical bonding. Eventually they gave birth to modern, scientific chemistry, whose mathematical certainties made it senseless to speak of the souls and spirits of sulphur, mercury, and water.

The modern world began in the last quarter of the Age of Pisces, when Lavoisier isolated oxygen and Isaac Newton emerged from his alchemical laboratory and laid the mathematical foundations for modern physics. Marvels of a purely natural order succeeded and overshadowed those of the visionary realm, leading to technological inventions unimaginable a few centuries before. The industrial revolution led to the growth of new cities, with a concomitant renewal of chaos and anonymity. Cosmic consciousness was all but forgotten again.

The history of philosophy in the second millennium of Pisces provides the clearest evidence for how mystical claims have become more and more problematic for us. Back at the beginning of Pisces, Christian theologians borrowed Plato's distinction between the sensory world and the eternal world of ideas and renamed the latter Heaven and its guiding principle, God. They borrowed from Aristotle some more scientific-sounding notions. God was the "Prime Mover" of the cosmos and the "First Cause" of everything that exists. These conceptions went unchallenged for most of the Age of Pisces—refined perhaps, but never seriously questioned.

The rise of mathematical science, however, brought about monumental changes. René Descartes made significant contributions to both philosophy and science. He founded analytical geometry and advanced algebra. We are still learning his ideas in our junior high schools. But his most radical views are found in philosophy, where he introduced the notion of "universal doubt." Challenged by recent discoveries in mathematics and science, he wondered, "What can I know for certain?" The one thing he could not doubt was doubt itself. From this arose one of the most famous conclusions in history: "I think, therefore I am."

His goal was not to deny God, Heaven, and the afterlife, but to give them a firm and reliable foundation. So, from his unshakable certainty that he existed and was thinking, he moved step by step to admit the existence of God as the First Cause and the reality of the physical world as a thoroughly mechanical structure entirely divorced from the mind. Subjectivity ("I think") and objectivity (the outside world) became two separate realms connected only by the intervention of God. An all-good God would not let us be deceived. A deep loneliness was implied in Descartes' philosophy. Our subjectivity isolated us from one another and from the clockwork world outside us. Only the somewhat ghostly notion of God could keep us connected.

Subsequent thinkers accepted the distinction between subject and object, but had problems with Descartes' invocation of God. Hume asserted that the only thing we can be certain of is the fact that there is an unbroken stream of subjective images and ideas. We cannot even be certain that there is something called a mind which contains them, for the mind itself is just another idea. This was "radical skepticism," and it awakened Kant from his "dogmatic slumbers." Kant demonstrated, in a manner that has never been successfully refuted, that the world we see, hear, taste, smell, and touch depends entirely on the nature of our perceiving apparatus. What we know is simply what appears to the senses: the "phenomenon," that which appears. We may believe that there is an actual "thing itself," independent of our sensing it, but we can never know what it is.

What a radical change has occurred! For Climacus, the real was the visionary cosmos, and the sensory world was a devilish distraction. For Kant, knowing certainty is limited to the sensory world, and the visionary cosmos is a matter of belief. Only morality requires this belief, not knowledge. Nietzsche represents the end-point of this modern development, which he called the decline of metaphysics. Aristotle defined *metaphysics* as that which lies beyond the physical world. Nietzsche announced the "end of metaphysics" and the "death of God." He argued that we can no longer pretend to know or believe anything that lies beyond the world in which we live. The Platonic world of ideas, which Christianity "baptized" as Heaven and God, is no more than an illusion to which we have been clinging for centuries in the vain hope that it would give meaning to our daily lives. It does not. We are being dishonest with ourselves if we think it does. In actual fact, Nietzsche declared, all we have is our daily life.

It would be a mistake to view philosophers like Descartes, Kant, and Nietzsche as merely a series of demonic pied pipers leading us all to perdition with their mesmerizing ideas. Great philosophers do not invent their theories out of whole cloth, but rather give shape to the consciousness of their time. They place in compelling literary form what everyone else has been thinking. The 19th and 20th centuries have inherited, not only the books left behind by these "dead white males," but a way of thinking and seeing the world that those books merely articulated. We may try to deny the secularization of our worldview by joining fundamentalist sects that reassert old dogmas as revealed truth. But even those who do so continue to live in a mechanical world put together like an intricate clockwork by a prime mover who is an object of belief rather than of knowledge. The philosophers who sank the ship of Piscean metaphysics have merely been our spokesmen.

THE AGE OF AQUARIUS

Like it or not, we are the children of that syphilitic young aesthete, Friedrich Nietzsche. Because "God is dead" for us, transcendence exists only here, in human creativity. Nietzsche's "Overman" *recreates himself.* Nietzsche, the self-styled nihilist and anti-philosopher, rehabilitated that ancient dissolute, Dionysus, the god of intoxication and frenzy, who lives within us all as the spirit of creativity. Having lost our God, Heaven, and the afterlife—at least in the sense that no one fails to doubt them any more, at least in our most depressed and honest moments— we search again for transcendence, hoping to be intoxicated with a direct experience of cosmic consciousness and thereby recreate ourselves.

Today, more than 10,000 *networks* of New Age groups (König, 1988, p. 30) are trying to recreate themselves in retreats, workshops, and training programs on such cosmic-consciousness themes as meditation, shamanism, and aura manipulation. Most remarkable are those that center their interests around UFO phenomena. By one reckoning (Vallee, 1988, p. 231), some nine *million* Americans have experienced abductions by extraterrestrials in flying saucers, some of them discovering in the process that they themselves are "part alien." Others claim to be in telepathic communication with benevolent aliens who are sending us rays of wisdom and love which we are to "download" into our DNA structure and thereby discover our cosmic identity. The gods of Taurus seem to have returned.

To be fair, however, it must be admitted that New Age enthusiasms for what lies outside sensory verification are not trying to stand on the limb that Kant so decisively sawed off 200 years ago. They are supported, at least in part, by a new form of science. Newton's clockwork universe, which stimulated "universal doubt" and "radical skepticism," has itself been identified as a misleading abstraction by 20th-century science. It still works, as long as we confine our interest to the movement of large bodies, like planets, billiard balls, and molecules. But if we want to look at what comprises molecules or at movement that approaches the speed of light, Newtonian physics is useless.

Matter itself has become questionable. It used to be the only thing we "knew" for sure—whether as the objects of scientific certainty or the devilish distractions of the flesh people. Now it seems that matter may be just a peculiar form of energy. Furthermore, when we observe matter, we seem to change it (Heisenberg's "uncertainty principle"). Subjectivity and objectivity are no longer two separate realms, as Descartes believed and as the vast majority of us still take for granted. They seem to be related aspects of the same thing.

At the end of the 20th century, all bets are off. In one sense, we know the world better than anyone on Earth has ever known it before, and we have the technological advances to prove it. No generation before our own was able to send people to the moon, cross the Atlantic in three hours, observe in real time events taking place thousands of miles away, or efficiently manipulate a mind-boggling mass of data with computers. But in another sense, we know this world perhaps no better than our pre-Taurean ancestors.

As a species, we have spent the last 6000 years suppressing a natural human faculty located in the right side of our brains in order to discover ourselves as conscious subjects. If the New Age has anything revolutionary to offer, it must be the possibility of integrating rational methods with the visionary observations of cosmic consciousness: opening up our critical minds to a world of much wider scope and applying our conceptualizing abilities to the domain of cosmic consciousness. This is a very exciting prospect, although a dangerous one. Cosmic consciousness was suppressed for good reason. We need to look very carefully at what it is and where its dangers lie.

Chapter

3   SOJOURNS IN COSMIC CONSCIOUSNESS

If I say, "I'm New Age," does it mean I'm seeking a deeper planetary aware-ness, the emergence of a holistically oriented world, and a compassionate, em-powering attitude toward others? Or does it mean I'm interested in tarot cards, aura balancing, channeling, crystals, past lives, and a narcissistic pur-suit of magical powers?

(SPANGLER & THOMPSON, 1991, P. 56)

You are bushwhacking through consciousness, and you will come to a place where the vistas are grand and you have completely new options about where to go both on and off this planet.

(MARCINIAK, 1992, P. 78)

I asked these spirit figures if I was seeing them *or if I was seeing what was in my own brain. They answered, "Both."*

(GARRETT, 1967, P. 5)

If Out of Body Experiences *are "real," if the things Mr. Monroe describes cannot be dismissed as an interesting kind of fantasy or dream, our world view is going to change radically. And uncomfortably.*

(TART INTRO TO MONROE, 1977, P. 17)

new age began for me one cold morning in 1962, during a "time of power," when the Sun was trapped behind the used-car lots and apartment buildings to my right. The sky was overcast. My Desert Boots padded softly through the grime and desolation of Livernois Avenue in Detroit, as I grumbled toward the lecture hall where, the moment the bell rang, a cheery little bald man would start filling blackboard after blackboard with organic chemistry equations. I slogged through a world of numbers and formulas in order to marvel at the complex symmetries of the human body's molecular rhythms as they appeared on paper. If you wanted to glimpse those symmetries, you had to pay the price. I figured that was what life was about: paying the price. Truth to tell, there were a lot of prices I had not paid. The guilt these debts spawned billowed about my stooped form like a crowd of raucous crows.

That world "stopped" for good thirty-four years ago without the slightest warning. Suddenly, I *saw* that I was walking about two inches off the ground, still on Livernois, but in a world that was luminous with meaning. Nothing in my visual field gleamed or glowed that winter morning, but a tremendous weight fell off me—a weight I had hardly known could be released. As soon as it was gone, I knew I had no need of it. My life was between me and God and bore no requirement that I conform to others' expectations for what I did with it. Life became simpler and more joyful, and has remained so.

Sometimes these things happen to an unconscious fool who is stumbling in the wrong direction without knowing it. Sometimes it takes seven years of standing at the gate, begging the prayers of everyone who passes through. There is no telling what will cause a big enough gap in our stream of consciousness, or when it will happen. In fact, however, at the time of that monumental event, I had been meditating daily for six years, and it had produced other, smaller gaps.

The meditation I had learned boiled down to placing myself in the presence of God and just staying there, doing whatever I was moved to do, for fifteen minutes. I was always at a loss standing before God, knowing only that my thoughts should not be too idle. It had to be a time that was different. I could share my anxieties with God and ask Him to give me the strength to live up to some of my obligations. I could discuss my latest notions about what to do with my life. It seemed pretty inconsequential, probably a waste of God's time. But it produced moments, more and more frequently as time went on, when I found myself, involuntarily and without warning, in God's presence.

In retrospect, it seems that meditation had been about holding open a gap for fifteen minutes, struggling with the distractions that threatened to close it, so that I could recognize other gaps when they occurred. A decade or so later I learned that finding himself walking an inch or two above the ground was precisely how the great D. T. Suzuki, who brought Zen to the West, described his own first experience of *satori* (Watts, 1957, p. 22). Standing daily in the presence of God, which I continued for another seven years, had been my *koan*—just as begging at the gate had been Isidore's.

Before that morning in 1962, if anyone had asked me how I had occupied my mind during six years of standing before God, I would not have known what to say, beyond the obvious fact that I had struggled with distractions. Now, with the momentous event of *satori* behind me, I could give an answer much like Isidore's. In the first year it was an unwelcome drudgery. I persisted only because the high school teacher who had taught me the simple technique seemed to embody, in his understated spirituality and centeredness, a goal I might someday achieve myself. Evidently, his way of being had alerted me to the reality of a power I had not known existed and lacked the words to articulate. In the second year, my thoughts had much less to do with him, because I had begun to think perhaps I really *was* in God's presence. This carried its own subtle reward, although meditation was still mostly a struggle with distractions. This was when I began to notice the tiny gaps in which God became momentarily present in the midst of an English class or as I stood at a bus stop outside the "greasy spoon" at Greenfield and Seven Mile Road.

My *satori* marked the third stage. At that point, I entered a world that was merely the "inside" of a vast eternity. Working out a strategy for how to live a life faithful to that monumental "outside" became my principal concern, one that has been pursued without harassment from the crows of guilt. My consciousness "shifted" from the pursuit of imposed duties to the discovery of what is most meaningfully satisfying.

According to Don Juan Matus, a world "stops" when we terminate the internal monolog that sustains it. Before he was assigned to the gate, Isidore's monolog had to do with his learning and social attainments. Evidently, he had achieved considerable success in Alexandria, the cultural capital of his day, but still longed for a way of life that could satisfy his soul. He rightly looked for it in the Sinai desert, but brought his Alexandrian monolog with him. His arrogance and cruelty correspond to my guilt and oppression. They constitute ingrained and unconscious *strategies for dealing with the world*. This is what C. G. Jung called *persona*.

Originally, the word *persona* referred to the mask donned by actors through which their voices sounded (*per-sonare*, to "sound through"). We all don masks, more or less unconsciously, when we present ourselves to others. We pose as we wish to be seen, as we would like to see ourselves, or as we believe we are condemned to be.

In Alexandria, Isidore had lived at ease in a world of art, philosophy, and rhetoric. He gave the orders there, and was probably not wrong in considering himself "enlightened." No doubt he was a good deal wiser than most of our politicians, for he had glimpsed enough of the life of the soul to be dissatisfied with the glitz and glamor of the city. Very likely, he had been shocked by what he found in the desert at St. Catherine's: monks who could not even read, much less appreciate the subtleties of a well-made argument, rude men he would have thrown in jail back in the city for thievery and murder, men so plagued by their sex drive that they starved and beat themselves in hopes of achieving freedom from their unruly flesh.

When he asked himself how these low-life creatures could imagine themselves to be on the same spiritual path he was following, his internal monolog was sustaining his Alexandrian persona. What a childish and primitive faith these men had! How did they dare aspire to a moment of *satori*? When he was sent to the gate, Isidore took this Alexandrian persona with him—only now it was turned upside-down. In the first year, he was oppressed with the sinful arrogance that had "sold" him into this "slavery." Just to be seen at the gate by those creatures humiliated him so that he had to croak out his words "in bitterness and blood": *Pray for me, Father, for I am an epileptic.* He was the lowest of the low. The God of excellence and superiority was punishing him for his sins, just as he had punished the lawbreakers in the city of his birth.

By the second year, his humiliation had greatly diminished. He no longer saw himself as a jailed convict, but likened himself perhaps to a drunken trouble-maker in the city who had given up his wine and become a faithful street sweeper. He imagined God would reward him, much as he would have rewarded the reformed alcoholic. His interior monolog had changed. He no longer saw himself as destined by his excellence to rule, but as deserving in his submission to a higher law. Still, the fundamental structure of his world had not been "stopped," but was still patterned after imperial decrees. He had only accepted a more humble station in that hierarchy. The gaps opened by his meek pose revealed a world of greater power than he had at first imagined, but that world continued to resemble the urban structure of his origins. In the greater scheme of things, he did not belong at the gate. His begging was merely an exercise designed to enable him to rise to a station that better suited his talents.

In the third year, the Alexandrian structure of his lifeworld broke up and fell away. His monolog changed radically, and the gaps appeared in an entirely new place. God was no longer the enlightened ruler of Earth, styled after the potentates of Alexandria. Now God appeared in those rude monks he had formerly disdained. He saw their devotion to the world of soul, that they really lived in that world, that they enjoyed an intimacy with God foreign to his earlier anticipations. Now God, in His Wholly Otherness, passed through the gate, clad in dusty, worn robes, shining from the countenances of those unlettered men: *I lost the courage to look anyone in the face, but lowering my eyes and lowering my thoughts even further, I asked with true sincerity for the prayers of those going in and out.*

He had heard "the sound of one hand clapping." The hand of God clapped silently in the glow of those simple monks. The gaps through which the world of soul gleams appeared precisely in the last place he expected to find them. The world of Alexandria had been "stopped" for good. Finally, he could take his place among those monks, but, for Isidore, there was now no point in doing so. The *koan* of begging at the gate had completed his life's work. He had learned why he had come to the desert and, indeed, why he had been born. He could die in peace and gratitude.

Thirteen centuries ago, the flesh world was clearly more than the beastliness of compulsive instinctual gratification. It was any life strategy that excluded the gaps through which soul might appear. In this sense, Isidore's battle with the arrogance of education and enlightened rulership was essentially no different from that of the crude sensualists. In both cases, short-sighted persona strategies and the monologs that sustained them distracted monks from the gaps.

If this all sounds archaic and primitive to us today, we have to be careful not to fall victim to a New Age arrogance in which our scientists, philosophers, and psychics have elevated us far above the world of the Ladder Man, blinding our eyes to the gaps all around us. Let us, therefore, imitate Isidore and stand at the gate of the New Age to see who is passing in and out. What kind of glow resides in the faces of our contemporaries, and how did they relinquish their own persona strategies? How has the contentious, ambitious, and frightfully insecure world of the 20th century been "stopped" for them? And what difference has it made?

THE COSMIC ADVENTURES OF ROBERT A. MONROE

It would be hard to find a better contemporary guide to the landscape of cosmic consciousness than Robert A. Monroe, a southern businessman and media executive who began taking out-of-body journeys in 1958, long before New Age enthusiasms had been dreamt of (Monroe, 1977,

1985, 1994). His experiences began without conscious effort or intention. In fact, he found the initial sensations frighteningly unpleasant: a painful tightness in the region of his diaphragm and uncontrollable vibrations in his body. Unable to get satisfactory advice from physicians, psychologists, or clergy, he decided to relax, stop fighting the sensations, and see what would happen. Improbably enough, he found that he left his body behind in bed and traveled to three distinct "locales." He took detailed notes of his journeys, mercifully eschewing wild speculation and leaving us a dependable set of organized data.

Monroe's "Locale I" is the world of ordinary experience, but visited "out-of-body," that is by "clairvoyance." Being a highly rational man, Monroe was skeptical of what he was *seeing* in his *imaginal* journeys, and so spent years performing experiments to verify the accuracy of these visionary events. Although he achieved a good deal of success in this rational "science," after fifteen or twenty years, he became bored with fact-finding travel and decided to let the *dream* take him where *it* wanted him to go. Thus began a series of adventures that took him out of this world—into "Locale II." He met spirit beings who have never been human and others who were the souls of men and women who had died. He acquired some remarkable and even grisly perspectives.

Monroe learned that a fleshly life trapped in the empirical world of space and time is nothing but a fight for survival by plants, animals, and people, each sustaining its own existence by devouring others. The creator of this savage prison derives nourishment from the energy released by all these deaths. When Monroe traveled out-of-body, however, and left the narrow confines of space and time, he arrived at a cosmic perspective that placed the myth of the dark demiurge in context. He discovered that his full (spiritual) identity took the form of a dome of luminous fibers, very much like the top half of the luminous egg Carlos Castaneda *saw* when he looked at a human being with shamanic eyes. Each fiber had its own color and, when touched, brought Monroe into *imaginal* contact with a unique alternate life. Some of these fragments of Monroe's wholeness were living on Earth in the past, present, and future; others lived in other worlds. It is the wholeness of the luminous dome that is essential. It sends aspects of itself to live a space-and-time existence on Earth in order to *learn*. When it has accumulated enough learning, the dome will return "Home" to the One.

"Locale III" appears to be our own world, but lived separately by the alter-egos which comprised Monroe's luminous dome. One of these was a woman struggling in vain to save her family from the bubonic plague, another was a 12th-century warrior killed by a spear in the back at age 18, and a third was a lonely and ineffectual architect-contractor in the 20th century, unable to sustain relationships or keep a job.

Monroe's journeys constitute a veritable encyclopedia of New Age experiences: clairvoyance, contact with spirit beings, the nature of the aura, "simultaneous past lives," a new interpretation of life and death, the value of *seeing* and *imagination*, and even shamanism. In his eighties before his recent death, Monroe made his main work the rescuing of the souls of people who had died but become lost in lower levels of the spirit world. This was one of the classic functions of the shaman in traditional societies: to lead the souls of the dead to their destinations in the other world.

Monroe's luminous dome bears a close resemblance to Castaneda's luminous egg, and his dark demiurge living on death has much in common with Castaneda's giant black eagle standing on the boundary between this world and the next in order to consume the souls of the departed. Only those who have perfected the power of *seeing* will have their wits about them sufficiently to avoid the eagle's beak and enter eternity with their individuality intact.

Robert Monroe and the many others who have traveled out-of-body insist their experiences cannot be understood as dreams. They give at least four reasons for this. First, their journeys have none of the arbitrary, absurd, highly personal, and easily forgettable qualities of the dreams we all have at night. They are encountering an incontrovertible *reality*. For example, lions may sometimes escape from their cages, both in dream zoos and in zoos made of iron and stone. If we are standing too close, our fear of the rampaging lion will be much the same in either case, because the dream lion is as objective and dangerous for our dream-ego as any flesh-and-blood lion in our waking experience.

But Monroe's journeying is different. When he travels out-of-body to a zoo in "Locale I" and finds a lion escaping from its cage, he has to hurry back to his body and place an emergency phone call, because he knows beyond any shadow of doubt that a flesh-and-blood lion is actually on the loose inside a specific iron-and-stone zoo. This kind of reality is very rare in ordinary dreams, but not in Monroe's journeys. His painstaking experiments in clairvoyance have repeatedly, though not uniformly, demonstrated such empirical facts. Ordinary dreams may reveal private, psychological facts about the dreamer; but out-of-body journeys may gain access to verifiable public facts.

We have a language for this kind of knowing. We say that out-of-body journeys are *imaginal* events: *dreams* rather than dreams. Unimpressed, Monroe urges us not to limit our attention to clairvoyance, citing the second reason why these experiences cannot be dismissed as dreams. Monroe is journeying for us all, discovering the features of an objective cosmos. He does not want us to accept this as an article of faith, but rather as a possibility that can be experienced by everyone.

In this regard, Monroe's journeys closely resemble the *dreams* that C. G. Jung calls "big dreams." In *Memories, Dreams, Reflections,* Jung describes his trip to Mount Elgon in East Africa, where he found that the Elgonyi distinguish little, personal dreams from those that have significance for the whole community (Jung, 1961, pp. 258–272). "Big dreams" might advise the people to move their village, to hunt for game in a certain distant valley, or to beware of enemies approaching. They belong to the inborn human capability we have called cosmic consciousness. Out-of-body journeys surely seem to be a kind of "big dream."

In contrast to Monroe's optimism that anyone can gain access to these experiences, the Elgonyi find that only specially gifted individuals are able to *dream* for the community. In fact, they declined to tell Jung any *dreams* at all because, now that the English colonial governor was in charge of their daily lives, they said *he* had all the *dreams*. Apparently a "big dreamer" only emerges when the community needs direction. The Elgonyi thus may not have considered "big dreams" as a universal possibility.

In the last analysis, this is not so different from Monroe's view. Monroe presents himself as the exceptional individual who has managed to escape from Plato's cave. To show us that the ordinary world we take for granted is only a ghost of the larger reality of human life, Plato used a parable about a group of individuals chained from birth inside a cave, with their backs to the opening. What they can see are shadows of worldly events taking place outside the cave and cast upon the wall before them. Since they have never been outside the cave, they take this shadow-play as the whole of the world. One of them, however, manages to slip his bonds and escape. He brings back a report of three-dimensional men, animals, and trees, all alive in glorious color, and of a Sun that rises in the morning and sets in the evening. The captives refuse to believe his story and even consider putting him to death for his dangerous ideas—a fate similar to that of Plato's teacher, Socrates (Plato, 1961, pp. 747–751).

This brings us to Monroe's third claim, that his journeys are not dreams because the realities he encounters in them are so overwhelmingly vivid and "real"—more compellingly real and filled with significance than even his waking life. Indeed, the greater cosmos of "Locale II" is a larger reality, and our empirical world merely its shadow. He cannot prove this to us, any more than Plato's escapee could prove his findings to his enchained companions. But he asserts that the *experience* of that cosmos will convince anyone by its vividness. He knows he risks our ridicule in taking such a position and does not wish to force it on us. His attitude is similar to that of Don Juan Matus or John Climacus: Once you have *seen* the *nagual* or the world of soul, you cannot doubt its reality; beforehand it seems absurd. Thus, if we wish to continue to call Monroe's journey's *dreams*, we will have to recall that the *imaginal* world is more vivid and "real" for its sojourners than the sensory world is for us.

The fourth reason Monroe gives for not viewing his journeys as dreams is that he retains his ordinary consciousness while out-of-body. He knows he is in non-ordinary reality and never forgets his body slumbers at home in bed. "Little dreams," by contrast, so thoroughly submerge us in the dreamscape that we lose sight of the fact that we are no longer awake. We think there is a flesh-and-blood lion after us, about to snap off our hind leg at the knee. Should Monroe face a lion while out-of-body, he would be more terrified—if possible—than we. He knows it is not a bodily lion and so has no fear that his sleeping body will be mauled. He quakes for the journeying body—his greater reality. For when the fleshly body dies, the journeyer lives on. But if the journeyer should die, it is all over.

Thus the cosmic journeyer claims, not only that his *dream*scape is a larger and more complete reality than our everyday landscape, but that the Robert who enters that world is a larger and more complete Monroe. At first glance, this seems to echo what psychoanalysis has been telling us for a hundred years. Our conscious, waking identity is only the smaller part of ourselves. When we take our dreams seriously, we discover aspects of our unconscious identity that fill out and complete our understanding of who we are. The lion in our dreams is part of that larger Self—a raging, aggressive part. If the lion devours us, we fall into a state of blind, uncontrollable rage and do damage to ourselves and others. On the other hand, if we can find a way to "integrate" that lion, we become more effective personalities, more assertive, perhaps, and in touch with our instincts.

Again, Monroe responds that we have missed the point. We are still trying to find a way to be more comfortable in our Earthly chains by interpreting the shadows on the wall. The denizens of the cave are never in danger of being devoured by the shadow lion. But the cosmic lion (or in Castaneda's imagery, the eagle) threatens us with a real and ultimate *death*. We will never grasp the significance of out-of-body journeys until we dare to face our own demise.

THE GUARDIAN AT THE GATE

In fact, there is no "cosmic lion" in Monroe's books, but there is a great pseudo-god, a demiurge, who lives on death (Monroe, 1985, pp. 162–181). This unnamed being of unknown gender has turned the Earth into that balanced ecology of death we call the food chain. All of us, from one-celled organisms to philosophers and mystics, kill one another to nourish ourselves. In the beginning, the demiurge (or "partial power," "lower potentate," what the Gnostics called an Archon) was interested in death itself, in any form in which it occurred; for the energy released at a being's death supplied an essential force to enhance the tyrant's own existence. But as time passed, the demigod discovered that the highest quality energy emanated from the death of sentient beings. The higher the consciousness attained by a bodily being—the more aware it is of its tenuous hold on life and its terror of death—the more valuable the nourishment released at its demise. The clinging to life, the panicky struggle to survive, the longing and desolation occasioned by the passing of loved ones, the cruelty and aggression that drives off competitors—all these emotions enhance the death energy and delight the demiurge.

Monroe was shaken and appalled by this vision, but unable to evade its truth. It surely describes the bottom line of fleshly existence. Humans are, by and large, flesh people, obsessed by their survival drive. From the moment we are born, we are on our way to death. Although we suppress this knowledge in a bad-faith attempt to shake the horror residing in our hearts, we act from it constantly. It blinds us to the gaps through which soul might appear. We are the inmates and guards of our own fleshly prisons, snarling at threats both real and imagined, and poised to pounce on every opportunity to enhance our precarious and illusory security.

Human existence is "Being-toward-death," says Martin Heidegger, the most important philosopher to write about ultimate things in the wake of Nietzsche's proclamation of the end of metaphysics. Neitzsche himself depicted the Earth as a great ball of death. The soil of our planet is comprised of the decomposing corpses of those who have gone before us, the plants and animals that flowered, swam, galloped, and soared through a few exceptional moments before succumbing to the inevitable fate of providing inanimate fodder for those to follow. Life is the exception, death the constant.

Monroe's vision of the demiurge who lives on death brings us vividly back to the barren Sinai desert of the seventh century, where the

Ladder Man's disciples fought their fleshly compulsions by fasting, flagellation, all-night prayer, and standing at the gate. Death lies at the center of the teachings of Don Juan Matus as well. Stretch out your left arm to the side, straight from the shoulder. Don't look! Your death is standing there, less than three feet away, watching, waiting, ready to strike at any moment (Castaneda, 1971, p. 238).

Flesh people cringe when they glimpse death out of the corner of their eye. A "warrior," however, profits from death's constant presence. The instant we stop fleeing the certain knowledge of our impending demise, death becomes our "advisor." We act with the constant knowledge that our time on this Earth is limited, and we begin to attend to essential matters. We stop wasting our time. We get down to the business of our own unique, never-to-be-repeated life. We live it, in the imagery of Nietzsche, as though our existence were condemned to be repeated over and over for all eternity. What would I do right now, if I knew it were my last moment on Earth? What would I do if I knew I would face this moment again in lifetime after lifetime, and my act would determine the quality of this moment for all eternity? I would choose the act that best enhances my existence—the most powerful act, the most compassionate, the most far-reaching. The blinders would fall from my eyes. Life would be simpler and more convincing.

Death has been the underlying theme in everything we have examined in our survey of six thousand years. The Mayoruna burned their village every morning in order to get to the aperture between the worlds and renew their essential existence as soul people who live in a greater cosmos. What a difference between them and the Bosnian Serb I heard interviewed on the radio this morning. That man, driven by survival fear, hatred, and illusions of ethnic superiority, calmly stated that he was moving to Serbia and would burn his house when he left so that no Muslim could ever occupy it. He is caught in a panic-driven cunning that originated in the Age of Aries, all but extinguishing cosmic consciousness. The Gnostics, at the dawn of Pisces, scorned their own mortal flesh in a quest for the deathless realm of soul and spirit. The story of Jesus depicts a man who embraced death in fear and trembling in order to be faithful to his divine identity and be resurrected in a body that passed through walls and ascended into Heaven. The Victorian table-rappers and channelers communed with the souls of the deceased to reassure themselves that life will survive death, even the death of the 19th century. Our own anxieties belong here, too, as we face the death of a millennium and a zodiacal eon, hoping for a more satisfying and meaningful existence in the New Age.

That death lurking an arm's length from Castaneda's left shoulder is poised to enter through his abdomen. In order to *see* with the eyes of his soul, he has to open a gap in that region of his luminous egg. He stretches out luminous fibers through that opening to manipulate the *imaginal* cosmos, but must stand guard every second, prepared to slam the gap shut before his death slips in. Shamanizing treads a narrow line marking the boundary between the everyday world of space and time and that monumental world that most of us enter only after our last breath. The shaman plays with his mortality, tempting death, in order to steal the greater secrets that lie beyond what our fleshly eyes can see.

Monroe was all too familiar with that deadly game. When, in 1958, he stumbled involuntarily over the line and found himself hovering near the ceiling, looking down upon his sleeping body, he thought, "I am dying, this is death." He became afraid to sleep, even to lie down, because the next time he might not make it back. His waking life was filled with panic-driven visions of brain tumors and insanity. Medical specialists were puzzled. Christian ministers spoke as politely as they could of demonic possession. The vibrations and tightness in his diaphragm, premonitory signs of departing his body, would not go away. It was quite a while before he could contain his survival panic long enough to remain separated from his body for a few seconds at a time. He feared each episode would be his last moment on Earth. There was nothing rewarding about this experience. It was a torment of terror and completely out of control.

He came to call this fear his "animal panic," because it was totally involuntary and instinctual, a last-ditch clutching at life in the face of certain death—like a mouse in the jaws of a cat. He had been journeying for some fourteen years when he published his first book, *Journeys Out of the Body* (1977), but still he had to remind himself before every sojourn that he had not died yet and would probably not die this time either. The reason and logic of his left brain provided little security against the timeless visions of the right hemisphere.

The reader of Monroe's books, sitting in an easy chair, sipping a favorite beverage, may well become impatient with his constant references to the fear of death. What is wrong with this man, we want to say. Does he not realize this is just a *dream*? When we react like this, we are missing the point. This is precisely why Monroe insists his journeys are not dreams. He is encountering more awful realities than our left brains will tolerate, realities that begin with the first fundamental fact of his conscious fleshly existence: that he is Being-toward-death.

Monroe's journeys are not reflections on death. They are encounters with death. By the time his first book appeared, he had faced death at least a hundred times a year for a decade and a half. It is only in his second book, *Far Journeys* (1985), however, published almost three decades after his sojourns began, that he says: "Once the *fear* barrier is crossed, the individual begins to know, rather than believe, that he does survive physical death" (Monroe, 1985, p. 30). It is reasonable to guess that he had journeyed more than twenty years before he had that moment of enlightenment, when the weight of his "animal panic" fell away.

Let us put John Climacus' question to the Robert A. Monroe who emerges from the pages of his three books: *How did you occupy your mind during those twenty years of staring death in the eye?* In the first year, he did his best not even to glance in death's direction. It had not been his idea to leave his body in the first place. He just found himself thrust out. One moment he was lying in bed, trying not to fight the tightness in his diaphragm, and the next moment he was floating, looking down in horror at the body asleep on the bed. He knew death was nearer than she had ever been, and he did not want her to get any closer. So he immediately dove down at the slumbering form below him, and the next moment was relieved again to find the covers on top of him, the mattress underneath, and the ceiling back up where it belonged.

In the second year, he tested death. What would she do if he hovered for a few seconds before scurrying back to safety? What would she do if he floated over to the door and took a peek into the hallway? Would the stairs be in their usual place, or would he find himself in one of those topsy-turvy dream-houses? He floated furtively, alert for the slightest indication that death might be sidling closer—and not at all sure that he would be able to detect such a thing. He tested death's limits, cautiously and with his heart in his mouth. When he could bear the tension no longer, he would zip back to his body, relieved that he had eluded death one more time. In this second year, he never ventured more than ten feet from the bed.

In the third year, he decided somewhat uneasily that death was not particularly interested in how far he traveled. He still journeyed anxiously, but he dared to visit the houses of friends and set up experiments to determine the accuracy of his out-of-body observations. Was he *seeing* what was really taking place at the party in his friend's living room, and precisely at the moment it was happening? He would call his friend the next day to find out. In this phase, he was still eluding death, failing to look her in the eye. He was distracting himself with his experiments, pretending death did not care what he did. But it was a bad-faith assumption, an attempt to deny the soul-shaking dread that pursued him, both in this world and in that.

It was some twenty years before he had his *satori* and the weight of his dread fell away for good. He was on one of the mid-level spheres of "Locale II," the world of soul, meeting with one of his non-human friends, discussing the nature of the cosmos. This was when he received the legend of the demiurge who lives on death. He was horrified and depressed for weeks, as he turned the grisly details over and over in his mind. He found it was true. The bottom line. As soon as he knew how unavoidably accurate the legend was, it dawned on him: survival from impending death is the law of the *flesh world*. That is what keeps it going. Flesh people are trapped in the world of space and time by their terror of death. They are so preoccupied with survival that they cannot see the greater cosmos through which Monroe sojourns so regularly. Yes, he will die, and he would rather it not be too soon, for he still has much to learn. But when his body dies, his identity will survive and continue its sojourns.

Now, for the first time, he can really look death in the eye. He *sees* that he has not been cheating her and could never have done so. Furthermore, he no longer wants to. Death is inevitable. She will come when she will. Meanwhile, he will make the most of what time he has left to learn what he can, enhance his existence in whatever way he can discover. His time is now as precious to him as to anyone who has looked death in the eye and been granted a few more years to live life more earnestly and enthusiastically.

LEAVING THE BODY

Monroe, who had a high respect for statistics and careful experimentation, estimated that 25 percent of the American population has had at least one out-of-body experience (Monroe, 1985, p. 4). Many of these occur at times of physical and psychological crisis, such as automobile accidents and surgical operations. Celia Green's dry catalogue (*Out-of-the-Body Experiences*, 1968) details many that occurred in unexceptional circumstances, as when walking down a familiar street or while gardening. But most seem to have taken place during some period of stress in the individual's life—perhaps during a frightening dream or, more likely, during a mid-life crisis.

It is evident, that in 1958, when Monroe's involuntary departures from his body began, he was in the midst of a mid-life crisis. Few details are provided, but he reports a tension between his wife and himself over religion. She was a devoted Catholic, while he was a confirmed agnostic. His first out-of-body experiences, in fact, occurred on Sunday mornings when his wife and daughters were attending Mass and he was home alone. His wife was deeply disturbed by his accounts of what had been happening to him, believing there was something forbidden and anti-Christian about her husband's experiences. In his second book, we learn that Monroe has left his wife and married Nancy Penn, a woman familiar with "psychic" experiences and an enthusiastic supporter of his researches in non-ordinary reality. Monroe also quite frankly reports in his third book, *Ultimate Journey* (1994), written after Nancy's death, that this second marriage has had an erotic and spiritual dimension that had formerly been unknown to him. The reader of my earlier book on the spiritual and transcendent dimensions of erotic love (*Divine Madness*, 1990) will not be surprised to learn this, for Eros affords us a readily available doorway into the world of the soul.

Although New Age enthusiasts with a poor sense of history, like R. M. Bucke (*Cosmic Consciousness*, 1977), are inclined to see out-of-body journeys as evidence of a new development in the evolution of human consciousness, studies in the history of shamanism will dispel this notion. It is beyond question that shamans have been leaving their bodies to journey in the greater cosmos for tens of thousands of years. Mircea Eliade's classic summary of the evidence (*Shamanism: Archaic Techniques of Ecstasy*, 1964) makes the out-of-body experience definitive of shamanism. Ecstasy (*ek-stasis*, to stand outside oneself) is what distinguishes the shaman from other practitioners of the sacred.

Shamans are typically "elected" by the spirits during a life-threatening illness during which they leave their bodies and travel to the "underworld," where they watch their body being dismembered by spirit-shamans. Perhaps the flesh is ripped off their bones or boiled in a great pot. Then their bones are reassembled with a significant difference. The new bones may be made of stone or crystal or connected to one another with bands of iron. In this way, they acquire a new journeying body, one that is stronger and capable of monumental feats in the world of soul. Shamans generally heal the sick by traveling in the greater cosmos to recover the errant soul of the patient and restore it to the body. They also conduct the souls of the dead to their "home" in the other world. In this ancient tradition, cosmic consciousness gains access to an invisible realm, greater than the world of space and time, that has causative effects upon our ordinary world.

Monroe's twenty-year struggle with the *koan* of staring death in the eye corresponds rather well with the traditional shaman's experience of dismemberment. Furthermore, Monroe was inclined to believe, although reluctant to say, that he had discovered the reality of the soul. Because *soul* seemed a theologically dubious word to him—tainted as it was with Christian conceptions he could not accept—he preferred to speak of the "second body." Unwittingly, however, he has touched here upon another strand in the history of religion. In 1871, Sir Edward Tylor published *Primitive Culture* (1974), in which he argued that all religion derives from early humans' dreaming experience. Because dreams seemed to be a kind of sojourn in another world, while the body remained asleep at home, Tylor reasoned that primitive humanity was led to postulate the existence of a soul that could roam free of the sleeping body, and that the plants, animals, people, and even stones met in their dreams were understood to be the souls of those physical beings. Tylor called his theory "animism," the idea that everything in the world possesses a soul (*anima*) which "animates" it and gives it invisible power.

Tylor's animism provides an interesting bridge between the cosmic consciousness of our pre-Taurean ancestors and the experiences of New Age pioneers like Monroe. Still it has not been a widely accepted theory, as it seems to turn our primitive forebears into 19th-century philosophers, constructing a metaphysics of the soul and the greater cosmos that requires a great deal of left-brain thinking. Very likely, Tylor was too much of an armchair philosopher. But it seems to be a fact that our ancestors many thousands of years ago did live in a world more animate than our own and paid a great deal more attention to their dreams. Surely shamans, since time immemorial, have been living in the world Tylor describes.

A final piece of evidence: the alchemists, too, seem to have lived in the world of animism. The objects of their proto-science were all conceived of as ensouled. They spoke of working with the *souls* of mercury, salts, metals, and water; and not a few of their experiential reports suggest out-of-body journeying. For example, one of the very earliest alchemists in the Western tradition was a certain Zosimos of Panopolis, who lived in the third century of Pisces, when the flame of Gnosticism had not yet guttered out. Zosimos was both a Gnostic and an alchemist, who left behind a record of his visions. In one of them, he meets a priest who tells him that the first step in personal transformation is "casting away the grossness of the body":

> I submit myself to an unendurable torment. For there came to me
> one in haste at early morning, who overpowered me, and pierced
> me through with the sword, and dismembered me in accordance

with the rule of harmony. And he drew off the skin of my head with the sword, which he wielded with strength, and mingled the bones with the pieces of flesh, and caused them to be burned upon the fire of the art, till I perceived by the transformation of the body that I had become spirit (quoted in Jung, 1967, p. 60).

In another vision, a barber appears to him and says, "Those who seek to obtain the art enter here, and become spirits by escaping from the body" (Jung, 1967, p. 60).

In the 17th century, one of the last of the alchemists, Gerard Dorn, described the sought-for transformation as a three-stage process (discussed in Jung, 1963, pp. 457–552). The first step is a kind of death, in which the soul separates from the body, for in the natural, fleshly condition, the human soul is too much under the influence of the body's sensory and instinctual compulsions. After separation from the body, however, the soul falls under the higher influence of the spirit and forms with it a "mental union" (*unio mentalis*) which opens the soul's eyes to greater realities. Once this has been achieved, the spirit/soul union is rejoined to the body (stage two). Now the individual is a bodily being who is open to spiritual realities. In the third stage, the body/soul/spirit of the alchemist is united with the "unitary world" (*unus mundus*), which is the world as it existed "before the first day of creation." This is surely what we have been calling cosmic consciousness, an awareness of the greater cosmos as it exists in itself outside of space and time. For space and time did not exist until the creation of this material world.

Thus, there is a tremendously rich and continuous tradition in human history wherein spiritual transformation requires some kind of out-of-body journeying. Very likely, most of those who left their bodies were individuals who had reached some kind of crisis in their daily lives: a profound physical shock, such as an accident or surgical operation; a crisis of identity, such as most people undergo at mid-life; or a crisis of worldview, the kind of thing that may have led Isidore to leave Alexandria for the Sinai desert or influenced a psychologist like Lawrence LeShan who has become a psychic healer, or modern physicists like Fred Alan Wolf who immersed himself in shamanism, and Wolfgang Pauli who tried to complete the theory of quantum mechanics with the psychology of C. G. Jung.

How are we to make sense of this universal human capability of taking leave of the body and journeying through a greater cosmos as a soul, "second body" (Monroe), or "double" (Castaneda)? Do we take it as a *literal* fact that we each have some kind of "subtle body" which resembles our "gross body" in all respects except its physicality? Or do we take it as a *symbolic* fact, suggesting that the greater cosmos is not a "place" at all and the subtle body not a "thing" at all, but rather that the journeys are dream-like experiences? In calling them *dreams*, in the spirit of Castaneda, we take a middle position. They are symbolic events that are also objective. They are "bigger" than personal dreams because they bring the journeyer into contact with realities that exist outside of what can be verified by the senses. Because *dreams* gain access to *imaginal* truth, Monroe may indeed have been journeying for us all.

The *sight* of the body lying on the bed is surely a clairvoyant vision, essentially no different from Monroe's journey to his friend's living room. In both cases, the fleshly eyes are closed and remain ensconced in the head resting on the pillow. The *seeing* of the body is an *imaginal* event: true, objective, and indubitable, but non-sensory. No fleshly eyes see it. The body is an *imaginal* representation available through the cosmic consciousness of the right brain, a point of view that Monroe explicitly accepts. But because the experience can be questioned, remembered, collated, and conceptualized, Monroe's left brain is also at work. In short, the whole brain that is encased in the head on the pillow is receiving and processing the image of the body, as well as the *dream*scape of the greater cosmos.

The ego of Monroe's left brain and the "collective unconscious" of his right brain cooperate in his visions. Monroe believed he had proven this to be the case by developing a method to help others to leave their bodies and enter cosmic consciousness with their egos intact. He had a laboratory in Virginia supplied with waterbeds and headphones (Monroe, 1985, pp. 16–25). The subject relaxed on a bed, while tones of separate frequencies were sent to the two ears, each neurologically connected to its separate side of the brain. The whole brain "heard" neither of them, but rather a third frequency, located midway between what its right and left halves were registering. It is this third, *imagined*, frequency, Monroe believes, which enables the soul to leave the body. His procedure parallels what Castaneda experienced when he learned to enter the *nagual* (cosmic consciousness) while his two guides, Don Juan and Don Genaro were whispering incompatible messages into his separate ears (Castaneda, 1974, p. 261). Castaneda felt himself undergoing a disturbing split whereby he seemed to be simultaneously in two worlds, until the visions coalesced and he entered the monumentally shocking world of the *nagual*.

We might speculate that our ordinary "little" dreams rely primarily on the right brain, while ordinary waking consciousness relies primarily on the left hemisphere. We can postulate a spectrum of human consciousness in which the far-left region (corresponding to the left brain) is devoted to waking consciousness and the far-right to the dreams of ordinary sleep. In the middle section, rarely or never visited by the majority of us, are the "waking dreams"—visionary experiences entertained by an observer who retains her ego-functions of questioning, discrimination, and choice, together with the memory that her body lies asleep.

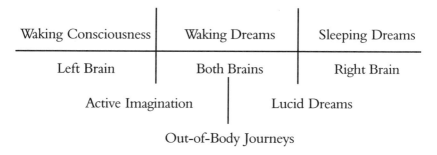

Figure 1. Spectrum of human consciousness.

The waking dreams within the central portion of this spectrum may be of several types. Perhaps the simplest type occurs through the process Jung calls "active imagination." This takes place on the boundary line between waking consciousness and waking dreams. Subjects remain awake, but in a light trance. Beginning with a spontaneous fantasy, or more likely a scene from a "little" dream of the night before, he deliberately withholds the critical faculties of his left brain to allow the fantasy to develop. Never losing his awareness that this is an imaginal experience and that he is seated in his living room, the user of active imagination retains the understanding and will of his ego. He can leap into the raging torrent to save the maiden in distress, or he can stand helplessly on the bank and watch her being swept away.

My own experiences with active imagination confirm what most people report, namely that we suspect we are "making it all up." The critical faculties of the ego resist the reality and validity of what is being seen. We can test the validity, however, by trying to force the imagery to follow our conscious will. If the fantasy process obliges us, Jung says, we are not doing active imagination; we are simply daydreaming. Only when the process retains its unconscious integrity can this experience be called a waking dream.

I once pursued an active imagination process over the course of several weeks, devoting a half-hour a day to observing, participating in, and recording the story unfolding in my waking dream. At one point, I found myself in an underground room piled high on all sides with unmarked cardboard cartons. In the center of the room was a large birdcage containing a fierce hawk. Without thinking, I walked directly toward the cage, intending to pick it up and carry it back outside to the open air, when suddenly I stopped, wondering what was in the cartons. I lifted one of them down to open it, but was surprised to find that it disappeared as soon as I set it on the floor. It had returned to its former position, stacked against the wall. I lifted it down again, and again it disappeared. After three or four attempts, I gave up. Clearly, my waking dream was uninterested in the cartons. I therefore proceeded to the birdcage, where the real interest lay, and my active imagination continued. Evidently, too much willfulness on the part of the ego interrupts the integrity of the dreaming process.

At the other end of the waking-dream spectrum, where the fantasy process shades off into sleeping dreams, reside what have lately been identified as "lucid dreams." Lucid dreams begin in sleep, but at some point the dreamer becomes aware that she is dreaming. Most people have some recollection of lucid dreaming, usually from childhood. Today, there is a small library of books available that describe lucid dreams and give procedures to encourage them.

Castaneda began his dreamwork by developing a capacity for lucid dreaming. Following Don Juan's advice, he sought to awaken his ego-consciousness in the midst of a dream by deliberately looking at his hands in his sleep. Once he knew he was seeing his hands in a dream, he would have the conscious will power to attend to any image in the dream that he chose. Castaneda says it took many years of trying before he could remember to look at his hands in his sleep. When he was able to do so, however, he was presented with a new problem. Either he got so excited at having succeeded that he woke himself up, or else the dream suddenly became so interesting that he forgot he was dreaming and became immersed again in the sleeping dreamscape (Castaneda, 1974, pp. 18–20).

Thus lucid dreaming constitutes a precarious balance between the conscious functioning of the ego and the unconscious integrity of the dream. Lucid dreams seem to appear as gaps in dreaming consciousness, moments when the ego slips in—just as the gaps in our waking consciousness allow the *dream* to slip in. Unlike active imagination, lucid dreaming never seems to be vulnerable to the suspicion that I am making it all up. It is vulnerable rather to a different problem: the incompatibility between the waking world of the ego and the compelling imagery of the dream.

These problems do not seem to arise in out-of-body journeys, where ego and dream, left and right hemispheres, are cooperating in balance. For this reason, I locate out-of-body journeying in the center of the waking-dream spectrum. What brings Monroe back from his sojourns in the greater cosmos is not the ego's excitement ("Oh look, I'm dreaming. I've finally done it, isn't it wonderful!"). Rather it is some discomfort in the sleeping body, a full bladder or the shutting off of circulation in a limb—the same sort of discomfort that wakens us all from our nocturnal dreams. Or sometimes it may be that the dream events become so scary that the dreamer retreats to the body to escape—just as we may unconsciously retreat from an ordinary falling dream by waking up before we touch bottom.

The defining experience of out-of-body journeys seems to be the vision of the sleeping body from an outside vantage point. On the one hand, we can understand this as a mere matter of fact. It is "nothing but" another dreaming vision. If my dream can take me to Central Park in New York City or to the home of my childhood in Detroit, why not to the room in which I am sleeping? What is so extraordinary about *seeing* myself asleep? Do I not have numerous dreams in which I am both the actor in the dream and also an outside observer?

Monroe and Castaneda could not be so sanguine. Observing their bodies asleep constituted a monumental shock for them. We will never understand the nature of out-of-body journeys until we grasp the emotional power of that shock. To *see* that body is to know that *it is not me*. Such knowledge disrupts everything I have known about myself from earliest childhood until now. We all take it for granted that we are the person we remember and perceive ourselves to be. Our awareness of ourselves is completely bound up with the history of that body, all the things that have happened to us and all the choices we have made. The world we live in is an assemblage of all we have learned while walking about in that body.

To stand outside my body and *know* my vision is real, is to be exposed to the unthinkable. The world cannot be as I have constructed it; it is unimaginably different. It constitutes the death of everything I have come to know and depend upon. I am not who I thought I was, and the world is not as I assembled it. I have entered a realm that is Wholly Other, and I have not the faintest idea what it is or how to negotiate it. The habitual monolog that sustains my world is centered in the body, and the body is over there, lying on the bed, while I stand here in the doorway. I no longer know who I am. I have lost all certainties. Nothing is dependable. Anything can happen. I am a powerless mote blown willy-nilly in an endless ether.

I have passed through the gap. The flesh person I always knew myself to be lies immobile on the bed. I do not know how to be a soul.

STRUGGLES WITH THE FLESH

Death may have been Monroe's Guardian at the Gate that leads to the other world, but lust was waiting for him just over the brink. He warns his reader about the overwhelming emotional pressure of unconscious drives,

> because you are no longer just a conscious, intelligent self. You are, perhaps for the first time, an entirety. Every part of you will be heard from, and must be considered in any action that you take. The trick is to keep the conscious, reasoning you (the one most cognizant of the physical world) in a dominant position. It isn't easy (Monroe, 1977, p. 223).

As soon as the fear of death had become manageable enough that he could feel other emotions, Monroe found himself assailed by that chaotic bundle of instincts and drives he called his "entirety." It may have been "entire," but it was hardly a whole. There was nothing unified about it. He was torn in all directions at once. All the impulses he had harnessed in becoming a successful businessman and adventurer broke loose from their habitual confinement. The most threatening of all for Monroe was the sex drive.

Paradoxically enough, Monroe had to leave the body to experience the power of what Climacus and his followers called the "flesh." The flesh is not so much the body but might more accurately be described by Freud's notion of the Id, that turmoil of animal drives we try to conquer by repression. The monks of the Sinai struggled with this reality while still in their bodies. Possibly, the fact that Monroe had to leave his body to experience it demonstrates what Western civilization has accomplished over the past thirteen centuries. We have learned to maintain an ego by which we know ourselves and analyze the world with reasonable dependability. But our Id still lies coiled in the psychic basement, every ready to raise its Hydra heads to devour our flimsy conscious attainments from all sides at once.

In one of his earliest disengagements from the body, Monroe *saw* his sleeping wife as an irresistible sex-object (Monroe, 1977, p. 191). Hardly recognizing her as the person he knew intimately, he tried in vain to waken her with his "second body" so he could satisfy his uncontrollable lust. When, in desperation, he returned to his body to unload his desire, his need evaporated. On another occasion, he had barely lifted out of the body when he felt himself attacked from behind by a naked male sex-fiend, clutching him tenaciously, scratching his neck with his beard, panting his lust into his ear (Monroe, 1977, p. 168). The homosexual assault terrified and disgusted Monroe and he battled in panic for some time before he realized his adversary was his own sex-charged body.

Sex in this stage of his journeying had no connection with love-making for Monroe. It was an impersonal drive seeking release, humiliating him by its intensity, and growing exponentially with his nearness to the object of his momentary obsession. He had to flee the out-of-body state when he met a woman there, lest he be unfaithful to his wife. He cites Gurdjieff's statement that, "if there had been *two* obstacles as formidable as sex," he would never have achieved the mystical state (Monroe, 1977, p. 191).

Powerless in the face of a lust that refused to be banished, Monroe finally resorted to his waking-world monolog and tricked the drive by promising it gratification—but later. Everything in good time. Fobbing off his drives with promises enabled Monroe to control himself on his sojourns. He would politely ask a woman met in a dreamscape if she would like to enjoy sexual congress with him; and he could respect her wishes when she declined. Evidently, two developments had occurred. He had gained a precarious balance with his lust, and he seems to have changed his mind about remaining faithful to his wife. Had he decided that *dream*-sex was permissible? On what basis, given its incontrovertible reality—even its susceptibility to the old monolog? Did it seem advisable to gratify the drive in order to stay on the journey? Or was his marriage already in serious trouble?

During this whole period, Monroe saw himself as conducting experiments. He left the body each time with a definite plan to test the clairvoyant accuracy of his *seeing*. To do so, he had to exercise an impeccable will and clarity of thought. The moment he allowed himself to be distracted, he would find his "second body" whisked away to some unintended location and the experiment spoiled. Most significantly, he had little interest in "Locale II," the untestable world of the soul. He generally found himself there by default, as a result of a failure to control his journeying.

It was by default, therefore, that he learned that sex in the out-of-body state was not a genital experience at all, but a transcendent experience of merging.

The "act" itself is not an act at all, but an immobile, rigid state of shock where the two truly intermingle, not just at a surface level and at one or two specific body parts, but in full dimension, atom for atom, throughout the entire Second Body. There is a short, sustained electron (?) flow one to another. The moment reaches unbearable ecstasy, and then tranquillity, equalization, and it is over (Monroe, 1977, p. 196).

This is an experience we can all have without leaving the body. When we get beyond the pure physicality of genital release and attend to the interpersonal communication occurring between ourselves and our beloved, we will feel this same merging that Monroe describes. The boundaries between my "I" and your "you" dissolve, and we enter one another ecstatically. We feel it throughout our whole body, as a oneness that is no longer "mine" and "yours," but "ours." We find we meet our beloved as never before, in unimaginable intimacy, coming to know ourselves and our partner more thoroughly than we had ever dreamed possible.

Evidently Monroe had been unaware of this possibility before his out-of-body visits to "Locale II." Probably it points to something unexplored between himself and his wife. Surely it helps us to understand one of the prime motives in his attraction to Nancy Penn, for it seems that the resolution of his struggles with the fleshly power of sex was taking place in two realms at about the same time. In his waking life, he had found a partner with whom he could share his soul work. In his journeying life, he was learning the emotional richness of sexuality.

The experiences in his second book all take place during his association with Nancy. Among them is his profound symbolic encounter with sex. In one of his "Locale II" journeys, while afflicted by a sudden crisis of lust, he came upon a great heap of living flesh that he likens to the intertwined and squirming ball of night-crawlers a fisherman finds at the bottom of his bait can (Monroe, 1985, pp. 88–89). This mountain of writhing forms rose as high and as far to either side as he could see. It was in continuous motion, slimy wet tubes of flesh flowing in and out of the mass in a relentless search for unattainable satisfaction. Suddenly, he was shocked to realize these "worms" were human arms and legs, male and female, seething with restless life. But they were all dead. These were humans who had left their bodies at death and, instead of sailing off into spiritual bliss, had become trapped by the lust they had not resolved during their lives. It seemed as though they would spend an eternity in this hell of unrequited lust. Monroe knew he could join them if he wished, but was repelled. He grabbed a hairy leg and pulled out a handsome, dark-haired man, who lay gleaming in his sweat, struggling to crawl back in.

> From that point on, I had a new technique to control any surfacing sexual drive. All I need do is think of that wriggling, writhing, mindless pile of humanity. That does it (Monroe, 1985, p. 89).

If the confrontation with death was Monroe's first *koan*, the struggle with sex was his second. In both cases, he needed to gain an outside perspective, a symbolic representation that placed the fleshly compulsion in context. Twice, he arrived at a point where he could say: "So *this* is flesh, this panicky drivenness, this almost deliberate blindness, this slavery to base instinct. I am *not* this." He begins to realize what it means to be a soul person.

The Ladder Man's monks *knew* they were flesh. The reality of instinctual compulsion was obvious to them all, and not only to those who were reformed rapists, murderers, and thieves. A gaunt and holy man could sincerely convict himself of gluttony—not because he ate too much, but because *thoughts about food* distracted him from the gaps through which soul might appear. Now, at the end of the Age of Pisces, this way of thinking is almost incomprehensible. We worry about gaining weight rather than gluttony, but our preoccupation with our figure serves the same distracting purpose.

Monroe saw his experiments in clairvoyance as a noble, scientific endeavor. He was *dreaming* for us all, and very thoughtfully taking the trouble to back up his *dreams* with numbers. Above all, he *needed to know* he was not fooling himself with his out-of-body hobbies. If what he was *seeing* was really there, the world we have been bumbling around in for the past three or four millennia is but a broom-closet. The shock was too much. Despite its convincing vividness, he feared it might still be an illusion. Therefore, as scary, disgusting, and humiliating as most of his experiments were, he kept at them. Journeying was so compelling he could hardly bear to be sick—not because of the sore throat or aching muscles, but because he would not have enough energy to get out of his body. He was as obedient to his sojourns as Castaneda was to Don Juan or Isidore to Climacus. Was it all foolishness, or was he discovering the secrets of the cosmos and of the human soul?

These are the kinds of thoughts we have when we begin to meditate upon our master's question: *What is the sound of one hand clapping?* Why did he give me that one? I'll just have to *pretend* to think about it. It's too absurd. Zen must be about something else. As long as we fight the *koan*, there is no hope of finding any gaps. Gaps appear when we stop distracting ourselves. Monroe distracted himself from the world of the soul for some two decades by preoccupying himself with proofs.

The "second body" he entered during those twenty years was not really so different from the physical body back on the bed. Not only did it have the same shape, but the Robert Monroe who occupied it brought all of his everyday preoccupations along with him. He kept up the same old monolog: *The trick is to keep the conscious, reasoning you (the one most cognizant of the physical world) in a dominant position. It isn't easy.*

Around the time of Monroe's *satori*—while walking two inches above his "second body," when he encountered the legend of the demiurge and the image of the writhing pile—he discovered there was a "third body." The "third body" was his gap. He slipped out of his monolog, dropped the weight of his guilt and terror, and entered the world of soul. He discovered it was no longer interesting to make out-of-body space probes to Mars. There is something out there that was monumentally more important.

4

THE SEARCH FOR A COSMIC COMPASS

What you call past lives are simultaneous. You are forming past, present, and future simultaneously.

(ROBERTS, 1970, P. 164)

If you want to prove—to yourself and to no one else—that we survive physical death, you can learn to move into the out-of-body state and seek out a friend, relative, or someone close to you who has recently died.

(MONROE, 1994, P. 11)

Although I met hundreds of people who'd had near-death experiences, I met very few who experienced all the things that I did. Most people went to what I call the first level, in which they go up the tunnel, see Beings of Light, and have a life review. Very few went to the city of light and the hall of knowledge.

(BRINKLEY, 1994, PP. 131–132)

For nearly twenty years, I have been on the look-out for gaps in people's awareness, the apertures through which another world is trying to appear. Whether they know it or not, people enter Jungian analysis, or any sort of therapy, in order to have their habitual world "stopped" and reassembled in a manner that will allow them to live a more satisfying and meaningful life. Don Juan Matus is right: We unconsciously maintain our world and prevent it from changing through an internal monolog that tirelessly reasserts a few central features and distracts us from any evidence that the world can be seen differently. That monolog becomes auditory in the gaps of our everyday speech.

Anyone can detect the gaps in another person's conversation by making a very slight "shift" of attention. It is a bit like watching a movie from the perspective of the projectionist. The man in the projection booth is free to watch the unfolding drama of the film if he chooses. In doing so, he joins the audience and becomes immersed in the dream-like story playing out upon the screen. This corresponds to the way we listen with interest as our companion tells the story of a recent argument with her boss. We become immersed in the narrative by identifying with our friend or perhaps by becoming a fascinated third party, standing off to the side as the two of them trade complaints, pleas, and claims of injustice.

At the same time, however, the movie projectionist has to be on the lookout for a signal in the upper right corner of the screen—usually a smudge of incoherent color that blinks precisely ten seconds before the end of a reel of film and then flashes again ten seconds later. Because the audience allow themselves unhindered involvement in the cinematic drama, incidental blots on the screen become irrelevant to their experience and are ignored. But the projectionist is paid to watch for that spurious blob of color, for, without it, he will not know when to start the next roll of film. His action has to be precisely timed so that the audience can remain immersed in the continuous flow of image and sound.

Once we have seen and recognized that signal, we will rarely again be able to watch a film without noticing the reel changes—even as a paying customer. Listening for the gaps in a person's conversation is very much the same. When we have heard what they sound like, we begin to notice them all the time. The most common type of gap takes the form of a brief phrase in which the emotional stream of speech is broken and a few words are pronounced flatly, with an emotional deadness that contrasts sharply with the words that precede and follow it. It is in these emotional gaps that a fragment of the speaker's internal monolog appears: *My boss is just like all the rest.*

In the gap occupied by this cliché-like phrase, the story suddenly loses its personal vitality. For a brief instant, we are no longer listening to a tale of two unique individuals battling over a painful misunderstanding. In the moment of the gap, the story flattens out and becomes impersonal. We encounter one of the inflexible constants in our friend's lifeworld, one of the matter-of-fact pillars or struts that holds it all together. Her argument with her boss has become, in this instant, another "same old thing"—what she expects to encounter repeatedly throughout her life. She may consciously hope that life can be different, that someday she will have a boss who is truly unique and an admirable person. But this one is *just like all the rest*.

When, as usual, we fail to notice that a gap has occurred, the matter-of-fact tone of *just like all the rest* draws us into an unconscious agreement. We nod and bemoan the fact that people, particularly bosses, are so lamentably predictable and unworthy of the hopes we want to place in them. If, on the other hand, we notice the phrase *as a gap*, we are not so ready to agree. We are pulled up short. We want to fire up another reel and say: "Wait a minute. What are you talking about here? Who are *all the rest*, and what are they *like?*"

These are challenging questions that ask the unthinkable. Our friend never examines the absurd "givens" of her life. She takes them for granted. She weaves them together into a coherent, rigid structure—the monolog that provides a context of meaning for every incident that occurs. She does not want us to challenge them. If we do so, she is sure to become confused and irritable; for they are what gives her life its regularity and dependability. It may be a miserable and oppressive dependability, but without it she does not know who she is or how to negotiate the world.

For this reason, the phrases that appear in the gaps of her conversation are pronounced with a regretful shrug that says, *This is the way things are, and nothing can be done about it.* They make an emotional demand on us to agree, to shrug along with her, to shake our head, cluck our tongue, and implicitly support her worldview: yes, indeed, the world is filled with hopeless, benighted, and vicious individuals who may pose as our supporters; but, sure enough, they will eventually show their true colors and stab us in the back, *just like all the rest*.

Once we begin to notice such gaps, we learn that people use them in a variety of ways. Some who are perhaps almost aware that the clichés filling their gaps consist of dubious propositions lying nakedly open to unwanted challenge, couch their monolog fragments as jokes. Witticisms express the truth in a diverting manner. We are invited to laugh at the supposed truth that *all bosses are alike.* When we recognize the joking statement as a piece of monolog—on account of its flat, earnest tone— we know our friend is not really joking. She means it. But the wittiness of the joke draws us into a collaboration with the jokester. Our laughter implies our agreement that this is nothing but a joke. We are pressured not to be so "humorless" as to ask, "What do you mean? *How* are all bosses alike?"

The monolog fills the gap like a plug to shield us from the shock of discovering that the world and ourselves are not as we have been maintaining them. We scrupulously—albeit unconsciously—hide from ourselves a secret longing to have our world "stopped," our monolog challenged and opened up to revolutionary notions that will make our lives more satisfying. But because we are scared to death to face the loss of our dubious certainties, the Don Juan Matus who is going to "stop" our world must be cunning.

Hypnotist Milton Erickson stealthily worked to pry open the internal monologs of his patients so they could accept new ideas. For example, a young man, whose miserable refrain insisted he was seriously retarded and unfit to live, was led to ask himself how profound his stupidity really was. He agreed to test his self-evident retardation by seeing how long it would take him to flunk out of a college English course. When he finished the course with a passing grade, he set out to prove that he was not smart enough to handle two courses in the same semester. Eventually, the young man finished graduate school without discovering the limits of his stupidity (Haley, 1973, pp. 130–135).

No doubt many had tried to reassure the "retarded" young man, by telling him he should go easy on himself, that he was much smarter than he realized. But his monolog on stupidity discarded such sensible encouragements as well-meaning "lies." Our gaps are well-defended. People like Don Juan and the Ladder Man had to resort to cunning. Erickson did, too. His first principle was never to deny or directly confront anything his patients said. Ostentatiously, he would accept his patient's claim at face value, but at the same time insert a tiny, innocent doubt.

If he had said, "That's all nonsense; I want you to take an English class, pass it, and prove to yourself that you are smart," the man would have walked away feeling misunderstood. Instead, he said: "I want you to try something we both know you're going to fail at. What we want to know is how long it takes you to fail. Maybe you'll fail in the first week, maybe in the second. Perhaps you'll get all the way to the middle of the term before you fail." The young man was encouraged to take his internal monolog with him to English class and to compare its message with what was actually going on. Here is where Erickson's genius shows. Internal monologs remain the same until they are brought out of the dark and tested against reality. He designed a *koan* for the young man, to trick him into challenging his own monolog.

Monroe's *dreams* performed a similar service. His life-long internal refrain about death and survival must have run something like this: "These are dangerous stunts you're performing. You're tempting death every second you roam outside your body. You better be on guard. Never forget, your survival's at stake." When, after nearly two decades, the vision of the demiurge was able to slip in through the gap, it started out by confirming the old monolog. It said: "Yes, you're right. Just look down upon this fleshly world from outer space. Everything dies. Everything is scrambling for life with every ounce of its strength, because somehow it knows that it's destined to become the food and fertilizer for generations to come." It is the same old monolog, but with a twist. Now he is looking down from outer space. He is no longer in it. He has glanced at the upper right corner of the screen and seen the smudge of color. That smudge is flesh—the *flesh* that dies, and fights to live. It dawns on him that, somewhere along the line, he has come to accept the reality of his journeys. The world of flesh and survival has "stopped" for good. He finally gets it. Flesh is the broom-closet.

Monroe struggled to stare death in the eye for twenty years, because he still had a life ahead of him. When he first left his body, he was 42, in good health, a fabulously successful businessman who had tried his hand at just about everything. He was an architect, a broadcaster, a company president, a sailor, a pilot, and anything else that caught his fancy. He was immersed in a very rich life in this garden of death.

NEAR-DEATH EXPERIENCES

People who are facing death as an immanent certainty, however, and not merely as a strong possibility, have quite a different experience. When our heart has stopped and our brain waves flattened, there is no longer anything to deny. Death is here, the fleshly journey over. Those who sincerely believe they are dying and have momentarily been pronounced dead by their doctors may enter a greater cosmos that has much in common with the realm through which Monroe has been journeying for the past forty years. But they do not see themselves as temporary visitors on an interesting excursion. The doubts that kept Monroe debating the "reality question" for twenty years and devising experiments to test it, play no role in near-death experiences. The dying do not have that luxury. The self-evident fact of their actual death stops the fleshly monolog abruptly. There is no going back. The cosmos inhabited by beings of light is all there is for them.

Raymond A. Moody, in *Life After Life,* calls the near-death journey a "wide-spread and very well-hidden phenomenon" (Moody, 1975, p. 5). People want to hide it because it contrasts so starkly with what "everybody knows" about death—namely, that dying is like going to sleep, like forgetting, or the final snuffing out of the conscious personality. These notions are so central to most people's internal monologs about death that they are intolerant of any evidence to the contrary. Many near-death experiencers have timidly tried to share their surprising adventure with friends, only to encounter ridicule or stony silence.

If this hostility has lessened somewhat in the twenty years since Moody's book first appeared, it is likely that a growing interest in New Age wonders is responsible. At the present time, a significant segment of our population is more open-minded about these reports, while the rest are puzzled or disdainful. A trivial and pointless debate about whether there really is a life after death distracts us from what is going on.

Enthusiasts of near-death journeys wish to take them as proof that death is not a snuffing out of consciousness, but rather a great awakening. The reports "prove" to them that a wonderful life awaits us after death. Twenty-five years ago, in fact, Elisabeth Kübler-Ross, whose *On Death and Dying* (1969) brought to our awareness the importance of the dying process and the famous five stages of grieving, spoke only cryptically of near-death journeys. She said she had a great mass of material which she refused to publish, lest people be encouraged to take their lives in order to enter the cosmos of light.

Those who pride themselves on their common sense correctly observe that no one has yet come back from death. People have only returned from *believing* themselves dead. The fact that they managed to rejoin the rest of us, clearly indicates that the "near-death" phenomenon must be counted as one of *life's* possibilities. Thus far, they are surely right. But if they go on to argue that the near-death experience is nothing but a wish-fulfilling delusion, they, too, are carried away by a prejudice that blinds them to what is going on.

These are the facts. Some people (but not all) who have been utterly convinced they are dying and actually passed several moments when medical professionals could detect no life-signs in them, have left their bodily pain behind and been overcome by a profound feeling of peace. Then began a *dream* in which they took leave of their body—some of them *seeing* it from the outside, very much as Monroe did—and passed through a tunnel that led to a region of light where they *saw* people who were glowing with light or actually seemed to be comprised of light. One of these light beings greeted them with profound warmth and love and introduced them to a detailed and emotionally powerful review of the lives they had lived from early childhood up to the point of the apparent death. After this, they gained the conviction that it was not yet time for them to leave their bodily existence forever and that they would have to return. Many of them were extremely reluctant to do so and begged to be allowed to stay in the world of light, but to no avail. Upon their return and recovery from their physical crisis, they began to live differently than they had before. They had undergone a transformation of personality and found life substantially more rewarding and meaningful than it had been prior to their close brush with death. About 95 percent of near-death experiencers report this as a profoundly blissful interlude. The other 5 percent were terrified (Moody, 1975, p. 17).

Moody emphasizes that not one of the people he interviewed expressed the slightest doubt that the figure encountered in the experience was a *personal* being, a being of light, and that the love and warmth emanating from this being was utterly beyond words. These people also vigorously assert that "it was nothing like an hallucination" or even a dream. The events were too real and vivid to be understood as mere fantasy. It was not possible to doubt them. Their close associates, too, cannot overlook the evidence that something profound has happened to them. Their lives after the apparent death have taken on a subtle, quiet conviction. Their outlook has clearly been broadened and deepened. They have become more reflective and concerned with ultimate philosophical issues. They are utterly convinced there is a life beyond the grave and that they have experienced it.

The evidence suffices for *them*; they are the ones who *saw* the greater cosmos. We did not. We still have our doubts, and there is no reason to give them up. The near-death people have had an *experience*. They do not simply *believe* that earthly life is a brief episode in a larger cosmic existence. They *know*. They are like the sighted, and we the blind. Blind people like us do not know what it means to turn on a light to "see" better. But we know sighted people all do it. Evidently, lamps serve some useful purpose. There is no point in debating whether light really exists or is only a delusion. The fact of the matter is, it changes people's behavior. Sighted people seem to move faster, for instance; they do not have to tap their way through unfamiliar territory the way we do. They can drive cars, and they claim to appreciate paintings.

We would be wasting our time to debate the reality of a life beyond the grave. If, by chance, we could all agree that it did or did not exist, we would be talking about whether we *believe* it or not. *Belief* is beside the point. What is important, the near-death people assure us, is the experience, what it has done for them. Psychologist Kenneth Ring's books on the near-death phenomenon (1982, 1985) present convincing statistics about the nature of these changes.

The near-death journeyers' brushes with death shut off their internal monolog. The gap appeared as a tunnel with a realm of light at the other end. It gave them a new perspective on the life they had been living. When they returned, they found a way to incorporate their experience of cosmic consciousness into their new internal monolog. They now began to talk to themselves about the world of light and how it gives everything material and temporal a new significance. They began to act differently, because their old world had "stopped" and the new world had different priorities. Their monolog changed and began to support a new set of goals and principles. For all of them, the new world was shot through with gaps in which they encountered reminders of their monumental experience. For some, the gaps also gave them clairvoyant and other psychic powers.

What would an Isidore standing at the gate of the New Age *see* in these people? What is glowing in their faces? What kind of gaps would they open for that holy man who learned to *see* the world of soul in the dusty robes of every monk?

If Isidore and the near-death journeyer, Dannion Brinkley (*Saved by the Light,* 1994), had met before their respective transformations, they would have despised one another. The haughty and cruel Alexandrian would have seen Brinkley as a low-life thug and been astonished that a man like that could have been drawn to the desert. Meanwhile, the American would have seen Isidore as a self-satisfied and dangerously powerful aristocrat.

In 1975, the 25-year-old Brinkley was struck by lightning through the telephone he was holding. From the ceiling, he saw his body thrown across his bed, the melted receiver in his hand, his shoes smoking. While hovering above the ambulance that carried his body away, he saw a tunnel racing toward him "like the eye of a hurricane." He passed through to a bright realm, where he was met by a being of light radiating love so intense as to be "almost too pleasurable to withstand."

In his own glowing, bodiless form, he reviewed the ruthless cruelty with which he had bullied his way through school and become an assassin in Vietnam, following high-level "targets" in the North Vietnamese Army and blowing their heads off in front of their troops or dynamiting the hotels in which they spent the night. He relived the cold-blooded satisfaction of every "kill." But the worst part of the experience was that he was forced to feel the anguish, humiliation, and pain of his adversaries, including the effects their injury or death had upon their families and loved ones. He followed his career after the war, into his clandestine operations in countries friendly to the United States, delivering weapons and training assassins.

Evidently, Brinkley had spent his first twenty-five years in a kill-or-be-killed world. He must have talked to himself about how treacherous and undependable everyone else was—how they would "get" him, if he did not act first. He lived a scheming life appropriate to the chaotic and dangerous Age of Aries, in which the winners were devious and cruel, the losers naive and foolish. He would never be meek, never submit. Had he lived thirteen centuries earlier, he would have been one of the monks drawn to the monastery of St. Catherine because he had hit bottom in his sinfulness.

Confrontation with the overlooked emotions of his cruel past was the first step in Brinkley's spiritual rehabilitation. His life-review is reminiscent of a story John Climacus tells of a notorious robber who sought to enter the monastery. He allowed himself to be led before the 230 monks assembled for holy services clothed in a hair shirt and with ashes sprinkled on his head. The Abbott called out from the sanctuary in a voice of thunder, "Stop! You are not worthy to enter." Thinking it was the voice of God, the robber-monk fell on his face and began to confess

> sins of the flesh, natural and unnatural, with humans and with beasts; poisonings, murders, and many other deeds too awful to hear or to set down on paper. Everyone was horrified. But when he had finished his confession, the superior allowed him to be given the habit at once and to be included in the ranks of the brethren (Climacus, 1982, p. 94).

Later, Climacus asked the Abbott why he had imposed so severe and dramatic a penance. The cunning Director of Souls answered:

> So that this man, having confessed now in shame, might in the future be spared fresh remorse for those deeds, which is what hap-

pened. He did not rise up from the floor, Brother John, until he had been granted forgiveness of all his sins. Have no doubt about this. Indeed, one of the brethren who was present told me he saw a terrifying figure holding a book and a pen and crossing off each sin as it was confessed (Climacus, 1982, pp. 94–95).

To "stop" the penitent's world, the Abbott had to silence the poor man's guilty monolog. The way to do this was to rip the memory of those crimes out of his heart's hidden closet and bring them to public knowledge. Otherwise he might have brooded over them for the rest of his life, plugging all the gaps with his overwhelming remorse. The Abbott *saw* that his soul was more in danger from the burden of his guilt than from the sins themselves.

Similarly, Brinkley had to tear his cruelties loose from the trivializing monolog that hid them. He had to *see* them in three dimensions, in full emotional color. Flat banalities that "everybody knows" had kept those atrocities hidden. The dead were enemies of America. Killing them saved innocent lives. Passersby were guilty by association. He had shut off his own feelings fifteen years earlier when he learned how enjoyable it was to bloody his schoolmates' noses. His enemies had no feelings, were not really people. They were jerks, "s.o.b.'s," or "targets."

Not surprisingly, the first thing to flow through the gap opened by his "death" was emotion: the love too pleasurable to withstand and the cruelty too devastating to bear. He felt his own cold-blooded and isolating scorn and plunged into the lives of everyone affected, taking on the emotions of each individual in turn. The flat cartoon of the monolog could no longer hold back the vitality, passion, and devastation of real people dying, grieving, and panicking. Having finally understood his crimes at a deep emotional level, he was free of them. He *saw* the being of light beside him as an angel, looking on with "non-judgmental compassion," and advising: "We are each a link in the great chain of humanity. What you do has an effect on the other links in that chain."

The life-review is the most convincing and vital passage in Brinkley's sojourn. When it was finished, he was taken to a glorious Crystal City, where he attended classes and "only had to think of a question in order to explore the essence of the answer." He watched the light beings assembling electronic devices and witnessed a number of future Earth events on television screens set into the chests of humanoid figures.

During months of physical rehabilitation, he returned to his lessons in the Crystal City whenever he fell asleep. He felt himself alive and vital only in the midst of those *dreams*. Bodily life was a dreary burden. He could think of nothing but the greater cosmos and his longing to be there. Family and friends saw him as delirious and raving about Crystal City "like a retarded fundamentalist" (Brinkley, 1994, p. 84). He button-holed everyone he met to tell them of the wonders he had *seen*, inspiring embarrassment and evasion.

By clinging to his cosmic fascinations, Brinkley was refusing to come back to Earth. No doubt he had always felt like a misfit and had learned to deal with his strangeness by becoming a bully. But his cosmic journeys made it clear that his life as a professional assassin had to stop. He had to find a new lifestyle, establish new priorities, develop a new internal monolog.

His experience in this regard is not unique. C. G. Jung had an out-of-body experience after his heart attack in 1944. He, too, spoke of the vividness and sense of reality his visions provided. Indeed, his journey confirmed the truth of what he had been writing and holding back from publication for the past ten years, books and papers on alchemy, synchronicity, Gnosticism, and the like. After his return, he revised and published them. But the return itself was difficult. He said that, in comparison to what he had *seen* in the greater cosmos, this world carried all the conviction of a black-and-white newspaper photo. He called this the "gray box world," and returned reluctantly and against great resistance (Jung, 1961, p. 292).

Jung had a significant advantage over Brinkley. His out-of-body journey took up an on-going theme in his life and emphasized its importance. Brinkley knew only that he could not stay on his old path. Having no notion of how to proceed, he preferred to stay in the dream.

What reconnected him to life on Earth was a lecture by Raymond A. Moody that made human sense of his sojourns and introduced him to others who had left their bodies in a near brush with death. He learned that some who had been "monumentally shocked" like this and not found a way to get on with their lives had been sent to mental hospitals. Grateful to have been saved from that fate, he had numerous meetings with Moody, and a warm mentor/disciple relationship developed between them. Brinkley began to accompany Moody on his lecture tours, where he considered himself the star witness for the reality of near-death sojourns. His visions were the most detailed and extravagant of all. Furthermore, he could read minds and predict occasional future events with remarkable accuracy. Even Moody was impressed and admitted to being "stymied" by Brinkley's abilities.

At this point in his "return to planet Earth," Brinkley became a kind of side-show freak. He had to catch planes and follow the clock like the rest of us, but when he got to his destination, he played the role of a kind of Martian visitor, speaking of his extraterrestrial adventures and demonstrating his powers of clairvoyance and mind reading. His out-of-body sojourn was still cut off from everyday life. He could only talk about it; he had not yet found a way to live it.

New Age interests in the greater cosmos are often side-tracked by amazing, "non-ordinary" visions, leading to metaphysical speculations about what may be "out there." In India, the yogis have been reporting these wonders for millennia. They take them as matter-of-fact human capabilities that can be achieved by anyone who pays diligent attention to the gaps that can be opened up in our consciousness through meditation. But they do not brag about them. They warn us that marvelous powers (*siddhis*) can be a dangerous distraction. Just as obsessions with food, sex, money, and power keep us imprisoned in the survival world of the flesh, fascination with *siddhis* can blind us to the spiritual significance of soul. We can come to believe we are specially gifted, an aristocratic sort of human being, elevated above our fellows and deserving of applause. When we begin to seek honors for the *siddhis* that have simply fallen in our lap, we turn our psychic powers to our own self-aggrandizement and miss the point.

The point is that these amazing possibilities represent opportunities to grow, to understand ourselves more completely, and to become more effective human beings. It is surely interesting that Dannion Brinkley can read minds and predict a few major world events. But the essence of his story is the monumental change whereby a professional killer learns compassion.

In his life outside the lecture circuit, Brinkley knew only one thing for sure. He had to avoid cruelty unless he wanted to suffer its effects at his next life-review. He was like a child learning not to touch a hot stove. He gave up assassination and cruelty but retained his opportunism, using his new-found psychic powers to succeed at gambling and business ventures. Life was still a competitive, survival-oriented place, but now he restrained himself. No overkill, no gratuitous insults. It had not occurred to him that he might sympathize with people and come to understand them. His primary concern was still to avoid pain himself. His new monolog included an important motif derived from his near-death experience: "Be careful what you do in life, because you have to see yourself do it again when you die. The difference is that this time you are on the receiving end" (Brinkley, 1994, p. 82).

Brinkley was tinkering with his old lifestyle, trying to find a way to accommodate it to the wisdom he had found in his near-death journey; and he was failing. Fortunately, his new monolog was a poorly assembled patchwork, full of sloppy gaps. Emotionally charged thoughts "beamed" in from other people's minds, along with images of future events. They were so fascinating that Brinkley had a hard time attending to his faulty life-strategy. He became as preoccupied with these marvels as Monroe had with his statistics—being much less disturbing to contemplate than the images and thoughts of kindness that assailed him.

At first the notion of kindness puzzled him, and he worried that he had not found a way to include it in his life. He had no words for it in his internal monolog—or indeed in his book. It had not dawned on him that he might do everything with kindness, that kindness is a way of being, not something for which to find an outlet. Brinkley was not a reflective man. He thought exclusively in terms of goals and tasks. Although emotions and feelings had been the central theme of his life-review, he had no place for them in his daily life. He did not notice his own feelings unless they were painful, and he had no thought that other people might have them.

The failure to notice feelings had doubtless been an advantage for Brinkley, the assassin. The new Brinkley was confused. He decided it was unkind to use his psychic powers opportunistically and stopped. Then he began volunteering his services at a hospice for the dying, where he listened to the stories of the terminally ill, sometimes encouraging them by speaking of what *he* had *seen*. He began to learn something of the pain and stress these people were suffering and tried to do something about it. But it was still only an exercise, one more duty in a hectic life of business deals and travel. He was trying to live two lives. His body, which was still badly hobbled from the lightning strike, was having a hard time keeping up. He walked with difficulty, and his heart was only half as effective as it had once been.

In 1989, fourteen years after his first "death," he suffered heart failure and left his body again. This time, when he reviewed his first twenty-five years, he found it a "wonderful" experience, the story of a man whose life had turned around. His monolog about avoiding cruelty had worked, but there was more to the life-review. He was shown the angry, vengeful attitude he carried toward people who had bested him in business dealings or insulted him personally. He had a new, more subtle failing to understand.

We are not able to follow this new development in Brinkley's life, because the book's narrative ends shortly after the second life-review. Nevertheless, the second sojourn gives us some valuable information on Brinkley's volunteer work. In reviewing the hospice scenes, he feels the emotions he missed at the time. His out-of-body state has access to feelings of bonding and affection in this second life-review. Just as in his first sojourn fourteen years before, Brinkley is immersed in the emotions of all the participants.

He sees himself lift a frail old woman from her bed so it can be made up with fresh sheets. He carries her from room to room of the hospice, showing her the views from the windows. In his near-death *dream*, he finally feels the love he had had for that old woman, the delight he took in showing her the neighborhood, the bond of affection that coursed through the two of them while all this was going on.

He accompanies a young man home to announce that he has AIDS. Brinkley feels his own confident hope for a glowing family reunion and the young man's terror. The meeting is a disaster. The young man's announcement is greeted with hostility and abandonment from every member of his family. Brinkley knows he is responsible. He had pushed his naive and sentimental hopes despite clear warnings from the young man. When he had lived through this scene in his fleshly body, he had felt primarily his own anger at the failure of his hopes. But now, in review, he *feels* the emotions of all the participants and *sees* that he has to tie his feelings to reality and not conjure up a delusional world of how things *should* be.

He has to learn to assess what is going on between people by accurately taking note of the feelings being expressed. Apart from anger, vengeance, and greed, feelings had never before been part of his conscious world. Now he is being shown the missing piece. If he can remember these scenes and use them to open emotional gaps in his continuing work as a volunteer, a change of great moment is portended. Far from taking him out of the world, then, Brinkley's near-death journeys have been preparing him for a more human life within the world.

WHO IS THE JOURNEYER?

Under the influence of a tradition at least 2000 years old, we have accepted the idea that the Brinkley or Monroe who leaves his body and sojourns in a visionary cosmos is the *soul* of that individual. We have not bothered to ask ourselves what, after all, a soul might be. We have attended only to a tradition that distinguishes three elements in the human being: a body limited to sensory knowledge, a soul with its visionary knowledge, and a spirit capable of *gnosis* or direct knowledge of the One. Everything we have seen has had to do with the relation of body and soul, or everyday consciousness and journeying consciousness.

The differences between the experiences of Monroe and those of Brinkley appear to have been determined largely by the two men's relation to bodily death. Monroe journeyed only when he was in good health, but believed he was facing death every time he left his body. For some twenty years, he maintained a tight control over his *dreaming*, by willing his destination and performing experiments to satisfy rational, left-brain concerns. When his willpower failed and he found himself willy-nilly in "Locale II," he was often afraid of getting lost. He had no compass to orient himself in a greater cosmos that was too vast and complicated to comprehend. His unfailing point of reference was the body lying in bed at home. He could always slip back into it when his journeying adventures became too scary.

Brinkley, by contrast, was for all practical purposes deceased when he set out on his cosmic journeys. He believed himself dead without a shred of doubt and had *seen* the ambulance workers pull the sheet over his face. There seemed to be no body to which to return. He entered the greater cosmos with no thought of going back and no sleeping body to serve as refuge. But Brinkley had no fear of getting lost. There was no orientation problem. Evidently, someone else had the compass and led the way. Knowing he was in good hands, Brinkley willingly followed where he was led.

It took Monroe almost twenty years to get to this point. Only when his fear of death had begun to diminish and he had become confident of his ability to outwit his sex drive did he notice that his ego-controlled journeys to test clairvoyance or to view the other side of the moon had become boring. The left brain had seen enough, but the greater Monroe was still unsatisfied. This is the point when he decided to leave his conscious agenda at home with his sleeping body and let the *dream* take him where *it* wanted to go. At this point, he, too, discovered he was in good hands. The sojourns became interesting again, and he learned the three mythic lessons of the greater cosmos: the heap of lusting ghosts, the demiurge of death, and the luminous dome.

Evidently, the key to entering the greater cosmos in earnest is the act—deliberate or not—of leaving behind one's conscious agenda. Monroe's experience shows how difficult this is to do when the sojourn is understood to be an interlude, a few moments' or hours' vacation from earthly existence. The gathering of data and testing of hypotheses had unwittingly been designed to subordinate his journeying to the themes of the habitual monolog of his waking life. Boredom was the gap in his scientific agenda. It told him to stop staring at the shadows on the wall. To make his exit from the cave of his conventional attitude, he had to submit to intentions of wider scope and deeper emotional intensity than his own, even though he had no guess as to what they were or where they originated. A frightening decision. This submission was easier and more comforting for Brinkley, for, because of his "death," he had no choice but to leave his conscious agenda behind. Whatever he had learned in a quarter century of struggle had been rendered useless by a single stroke of lightning.

Although the journeyer goes into a greater cosmos, a "Locale II," or a realm of light—someplace Wholly Other—once arrived, the traveler inevitably turns around and gazes back upon earthly existence. Clearly the life-review of near-death journeys has no other purpose than to look back at the individual's temporal life. But Monroe has turned his gaze back to Earth no less certainly. Nearly all his journeys in "Locale II" take place within the concentric spheres surrounding the Earth, from which the mental and emotional "noise" of human life is a disturbing or seductive song. The myth of the demiurge and the image of the orgiastic pile of ghosts are accounts of fleshly existence. Their purpose is to enable Monroe to see clearly the limitations and blindness of a bodily life lived in ignorance of "soul," or the possibility of journeying. The image of the luminous dome also serves to place bodily existence in context. It is a viewing point outside space and time and outside of Monroe's personal existence as well. What is *seen* from that vantage point is the multitude of earthly lives that are in some sense Monroe's. It is a view that reveals the interlinked nature and purpose of human life.

But *who is it* that embarks on this cosmic journey? Monroe and Brinkley simply call the journeyer "I": "*I* relived every kill"; "*I* saw a seething heap of flesh." But surely it is not the same "I." An old, habitual "me" was left behind on the bed. The assumptions, purposes, and concerns of that "me" were left behind as well. Furthermore, the "I" who reviews Brinkley's life sees and feels as that old "me" never did. Brinkley's old "me" was a cagey assassin who saw and felt only the threats and opportunities that enabled him to survive and advance. The "I" of the journeyer, however, was able to feel the loss, panic, fear, anger, and depression of his victims. The journeying "I" perceived the interlinked reality of human life and felt everyone else's emotions more strongly than Brinkley's old "me" had felt his *own* emotions. Even more significantly, the journeyer felt a bond of love between Brinkley and the old woman he carried around the hospice. Evidently, emotions had coursed through Brinkley's body at the time he was carrying the woman. Although they had remained unknown to Brinkley's old "me," the journeyer felt them fully.

Perhaps we should say the journeyer is a larger and more complete Brinkley or Monroe. The old "me" is stuck in a narrow perspective, defined and controlled by the internal monolog. It is limited to a single life-strategy and can see only what its eyes are focused upon. The journeyer, however, sees everything at once. Out-of-body travelers report seeing in 360°, as though they had eyes on all sides of their heads (Monroe, 1977, p. 184). They also experience every incident in their life-review as though seeing them from all perspectives at once, simultaneously. Brinkley's journeyer feels Brinkley's love and that of the old woman. He relives his "kill" and at the same time lives through its effects upon a whole community of affected individuals. If the journeyer is an "ego," it is unimaginably greater than any sense of "me" I can acquire in an ordinary state of consciousness.

Betty J. Eadie, in *Embraced by the Light*, says of her out-of-body journeyer, "This is who I really am" (Eadie, 1994, p. 30). Eadie is less a philosopher even than Brinkley, but she has articulated a profoundly felt truth in these six words. She is trying to say: I knew the moment I left my body that I had never been my full self before. I had allowed myself to be defined too narrowly. I had been unhappy and longing for I knew not what. In leaving my body, I discovered the larger *me* that had been hidden.

Eadie "died" at the age of 31, in 1973, of a massive hemorrhage in the night following a hysterectomy. She had been a sad, meek woman, raised as an orphan on Indian reservations, separated from her siblings by gender and age, abandoned, loveless, and downtrodden. Her internal monolog rehearsed all her woes: "Oh, my aches and pains. I'm not loved. Look at my sufferings. I can't endure this" (Eadie, 1994, p. 64).

In the out-of-body state, she learned that she was much more than she had imagined. She *saw* her husband and six children: "I felt their emotions and intents. I *felt* their love. I experienced their feelings. And this filled me with joy because they loved me so much." She also learned that each of her children was "an individual spirit like myself with an intelligence that was developed before their lives on earth" (Eadie, 1994, pp. 34, 35). She saw that her children were not "hers," as she had always assumed, but had their own life-agendas. Eadie had hers, as well: "I felt a mission, a purpose; I didn't know what it was, but I knew that my life on earth had not been meaningless" (Eadie, 1994, p. 132).

This is a sad story, as well as a happy one. It is heart-rending to see how thoroughly Betty Eadie undervalued herself. She had to leave her body and gain the perspective of the journeyer to learn for the first time—and really to feel and believe—that her own children loved her.

Clearly, she had not seen herself as an individual with a right and duty to live her own distinctive life. She had been tossed by life, like flotsam, far up on a beach, lonely and isolated, waiting for a storm to take her back out in the terrifying surf, where she might bump into another like herself. A momentary spark of fellow-feeling, only to be dashed by the next wave.

Out-of-body, she was empowered. Unfortunately, we do not learn how she put such a revelation into practice. We only know that the scales fell from her eyes while she *saw* her life from the perspective of the journeyer. She became a woman who is lovable and capable of loving, who can finally be a real person for her children, who is able to see *them* as the distinctive and powerful individuals they already are. Through Betty's "death," the world has changed for a whole family.

We do not know whether any of this will happen in a real-death experience. But it is hard to ignore the fact that, in a near-death experience, the *imaginal* event of leaving the body effects a revolution in our outlook. The journeyer seems to know everything we have been overlooking. It is tempting, in fact, simply to name the journeyer as our habitually unconscious wholeness, for it knows the feelings we fail to register, perceives clearly the interconnections between people upon which we can only speculate, and sees us, not as we wish to be seen, but as we really are.

If our internal monolog is the device we use to maintain our narrow, ego-centered identity, it must be our potential journeyer who is peering in through the gaps, inviting us to drop the arbitrary limitations we place on ourselves and discover our larger, more complete, and more satisfying self. The "monumental shock" that awaits us is the startling recognition that our narrow life-strategy has been a subterfuge and distraction to keep us in ignorance of our larger selves.

If we wish to call this journeying wholeness our "soul," it is not hard to see how the Gnostics of 2000 years ago arrived at the idea that matter is evil. For it seems to be the material, fleshly body, with its survival compulsions, that keeps us ignorant of the fact that we are potential soul people. Now, with the perspectives of the New Age at our disposal, we see that it is not so much the *matter* of the body that keeps us ignorant, but the narrow-mindedness of our internal monolog. When the journeying soul leaves the body upon a near brush with death, all this becomes clear. We drop our isolated perspective and *see* from all sides at once, drop our temporality and *see* from the eternal point of view.

Since Nietzsche, Western philosophy has been impressed with the fact that human consciousness is always "perspectival." It invariably sees things from a certain point of view. But the journeyer lives, as it were, in the Middle Ages, when the goal was to see things in a manner that transcends all perspectives: *sub specie aeternitatis,* from the viewpoint of eternity. Out-of-body journeying demonstrates that the eternal view is available to us all, as soon as we can shut off our internal monolog.

The near-death journeyers have been "lucky," in the sense that they had their monolog shut off for them. They did not have to discipline themselves with decades of meditation. Nevertheless, once the threat of physical death has passed and they are able to resume a healthy life, their task is no different from ours. The spiritual challenge of human life is to find a way to construct a life-strategy and supporting internal monolog that remains open to the larger reality of soul and respects the gaps through which the journeyer would assist us.

WHꙨ HꙨLDꙄ THE CꙨMPAꙄꙄ?

When Monroe let the *dream* (or as he called it, his "greater self") take him where *it* wanted to go, he traveled as a journeyer who had no idea where he was going, but found himself repeatedly in cosmic locations whose very existence had formerly been unknown (Monroe, 1984, p. 6). The journeyer sojourns through an unfamiliar *dream*scape, confident that someone else holds the compass and knows the destination. Monroe says, "I began to trust my unseen pilot(s) as I never would have trusted myself" (Monroe, 1984, p. 92). This is a major admission for Monroe, who avoids traveling on commercial airliners as much as possible because he believes the pilots are not as skilled as he is.

After a number of such blind but guided sojourns, Monroe's journeyer formed friendships with a few beings of light. These were denizens of the greater cosmos who seemed to know their way around. Most of them were apparently non-human. Monroe, with his maddening propensity to give everything a pseudo-scientific moniker, called them "inspecs," short for "intelligent species." He spent a lot of time with "inspec BB," whose home planet was "KT-95." It was BB who revealed the myth of the demiurge. On another occasion, BB led Monroe's journeyer on a multi-dimensional game of crack-the-whip, which raises some interesting questions about the nature of the cosmic compass.

He turned, spun off, and I stretched behind him. Focused tightly on his ident[ity]. It was like holding onto a greased pig on a sheet of ice, only the ice was three-dimensional—no, worse than that, it had many dimensions. It was whirling, stopping, starting, moving slow then fast, passing through strange flashes of percepts, into a brilliant sun and out the other side, dodging around clusters of forms who seemed startled at their percept of us. All the time I hung on to BB's ident much as the last skater in a crack-the-whip, in and out of clouds, bands of energy that were like gusts of hot and cold air, electrical shocks, straight through the walls of a magnificently spired city. *I was afraid I couldn't hang on to his ident much longer, afraid if I let go I'd be thoroughly lost.* He stopped suddenly and we were back again in the thin haze of outer earth environ. I was shaking (Monroe, 1984, pp. 157–158).

This is a bewildering story, and not just because wise and ancient "inspecs" like to play childish games. In accepting BB as his guide through unfamiliar reaches of the cosmos, Monroe's journeyer seems never to fear that BB will be lost—although: *I was afraid if I let go I'd be thoroughly lost.* On the analogy of ice-skaters playing crack-the-whip, it is not hard to imagine that the journeyer could be snapped off into another dimension with no earthly notion of where he was or how to get back.

But why is this frightening? Monroe has two dependable points of reference. The first is his sleeping body at home. He knows he finds his way back to it any time its bladder becomes full, its blankets slip off, or it faces any of the disturbing sensations that wake us all. If his body can bring him back, he surely could not stay lost for long—unless finding his body requires orientation. Does he have to know where he is and how he got there, in order to retrace his "steps" and find Earth, the Commonwealth of Virginia, his home, and then his body?

He tells us he can "find" BB by concentrating on BB's personal qualities, his "ident," at the time he leaves his body, and that this ego-willed intention will take him directly to BB. Can he not do this while lost in the cosmos as well as while ensconced in his body?

Because he "located" BB through an exercise of willpower, the entire crack-the-whip adventure must have taken place without Monroe's having invoked his "greater self," the Being holding the compass, his second reference point. Very likely, he was sojourning on his own when he played crack-the-whip, and was therefore at greater risk of becoming lost. But, if he had been snapped off into another dimension, some unfamiliar sector of the greater cosmos, without knowing how he got there, why could he not have placed himself in the hands of his "greater self" at that time? Is he not always in unseen connection with his greater self? Are not we all?

Near-death journeyers do not seem to have this problem. They never hold the compass themselves, but they also never doubt that someone holds it and that that someone is utterly trustworthy. Betty J. Eadie says she knew she "should" be terrified while on her near-death sojourn. But, instead of terror, she felt more calm and well-off than she had ever felt on Earth. Her tunnel, which raced toward her "like a tornado," turned out to be "filled with love, warmth, and healing." When she emerged at the other end, she was greeted by a being of light whose glowing aura merged with the light emanating from her own form, so that she knew she had "always been a part of him" and that he loved her in spite of her faults.

> It was the most unconditional love I have ever felt, and as I saw his arms open to receive me I went to him and received his complete embrace and said over and over, "I'm home. I'm home. I'm finally home" (Eadie, 1994, p. 41).

Dannion Brinkley does not call the Crystal City his "home," but it is clear that he felt a greater well-being and sense of purpose there than he did in South Carolina. Because he was transported there every time he fell asleep, it was many months before he could take the material world seriously enough to get on with his life. Furthermore, just prior to his second "death," he explicitly forbade the doctors to operate on his heart. He said if it was time for him to go, he was glad of it, and would prefer to live in the other world than in this one. He never had any doubt that the beings of light were utterly at home in their world and that they could be trusted fully to take good care of him, to offer dependable instructions, and to be well oriented in the greater cosmos. He does present another point of view, however, one that might be surprising in view of what we have learned.

Reviewing what we have learned, it seems clear there are three agents implied in an out-of-body journey. First, the everyday ego with its internal monolog is left behind. Second, the journeyer, who appears to be the individual's "whole self," leaves the realm of space and time and comes to *see* everything at once, from all sides, simultaneously. Third, there is someone—an even greater self—holding the compass, keeping us oriented, ordering our priorities, and doing so in harmony with the greater cosmos itself. These three agents correspond to the traditional three dimensions of human existence. The flesh is the agent who speaks the monolog. The soul journeys into the cosmos of its visions in order to grasp the larger picture which gives life its meaning.

The spirit is the compass-bearer, its needle unwaveringly drawn to the One, the center and emanation point of the cosmos.

The flesh seems so left behind and denigrated in this view of human nature, that it might be surprising to learn what moves these beings of light who seem so much wiser than we are. Secret agent Brinkley might be expected to have an opinion. He lived in a world where nobody does anything out of goodness of heart. There has to be something in it for the spirit beings.

> I had the amazing realization that these Beings were desperately trying to help us, not because we were such good guys, but because without us advancing spiritually here on earth, they could not become successful in their world (Brinkley, 1994, p. 57).

It may be strange to think that these "higher beings," who have the whole cosmos in which to roam about, who have their priorities straight and are evidently oriented to the One in *gnosis*, need fleshly beings like us. What can they derive from beings who can become lost in the obsessions of a moment or snarl up a lifetime with unresolved fears and narrow presuppositions?

C. G. Jung faced this question near the end of his autobiography, where he speculated that death takes us all back into the "collective unconscious," where nothing ever changes. Change occurs only on condition of our having a fleshly body. Only an ego tied to space and time can learn, for learning is a process of change through time. As fleshly beings, therefore, our contribution to the greater cosmos is the advancement of knowledge. What we, the least of intelligent beings, learn becomes immediately available to the greater cosmos, which floats in a featureless eternity. Earth is the temporal laboratory by which the cosmos comes to know itself and advance.

These conclusions are very close to what Monroe pieced together from his sojourns. Once he began to assimilate the significance of the luminous dome, he recognized it as his "greater self" and came to realize that most of the "inspec" friends he had made in the course of his cosmic journeys were alternate components of that same dome—each identified with a separate luminous fiber.

Over the course of several journeys, for instance, he and BB watched in horror as another "inspec," known as AA, gradually became fascinated with the fleshly world of survival and could not resist the impulse to dive in and become incarnate as an infant. AA's entanglement was boundless, and the poor "inspec" fell to the lowest level of survival compulsion. Monroe and BB did their best to get through the gaps in AA's monolog with bits of cosmic wisdom to halt the free-fall of fleshly ignorance. But all to no avail. AA would have to learn what every other incarnate being needs to know, would have to hit bottom and gradually find the way upward through lifetime after lifetime (Monroe, 1985, pp. 141–143).

From the cosmic perspective, it may seem a foolish enterprise to allow oneself such an entrapment. But Monroe learns it is the main activity of his luminous dome to send aspects of itself into the heavy, seductive atmosphere of Earth in order to learn. Several of its luminous strands are simultaneously engaged in separate earthly sojourns, the man known as Robert A. Monroe being only one of them. The dome uses its simultaneous multiple individualities to assist the several alter egos who are immersed in the earthly learning process. Among them, Monroe is unique in his ability to travel back and forth through the aperture between the worlds and see things from both sides. He is *dreaming* for his whole luminous dome, bringing cosmic wisdom and earthly knowledge together.

By the end of the three-volume account of what he has learned in his out-of-body journeys, Monroe has come to the view that his luminous dome is reaching the end of the incarnation process. It has learned nearly all it needs to know from several lengthy series of fleshly involvements and is almost ready to go "home" to the One. Monroe apparently has little idea what this "going home" is all about, but he has accepted it as the "ultimate journey" and is working to further this process by learning compassion.

It is surely interesting that the out-of-body dabbler, Monroe, and the "twice-dead," near-death journeyer, Brinkley—two fiercely agnostic, technologically-oriented masters of the survival game—should have come to the same conclusion, namely that compassion is the higher truth that bridges the two worlds. Furthermore, Monroe and Brinkley both exercise compassion in regard to death and dying. Brinkley spends more and more time in hospices for the terminally ill, trying to ease the final days of those about to leave their bodies for good. Monroe spends more and more of his time out-of-body, roaming through the nearer spheres of the cosmos, where fleshly energies from Earth have the power to mesmerize the souls of the recently departed and keep them stuck in remnants of their fleshly monologs.

In faithfulness to his cosmic identity, Monroe has become a shaman, searching out lost souls to convey them to a point in the cosmos where they can recognize their bodiless condition and choose the next stage in their larger destiny, whether this means to reconnect with their dome or to reincarnate for further lessons in temporality.

In faithfulness to his earthly fascination with technology, Monroe employed his waterbeds and headphones to teach twelve disciples to reach "Focus 27," the brain-frequency at which one enters the cosmic decision point, where a disembodied soul recognizes its cosmic identity and chooses what to do next. Furthermore, he started a "Lifeline Research Department" at the Monroe Institute, where data is gathered on the recently departed (Monroe, 1994, p. 252). He tried his best, in the out-of-body state, to ascertain the earthly identities of the souls he was guiding. Once back on Earth, he searched county records to verify that these shamanic journeys are *dreams* and not merely dreams.

He gathered and collated data from both sides of the aperture between the worlds, propelled by his nagging agnosticism, fighting a reality he could barely deny, worried perhaps that this was an insane thing he was doing, rescuing the souls of those who had died but did not know it. By the time he had reached his eighties, he had been journeying half his life; his earthly activities were almost exclusively devoted to the reality of the greater cosmos and the implications it has for both the living and the dead. His own death lay not far off.

Like Isidore, he was standing at the gate between the two worlds in humility and awe. But Isidore had no data bank and never learned the stories and preoccupations of the monks passing in and out. He presumably made no out-of-body journeys himself. Indeed, if invited on a sojourn, he would surely have refused and begged to be allowed to finish his days at the gate. It was enough for him to catch the hints of cosmic oneness he *saw* in the faces of those monks. Nothing more was required to rend the fabric of his internal monolog. Without ever leaving his body, he stood in two worlds at once.

Chapter

5

HINTS OF COSMIC ONENESS

The guides would stick tubes through my arms, down through my hands and into the body of the patient. Apparently, they use all the same equipment that a normal surgeon does—scalpels, clamps, scissors, needles, syringes, etc. They cut, scrape things away, cut things out, do transplants and sew things back up again. At one point, I saw a large syringe float down my arm and into the body of a patient whose spinal nerves were being rejuvenated and sewn back together. I looked up at my friend and asked, "Did you see that?" She said, "Yes," and went on to describe the same scene I was witnessing. Since then, we have done many healings together, always correlating what we see.

(BRENNAN, 1988, P. 219)

If this thing works, we want to know about it. If it doesn't work we want to know about it, even more so, because if it's a fake we want to stop doing it.

(EDGAR CAYCE IN SUGRUE, 1974, P. 32)

In a nutshell, shamanic physics consisted of all the experiences in conscious-ness that result from seeing the universe as a gigantic hologram or spider's web. By extending one's belief system, it was possible to reconnect with the whole universe—to become one with everything and be healed. Shamans did this through the observer effect; they altered everything by altering the way in which it was observed. Invariably they brought the mythic and death worlds into this one to do this.

(WOLF, 1991, P. 295)

One of the most succinct and lovely documents from the Gnosticism that flourished around the dawn of Pisces is "The Hymn of the Pearl," which may be found in the apocryphal Acts of the Apostle Thomas. Although there is nothing specifically Christian about the hymn, it is likely that a Christian Gnostic sect had taken over an earlier story and preserved it as a legend that gives a compelling account of what we soul people are doing here in the world of flesh.

An Everyman is sent out from his heavenly home on a mission to recover the One Pearl which lies surrounded by a snorting serpent in the middle of the sea in the land of Egypt. To make the journey, the hero must be divested of his heavenly robe of glory. Upon his arrival in Egypt, he puts on the robes of the Egyptians so as to preserve his anonymity. While waiting for the serpent to slumber so that he may steal the Pearl, the hero eats and drinks with the Egyptians and thereupon forgets his spiritual identity. At this point, his heavenly father, mother, and brother send an angel who appears to him in a dream, and he wakes up reminded of his origins and mission. Chanting the names of his father, mother, and brother, he lulls the serpent and seizes the Pearl. He brings the Pearl back to heaven with him and dons again his heavenly robe:

> As I now beheld the robe, it seemed to me suddenly to become a mirror-image of myself: myself entire I saw in it, and it entire I saw in myself, that we were two in separateness, and yet again one in the sameness of forms. . . . And the image of the King of kings was depicted all over it. . . . I saw also quiver all over it the movements of the *gnosis* (Jonas, 1963, p. 115).

The vision of the hero and his heavenly robe mirroring one another, suggests very strongly the relationship between the ego and the journeyer, who are also "two in separateness and yet again one in the sameness of forms." This scene is so emphasized in the hymn that we have to assume it was meant to express the point of the story. It tells us how Everyman profited from that Earth-mission. He has learned the difference between his fleshly little "me" and the completeness of his journeying soul. He traveled to Earth to immerse that little "me" in flesh and confine it to space and time, for the One Pearl can only be found in Egypt, the world of bodies, and only by a bodily being with a material hand to grasp it. We forget our mission, however, if we do not remember that Egypt is a land of exile and that we come from somewhere else and are called to return there.

Egypt is the perfect symbol for this fleshly world of forgetting and remembering. On the one hand, it is the land where the Israelites forgot themselves and became slaves and where the infant Jesus fled to hide his divine origins and destiny. In this sense, the garment of Egypt is the fleshly body and its refreshments (the "flesh pots" of Egypt) that nourish a bodily way of life correspond to the monolog that feeds our mind with bodily concerns and keeps us ignorant of our greater identity and sublime calling. On the other hand, throughout the Age of Pisces, Egypt has stood for the place where we try to remember. The Land of Egypt is the mysterious source of ancient wisdom, where more has been forgotten about immortality[1] and the magical secrets of our hidden powers than the rest of the world has ever known. For this reason, Egypt has been a "place of power," one of the spots on Earth where the chances of finding cosmic consciousness are better than average.

What is perhaps surprising about "The Hymn of the Pearl" is that, once the Pearl has been found, nothing more is said about it. The focus of the story turns to the robe that had presumably been worn for an eternity before our Everyman divested himself of it and donned the garment of flesh. Because so much attention is paid to the appearance of the robe, with its images of the King of kings and *gnosis*, we must conclude that Everyman had never noticed his *gnosis* until he lost it upon falling asleep in Egypt.

What has been brought back to heaven with the One Pearl is a new way of *seeing*. What formerly had been taken for granted is now recognized for what it is: *gnosis*, one-pointed orientation to the One. Probably, it is somewhat similar to the way we do not appreciate our good health until the day we fall ill. Perhaps those beings of light would be standing in an eternal trance, transfixed by the One and unconscious of themselves, if it were not for us flesh people bumbling around down here on Earth, discovering that two and two makes four and that love feels better than hate. Perhaps they wouldn't know what *life* is, if we were not fighting for survival.

The quest for the One Pearl represents the sacred mission of human incarnation. It is the reason Monroe's luminous dome sends its fibers of light down into the realm of death and survival, daring to forget the reality of the greater cosmos, in order to develop an ego-consciousness capable of learning and ultimately of advancing the realm of light. "The Hymn of the Pearl" is an allegory for every human life that needs to be awakened from its fleshly sleep, where it is lost in the never-changing coils of an internal monolog. Half of our own cosmic mission is already complete: we have forgotten. Now comes the more difficult part: wak-

---

[1] For example, the ancient secrets of embalming, by which the Egyptians of the Age of Taurus gave their kings immortality and made them gods.

ing up. The Aquarian Age, too, is about waking up from a materialistic and power-hungry sleep, to become aware of our cosmic journeying soul.

In the last two chapters, we have seen some pretty spectacular wake-up calls. Monroe, Brinkley, and Eadie were all ejected from their bodies in moments of extreme crisis. Most New Agers have experienced nothing so dramatic or life-threatening. Thus, while the out-of-body journeyers might be seen as astounding exceptions within the New Age population, they are the pioneers. They were the first to face the dangers of the unknown wilderness. They stared death in the eye, tamed the wild beasts of their Id, and left trail markers for the rest of us.

The reasons for beginning our survey of the New Age with Monroe and the near-death journeyers are three. First, none of them had any association with the New Age before leaving their bodies. They were refreshingly naive about the out-of-body state before they found themselves in it. They had no ax to grind, a fact that gives their testimony a believability it might not otherwise have.

Second, sparse though their accounts may have been, they each provided an autobiographical context for their monumentally shocking experience. This has helped us piece together the transformative effects their sojourns had upon their lives. In each case, they became New Agers of the most exemplary kind—that is, they did not just talk the New Age lingo, but made every effort to find a way to live it. There are no grounds to accuse them of an "airy-fairy flakiness" or a superficial infatuation with amazing rumors. Whatever the reader may think of them, their journeys were genuine experiences that forced them to come to terms with the most difficult issues in their lives.

Third, on account of the scope of their journeys, Monroe, Brinkley, and Eadie have collectively given us a kind of map of the New Age cosmos, a framework within which the various New Age marvels all have a meaningful place that relates them to one another and reveals the unity and complex detail of the Aquarian worldview. This chapter takes up some of those themes and shows how they fit in the bigger picture of the New Age.

"SIMULTANEOUS PAST LIVES"

The peculiar expression, "simultaneous past lives," that has been gaining currency in recent years, appears to be a typical example of New Age obscurantism. If the episodes of our supposed reincarnation are "past lives," would they not be serial rather than "simultaneous"? Simultaneous to what, one another or the present? Furthermore, these peculiar "past lives," we are told, might actually be "future" lives and not "past" at all. What a semantic confusion!

The idea that we have lived a series of earthly lives and can "remember" our former incarnations has a long tradition in Indian yoga. It became a popular notion in the West probably through the influence of Theosophy. Westerners have been going to mediums and psychic readers for at least a hundred years to learn of their "former lives." Now, at the end of the 20th century, there seems to be a new twist to this idea. Alternate lives lived by the same "individual" are still, by a kind of entrenched habit, referred to as "past" lives. Nevertheless, they are no longer required to follow one another in series, nor indeed to be finished and over with. Now, inspired by the idea that any of us can leave our place in space and time and journey through the eternal cosmos, we imagine this series of lives from the eternal point of view. Outside of space and time, all the episodes in all those lives appear to be taking place simultaneously. Theoretically, this gives us the option of making an *imaginal* "leap" into a past or future life without losing our bodily anchor in this life—as in the recent television series, *Quantum Leap*. Furthermore, popular extrapolations from the "new physics" suggest that past and future may be simultaneous but invisible "dimensions" of the present. The contradictory expression, "simultaneous past lives," therefore, seems to be derived from a conservative tendency to hang on to the out-moded notion of "past lives," but to update it with the rich haziness of simultaneity.

While not exactly a "lunatic fringe," believers in past lives have encountered a good deal of justified skepticism. Perhaps the most suspicious feature of life-readings is the way they tend to flatter the subject. Why were we never common laborers in by-gone centuries? Is it only the royal and famous that live again?

Although there is much that is suspicious about "past-life" reports, they often have an arresting aptness about them. Indeed, they very frequently appear to be exaggerated caricatures of some aspect of the individual's current life. Believers in reincarnation say that our present life is conditioned and influenced by that past life. Sometimes they speak as though they are simply condemned to repeat the themes of their past lives, as though they have no freedom of choice in the present. Meanwhile the skeptics argue that the alleged past life is merely a fantasy articulating one aspect of our present life—a dramatic representation of part of our internal monolog.

A woman in her late 20s, still living with her parents, who complained of an inability to keep boyfriends, was convinced she had been a princess in the court of Louis XIV, and spent a great deal of time studying the life and times of the Sun King. I could not help wondering whether this "past life" might not better be understood as a current fantasy, part of an internal monolog that made her too "special" to be involved with ordinary young men from the 20th century. Even if she *had* been a French princess, it seemed to be doing her more harm than good to know about it.

A man in his late thirties told me that, although he put little stock in the theory of past lives, to humor his wife he had gone to a "life reader" and been told something quite astounding. It seems that he, his wife, and his mother had all been contemporaries in Palestine at the time of Christ and that 2000 years ago the women who are now his wife and mother were rivals for his love. He found this an excellent explanation for why the two women despised one another so much today. I pointed out that he could dispense with the past-life explanation, for it was clear that his mother and wife were rivals for his love right now. He was thunder-struck. That idea had never occurred to him, but he saw it was accurate. Placing our foibles in "past lives" allows us to shake our heads and bemoan what fate has done to us, without ever having to face problems in the present—the only point on the time line when something can be done about them.

In his earliest book, Monroe tells the story of a man in "Locale III," a world which is parallel to and probably contemporary with this one (Monroe, 1979, pp. 96–99). Monroe could enter that "Locale III" landscape only by fusing his identity with that of a specific protagonist—just as he could enter this world only by fusing his journeying identity with his own sleeping body. The "Locale III" individual was a failed architect-contractor who lived on the second floor of a rooming house in a large city and took a bus to work. He was also conducting some obscure scientific experiments of dubious merit. Painfully shy, he fell in love with a widow who had two small children, but lost her because he was unable to express his feelings. This unnamed man seems to be a caricature of Monroe, who was a sometime architect, performing scientific experiments of dubious value on his out-of-body journeys, seemed to be very much a loner, complained of powerful feelings he was afraid to express, and had reached the end of a marriage that had been blessed with two children.

Narratives understood to be factual accounts of past lives are generally quite relevant to the present life circumstances of the individual and may be usefully interpreted as personal dreams (rather than objective *dreams*). We can put the question of objectivity in brackets and inquire into the contemporary emotional relevance of these stories.

In doing so, however, we fail to do justice to some of the dearest assumptions of the New Age. Like an idea whose time has come, the notion that we have a variety of lives—some prior to our present existence and some subsequent—and that all of these lives can be accessed through a journeyer who travels outside of space and time in an eternal cosmos, crops up over and over again. Twenty years ago, the theme was seen primarily in science fiction. Recently, the films of European director Krzysztof Kieslowski (*The Double Life of Veronique*, and the popular trilogy, *Blue*, *White*, and *Red*) all deal with contemporary lives that run strangely parallel to one another. Some kind of cosmic connection is implied, but never explicitly looked for. The films leave us with a sense of awe before an unnamable mystery. Terry Gilliam's movie, *Twelve Monkeys*, slides back and forth through time, and people "remember" events that have not yet taken place. Probably the most psychologically astute and conceptually consistent presentation of these themes is to be found in the "graphic novels" (long comic books) of Neil Gaiman, *The Sandman*, *The Books of Magic*, and *The Doll's House*.

What is experienced fully in the out-of-body journeys of Robert Monroe and the near-death experiencers has become a popular fascination. It appears that something in us believes that our world of space and time is the broom-closet of a greater cosmos and that the evidence for this larger reality keeps breaking through into our everyday world in the form of mysterious coincidences. It appears that Monroe has seen the whole picture, and the rest of us are glimpsing fragments.

ENCOUNTERS WITH ANGELS

Those who report visitations by angels have apparently glimpsed a momentary fragment of cosmic consciousness breaking through into their everyday lives. Nearly all of these incidents occur at times of extreme emotional crisis: people whose lives are in danger or who face extraordinary psychological challenges. The skeptic may dismiss such stories as nothing but overblown coincidences, the product of overactive imaginations. But, as with near-death journeys, the central issue is what this event has done for its witness. For, whatever has radically changed a person's life must have been a monumental event of enduring significance, one that has "stopped" an old monolog and fashioned a new one.

Authors of books on encountering angels generally have their own story to tell, plus a collection of similar stories gathered from other people. The effect of these anecdotes is to give a validating context for the experiences—as though to convince potential unbelievers that such events are so common that they cannot be discarded as the products of personal idiosyncrasies. There seems to be an "objectivity" to accounts that are echoed by a large variety of people from different backgrounds, negotiating different life circumstances, and even entertaining somewhat variant interpretations of what the coincidental events of mysterious power might mean. They encourage their readers, as well, to hope and keep their eyes open for similar monumental shocks in their own lives.

Unlike other cosmic consciousness-inspired reports, however, encounters with angels generate a good deal of religious argument, mostly from the Bible and Catholic doctrine, designed to prove that there is nothing "demonic," anti-Christian, or dangerous about such moving events. As much as half of each book on angels is devoted to proving that—far from threatening the Christian worldview—the appearance of angels actually constitutes support for following a traditional Christian way of life. A reader less concerned with Christian doctrine will surely wonder whether a breakthrough of cosmic consciousness has not been felt as a challenge to habitual Christian beliefs and that a great effort has been expended to maintain the theological underpinnings of an old monolog at the same time that visionary, *imaginal* events are forcing it to change.

Is there really any difference between the angels encountered by these highly Christian individuals and the beings of light met by New Agers of a less traditional mentality? Probably not. Those who report *seeing* beings of light without offering theological justifications are sometimes fiercely agnostic, like Monroe and Brinkley. Others, like Eadie, are convinced they have met Jesus and God the Father during their near-death sojourns. It is tempting to conclude that what is *seen* is in all cases very much the same—a bodiless, personal being emanating light and compassionate love. But that the *interpretation* of this bright figure seems to depend upon the monolog of faith that is habitual to the witness. Those who have *seen* angels, Jesus, or the Virgin Mary, appear to be strongly connected with a Christian worldview—even if only unconsciously.

New Testament accounts of encounters with the risen Christ have a similar character. Meanwhile, Buddhist texts speak of encounters with the "enjoyment body" (*sambhogakaya*) of the Buddha. In each case, the Buddha appears to his followers in precisely the form the devotees require at that moment in their lives to assist their advance along the spiritual path. It seems reasonable to conclude that fragments of cosmic consciousness may break through into the awareness of any human. When they do so, the "monumental shock" of the experience calls inexorably for a response, a change of life that incorporates the encounter as an essential dimension of one's lifeworld. If the appearance makes sense within the context of the subject's religiously-toned internal monolog, the being of light is immediately identified and named—just as the disciples of Jesus traveling to Emmaus after the crucifixion "recognized Him in the breaking of the bread" (Luke 24:13–35).

In the breakthrough moment of cosmic consciousness, the religious identification of the figure of light is immediate and unreflective. The interpretation is an uncalculated act of faith, pure and complete for the witness, who would insist there was no "interpretation" involved. The figure *seen* was self-evidently Christ, the Buddha, or an angel. For the witness in such a case, the visionary event was a confirmation of faith, not a faith-inspired interpretation of something unknown.

The history of Christianity—and, indeed, the Age of Pisces—has been filled with a fear of being led astray. "Even the Devil can quote the Bible to make his point." The fear of heresy is always present when strong convictions depart from everyday Christian experience, and the angel books are no exception. Thus, Sophy Burnham (*A Book of Angels*, 1990, pp. 34–35) provides three comforting "marks" by which angels can be distinguished from other, more dangerous, cosmic epiphanies. Angels always bring a calm, sweet serenity; their message is always "Fear not!"; and they always effect a change in personality. Cosmic consciousness is a dangerous thing, for demons, too, may startle us with visions.

Early in his mystical career, Ignatius of Loyola had a vision of a luminous serpent covered with eyes. For a time, he was comforted by this vision, believing it had come from God. Later, however, he concluded it had been a distraction cleverly placed in his path by the Devil. Partly in response to this deception, he included a substantial appendix to his *Spiritual Exercises*, "On the Discernment of Spirits." In contrast, the great mystic Teresa of Avila was ordered by her young Jesuit confessor to "give the fig" (in modern terms, "the finger") to her visions. She says she did so "in obedience," but she knew very well which visions were sent by God and which from the Devil; so she "gave the fig" to the Christ visions while weeping and apologizing.

The angel books, therefore, belong very clearly to a long Christian tradition holding that God can intervene in our lives at any moment with a visionary confirmation of our faith. But the same tradition holds that visions are dangerous. Very likely, the sojourns of Monroe would be viewed with the greatest skepticism, if not righteous scorn, by biblically correct Christians. But angel books also belong to the New Age, with its boundless optimism that the world is in the process of a monumental evolutionary leap forward. Thus Eileen Elias Freeman is convinced that angels are appearing more often today than in past centuries, in order to let us know that "heaven is not as far away as we think" (Freeman, 1993, p. 65) and that it is time for us to start transforming the world. Angels are, in this sense, agents of the "quantum leap" of the New Age.

The effect of angels upon Freeman's life is very similar to the effect of her near-death journey for Betty Eadie. Both women were extremely fearful and insecure from earliest childhood. Freeman describes her mother as a very pleasant and well-meaning woman who was totally incapable of emotional connection. Although Freeman did not appreciate her intolerable situation at the time, she lived in a vacuum of emotional abandonment and neglect from a mother who seemed the very image of diligent concern. Freeman was plagued, too, by death fantasies similar to those that oppressed Eadie—the idea that the soul was buried in the ground with the body and that a God who had ordained such a world must be even more cold and cruel, if possible, than her own guardians.

Before her angel first appeared to her, when she was 5 years old, Freeman lived in terror of the dark, the television, the telephone, the vacuum cleaner, most foods, and, above all, any momentary separation from her "loving older parents." These were the people who had been telling her that her grandmother, her kindergarten teacher, and her pet turtle, had all just "gone to sleep" before being buried in the ground for worms to devour. Little Eileen was terrified that she might inadvertently fall asleep in the wrong way and wind up buried in the cold soil along with those other innocent beings.

When the angel appeared in a mist of silvery light over Freeman's doll-crib as a strong, well-built man of light, he delivered a brief two-part message: "Your grandmother is not in a cold and dark grave. She is happy in heaven with God and her loved ones"; and "Always remember, there is nothing to be afraid of." Freeman says her mother never noticed that, from that moment onward, she showed no fear of the things that had formerly aroused overwhelming terror (Freeman, 1993, pp. 7, 9).

At the angel's second appearance, in 1970, Freeman was a senior at Barnard College and living a very sheltered and thoroughly church-centered life. Clearly, her early terror, while much reduced, had not departed entirely. This time she felt an invisible hand on her left shoulder, three times, as though in warning, and finally the angel's voice advising her not to enter her friend's apartment building. In her confusion at receiving such an unexpected and apparently baseless warning from an unquestionably trustworthy source, she entered a church to pray. When she re-emerged onto the street, she found her friend's apartment building surrounded with police cars. A murder had taken place in the building's elevator: "If my angel hadn't warned me, I might have been the one who was killed" (Freeman, 1993, p. 17).

Nine years later, her angels began teaching her about themselves, and over the course of the next three years she produced a 1200 page manuscript. Finally (the most important development in Freeman's mind) in 1992, twenty-two years after the murder incident, she started The AngelWatch Network and Newsletter, to collect, collate, and publicize people's encounters with angels. "To say that 1992 was a watershed year for general awareness of angels and their work in the world today may sound dramatic, but I believe it's true" (Freeman, 1993, p. xiii).

Although we learn few specifics of Freeman's life, it seems clear that a woman, so deeply wounded by unresponsive parents that she lived in a world completely devoid of security, has come to grips with life and gathered around herself a community of fellow believers, all occasioned by a series of breakthroughs of cosmic consciousness into her terrified lifeworld. Her life has been a sincere and largely successful struggle to incorporate cosmic realities into her internal monolog: first by making them theologically safe, and then by finding others who have had experiences that validate her own.

EDGAR CAYCE AND THE HEALERS

One of the most believable accounts of a proto-New Ager and staunch Christian who naively encountered cosmic consciousness without a theory to explain it concerns an inauspicious rural Southerner born in 1877, who was proud to say he had read the Bible once for every year of his life. Like Monroe, Eadie, and Freeman, Edgar Cayce had his first brush with cosmic consciousness while still a youngster. He was 13 years old and reading the story of Manoah[2] for the thirteenth time, when he looked up and saw a lady with wings on her back who offered to grant him his heart's desire. Cayce said he wanted to be helpful to other people, especially to children (Sugrue, 1994, p. 27).

---

[2] The father of Samson, Judges 13. An angel appeared twice to Samson's mother and once to his father to announce the birth of the hero who would save Israel from the Philistines.

The very next day, as he was struggling unsuccessfully with his spelling lesson, he heard the same lady's voice saying, "If you can sleep a little, we can help you" (Sugrue, 1994, p. 27). Following the words literally, he took a half hour's nap with the spelling book under his head and woke up knowing all the words. Two years later, the lady did not intervene when he was hit in the head with a baseball and went into a mild delirium. Reminiscent of sleeping on his school books, he prescribed an effective poultice while "out of himself."

Surprising knowledge acquired, not in the waking state, but in trance, became the central theme of his life in his 24th year, when his fledgling career as an insurance salesman was brought to a halt through an hysterical loss of his voice. Because medical doctors failed to do him any good, Cayce turned to an itinerant stage hypnotist and eventually learned autohypnosis to diagnose his own condition while "asleep."

> In the normal state this body is unable to speak, due to a partial paralysis of the inferior muscles of the vocal cords, produced by nerve strain. This is a psychological condition producing a physical effect. This may be removed by increasing circulation to the affected parts by suggestion while in the unconscious condition (Sugrue, 1994, p. 127).

He gave himself the suggestion to increase the circulation. Observers saw a reddening of the skin of the throat. When he regained consciousness, his voice had returned. For the rest of his life, he performed five or six cures a day by falling "asleep" and leaving his body through a self-devised hypnotic induction read to him by his father, wife, or son.

The lengthy, convoluted "diagnoses" he spoke while in trance give the strong impression he was journeying through the body of the patient, finding infections, growths, and imbalances. His prescriptions were odd by medical standards and often called for herbal, osteopathic, and other alternative methods. But he had a remarkable degree of success. He thought he might have had more success if he had been able to start a hospital, where his prescriptions could be carefully administered and followed up. In fact, he was not able to find even a single physician who would take his readings seriously. As a result, his patients rarely received the medically trained attention he thought they deserved.

The astounding thing about Cayce is that he made no sojourns in the greater cosmos. He traveled instead through people's bodies and souls. He experienced no vivid *imaginal* moment when he left his body, as Monroe did; and he retained virtually no recall of what he had *seen* and said during his trance.[3] Nevertheless, he had a clear *sight* of the surroundings through which his journeyer traveled—not only of the body of the patient, but sometimes of the room in which the patient's body was found or the landscape around the house. Physical proximity of the patient to the "sleeping" Cayce was unimportant. Sometimes, in fact, he gave readings on people who had only just posted a letter requesting his help, and before the letter arrived.

In his mid-40s, Cayce was persuaded by Akron businessman Arthur Lammers, a student of Theosophy, to answer metaphysical questions while in trance. He did so apparently without journeying *imaginally* through the cosmos, but just "knowing" the answer much as he had learned his spelling lessons by sleeping on the book. Cayce had been entirely ignorant of such notions as reincarnation and astral projection, and the metaphysical answers he gave while in trance caused him a great deal of confusion. He could find no mention of these things in the Bible, and believed there must be a reason for the Bible's silence. ←

He found himself in Monroe's position. The healings were by-and-large successful, demonstrating that his journeys through the bodies of his patients were producing reliable results. His journeyer seemed trustworthy. Did he dare extend his trust of the journeyer's work in "Locale I" (the bodies of his patients) to the vastly different realm of metaphysics ("Locale II")? If not, where might the line be drawn between *imaginal* truth and arbitrary fantasy? Cayce's own interest in cosmic questioning was primarily limited to seeking guidance in how to use his extraordinary talent. The answers were consistent, for example, that Virginia Beach was where he should establish the Foundation for Research and Enlightenment, accomplished in 1931, fourteen years before his death, and still carrying on his work today.

Despite his failure to journey through the greater cosmos, Cayce's talent surely belongs to the realm of cosmic consciousness insofar as he was gaining access to verifiable reality through *imaginal* means. We might speculate that the difference between Cayce and Monroe has to do with the mind-set (an aspect of internal monolog) of the two investigators. Cayce's mind was "set" by his exposure to itinerant preachers like Dwight L. Moody and the rural Christian mentality in which he was raised, but probably most of all by his request of the angel when he was

---

3 This is an instance of what Pierre Janet and the French hypnotists of the late 19th century called "complete dissociation," when what is experienced in the altered state remains unknown to the waking ego, as if two separate worlds can be accessed, one in the waking state and the other in trance.

13: *to be helpful to other people*. He evidently understood such a gift within the context of revival meetings and faith-healing. The content of his visions was not particularly biblical, but the mind-set within which he employed it was.

In contrast, Monroe's mind was "set" by the ideals of scientific exploration and technological application. He was guided by an internal monolog that constantly questioned how far he could go, how much he could learn, while Cayce humbly accepted the notion that his talent was given him to help other people in physical or psychological distress. Cayce was driven by a spirit of compassion from the beginning, while Monroe's mind was turned in the direction of compassion only after decades of metaphysical search and his mythic insight into the purpose of the luminous dome. We might conclude that Monroe and Cayce each had his own "predilection" for employing cosmic consciousness, and each has taught us a different lesson.

Edgar Cayce is one of the great—albeit unusual—examples of a psychic healer. Late in his life, he was shown a book by another uneducated American who had employed an almost identical gift fifty years earlier. Cayce said the similarities with his own life gave him "the creeps" (Sugrue, 1994, p. 289). Andrew Jackson Davis, of Poughkeepsie, NY, had begun his career by pronouncing diagnoses and prescriptions while in hypnotic trance, but gradually modified his technique to the point that he only had to place his fingertips on the palm of the patient.

Today, the New Age has produced psychic healers of all kinds, no doubt few of them using a "sleeping" technique like Cayce's, but all of them "shifting" their consciousness so as to take leave of their sensory awareness and enter an *imaginal* state of oneness with the patient. Aura-manipulators like Barbara Brennan (*Hands of Light*, 1988) speak of multiple "shifts," each bringing her into contact with another layer of the patient's aura. Different information is discovered at each of these levels, and different manipulations required.

Monroe and the near-death experiencers have gone on solitary, private journeys and learned about their own personal cosmic identity. Psychic healing implies something different—a real and essential, but generally unknown, connection between us all, self-to-self. If we think of this self-to-self connection between healer and patient on the model of out-of-body journeys, healers would be employing their journeyers (their larger and more complete selves) to encounter the journeying self of the patient. Just as Brinkley's journeyer was able to learn the full emotional reality of his fleshly involvements (as in the instance of his carrying the dying woman about the hospice), so the psychic healer's larger self engages with the larger self of the patient. In doing so, the healer is made aware of how the patient's larger self is being frustrated by the patient's conscious lifestyle, determined by an internal monolog.

Cayce's self-diagnosis and cure of the hysterical loss of voice would be a clear instance of this. His journeyer was able to *see* how the "nerve strain"—caused very likely by his pursuit of a livelihood in conflict with his essential calling, *to be helpful to other people*—had withheld blood from "the inferior muscles of the vocal cords." The "nerve strain" evidently represented a movement from his unconscious to prevent him from selling insurance and find a way *to be helpful.* The prescription, to increase the circulation by hypnotic suggestion, relieved the symptom and proved the accuracy of the diagnosis. But it did not reach the more essential situation, the source of the "nerve strain." The proof of this observation may be found in the fact that he continued to suffer loss of his voice from time to time during his life. In each case, he regained it by giving himself an hypnotic suggestion to increase the circulation.

The psychic healers of the New Age are often more aware than Cayce was of the distinction between conscious symptom and unconscious cause. Consequently, they are more apt to be on the lookout for the deeper psychological conditions underlying psychosomatic disturbances. Nevertheless, they are working with the same self-to-self connection which was the foundation of Cayce's healing.

Cayce's work implied an unconscious, cosmic oneness in which all individuals share—although not consciously. Cayce had to become *unconscious*, enter a trance, where he gained access to a unitary world, where the barriers between his journeying self and the journeying self of the patient dissolved. Only through the right-brained journeyer can this cosmic self-to-self connection be achieved. It runs counter to everything we Pisceans have taken for granted, and seems to be nothing more than rampant, harebrained mysticism.

Nevertheless, we encounter cosmic oneness between individuals all the time—even though our ordinary attitude relegates this data to the realm of the exceptional and meaningless. We are aware that mothers have an extraordinary ability to know when their children are in trouble before receiving news from a third party (particularly in war, knowing when their son died or that he is still alive, although reported dead). We are aware, too, of an intelligent but irrational connection we have with our pets, and they with us. Individuals who have visited gorilla colonies speak of sensing an intelligent connection with the animals and report feeling a great sadness upon leaving them. Is this evidence of "remembering" our pre-Taurean cosmic consciousness?

In *The Secret Life of Plants* (1974), Tompkins and Bird document an emotional connection between humans and the living beings we keep in pots in our living rooms and usually consider to be nonconscious. Recent discoveries in the area of particle physics carry this cosmic connection even to inanimate nature. Electrons separated by more than ten meters, where there is no known physical force acting between them, nevertheless have some kind of connection. It appears that common and scientific experience provides evidence of a kind of fundamental oneness among the objects and beings that comprise our universe.

It seems that our journeying self knows these things, even if they boggle our conscious minds.

MAPPING THE SELF

In *Journey to Ixtlan* (1971, pp. 243–250), Carlos Castaneda gives a puzzling account of *seeing* Don Juan's journeyer, or "double," as Castaneda calls it. The incident occurs early in his training, so that he does not quite comprehend what has happened. Carlos and Don Juan have met four young Mexican Indians in the Sonora desert, all of them apprentice shamans who know Don Juan, although Carlos had never guessed his mentor was involved in the training of others.

Apparently inspired by the fact that the four young strangers have been searching for quartz crystals, Don Juan builds a fire before a large rock and gives them a dramatic impromptu lecture on the shamanic uses of crystals. Then he leaves them for a short time, disappearing behind the rock. Evidently, he meditates or sleeps while out of sight, in order to leave his body; for when he reappears in front of the rock, the five young men, still sitting in a circle around the fire, *see* something incomprehensible.

Castaneda at first notices Don Juan is wearing a strange black hat. He puzzles over its bumps and points until it suddenly dawns on him that he is looking at a pirate's hat. Then he notices that Don Juan is dressed in a complete pirate costume, as though he had just stepped off a movie set. He even has a peg leg, and Carlos' attention is drawn to this detail so obsessively that he spends most of his time discussing within himself how the lower half of the leg could have been so perfectly hidden.

After this strange appearance, Don Juan vanishes again behind the rock and remains there until the fire has burned out and night has fallen. During the long wait, Carlos initiates a conversation with the other young men to get their opinions on how Don Juan created the illusion. He is shocked to learn that none of them *saw* a pirate. One *saw* a Mexican peasant in ragged poncho and battered sombrero, holding a basket. Another *saw* a wild man with long, unkempt hair, who had evidently just killed a friar and was wearing the dead man's robes. The third *saw* an armed *ranchero* in fancy riding dress. The fourth refused to reveal what he had *seen*.

We learn two important facts from this incident. First, the journeying self can sometimes be *seen* by individuals who are in a more-or-less ordinary state of consciousness. Surely the dramatic stories Don Juan had told before the event, some elements hilarious and others frightening, had upset and confused the young men. Their imaginations had doubtless been engaged, but they were still well-oriented in the everyday world, their internal monologs not completely "stopped." Second, when the journeying self is *seen* by individuals in a relatively ordinary state of consciousness, the *imaginal* event is rationalized and "deciphered" in a manner consistent with the internal monolog.

Castaneda is a cosmopolitan man, born somewhere in South America, raised on a wealthy *rancho* and, at the time of the incident, a citizen of Los Angeles where he was earning a doctorate in anthropology. He *sees* the journeyer in terms of the extravagant imagery of a Hollywood adventure film. Meanwhile the three Indians assemble the incomprehensible *sight* in a manner consistent with their own life experience. Still, there is a certain rough agreement in the visions. Each of them has *seen* a mysterious and dangerous character who might be expected to forcibly take whatever he wants, very possibly with violence, motivated by impulses the observer will not anticipate.

The story is consistent with several that Monroe tells about out-of-body journeys in "Locale I," the ordinary world, when he visited friends unannounced. In one instance, he enters the living room of a woman friend who is reading a newspaper. He *sees* that she looks right at him and says, "Bob, if that's you, please go home and don't bother me." Later he learns that what she had *seen* was a rag of gray chiffon floating in the air (Monroe, 1971, p. 171).

Monroe's accounts suggest that the journeyer is most apt to be *seen* by young children—who very likely have not lived long enough to develop an elaborate monolog capable of plugging all the gaps—and by adults with whom he has a strong emotional connection. Monroe insists on the emotional factor. He says his journeys in "Locale I" have to be directed to specific individuals whom he knows well enough that he can hold in his mind a kind of emotional picture of their personality and character (Monroe, 1971, p. 226). He requires some kind of self-to-self connection. Surely such a relationship was very strong between Don Juan and his five apprentices.

We can conclude from all this that a self-to-self connection between healer and patient is both open to the unitary realm of cosmic consciousness and at the same time involves left-brain schemata—schematic, structuring, interpreting imagery and concepts that belong to the habitual life of the conscious ego. We have to "schematize" what we *see* if we are to make conscious use of our visions.

Consider, for example, the stories brought back by camera-carrying explorers who have visited remote, preliterate societies. Very often, these high-technology Westerners have shown the natives a photograph, and a group of them has stood about puzzling over the shiny stiff paper with its gray shadings, until one of them traces the outline of a human form and they all suddenly "see" the photograph as a picture of themselves. We take photographs so much for granted that we forget that, at some point in our childhood, we had to learn how to "see" them. Similarly, biology students have to learn to "see" what is in a microscope slide. This is the reason so much undergraduate laboratory time is devoted to drawing and labeling the fuzzy granularity of what appears through the optics of the instrument. The higher the technology of the apparatus, the greater the effort involved in learning to interpret what has been made to appear.

Imaginal seeing involves the same kind of interpretive work. Aura-reading is a case in point. The luminous egg of the aura is a vision of the journeying self. But what is *seen* in that egg depends upon two factors. The first and more obvious is the *imaginal* sensitivity of the reader, the ability to "shift" consciousness and take advantage of the gaps in everyday awareness. The second has to do with the schematic interpretive structure the reader imposes over a luminous vision in order to derive highly differentiated information.

Professional aura-manipulators generally employ a standardized schema, so as not to have to "reinvent the wheel." Barbara Brennan (*Hands of Light,* 1988, p. 5) tells us that she had psychic powers as a child. She would sit in the woods for long periods of time without moving, until the animals resumed their daily activities and she was able to observe them. During this time, she realized she "knew" when a squirrel or a rabbit would emerge from the undergrowth *behind* her. She could detect each animal by a kind of *feel*. Having more opportunity than Monroe to verify these "Locale I" observations, she had no doubt of what she was *seeing*; and the more sensory feedback she got, the more differentiated her *imaginal* perceptions became.

As she grew older, involvement with the public world caused her to neglect her cosmic consciousness. But in her adult career as a therapist, she began to notice that she was *seeing* a glow around some of her patients. This led her to explore what others knew about auras through library research and training sessions with more accomplished aura-readers. Although she is aware that there are many different systems (organized sets of schemata) for *seeing* and interpreting the shapes and colors *seen* in an aura, she follows rather closely the system set forth by David Tansley (*The Raiment of Light,* 1984). In this system, the aura has seven basic layers, each generated from one of the traditional seven chakras identified in yoga. The lowest chakra (located between the genitals and anus) generates the layer closest to the physical body; the next (located in the abdomen) generates the second layer, a few inches further out from the body, and so on. Each of these has a distinctive color, reading from the lowest upward: red, red-orange, yellow, green, sky blue, indigo, and white.

In accordance with the schemata of this system, Brennan has learned to distinguish seven different "shifts" in her consciousness. She "tunes in," as it were, to the yellow light of the third layer or the sky-blue light of the fifth by aligning her consciousness with that same light frequency and chakra of her own journeyer. During a reading or healing of a certain layer of the aura, she has to "hold the color" of the intended layer throughout the entire work. She cautions that, if we wish to work on the red or blue layer, we cannot just "think" red or blue. "Thinking" belongs to the yellow layer and thought about any layer at all will place the aura-reader in her own yellow layer and limit her work to the yellow layer of the patient. To work with the blue layer, she has to "be" blue, that is, she has to "shift" her consciousness into her own blue area and attend only to what appears in the blue realm.

A real understanding of Brennan's system, which has been cobbled together from a variety of different sources, cannot be gained simply by reading her books. She is talking about *experience*, about how it feels and looks from these various "frequencies" of consciousness. She is using her journeyer in a highly differentiated manner to engage with aspects of the patient's journeyer. To learn to read auras as Brennan does, we have to submit ourselves to an extensive and highly disciplined training in order to find these very concrete and specific dimensions of experience.

We can understand this whole process in line with "The Hymn of the Pearl." Before he left his heavenly home, the Gnostic Everyman lived in his raiment of light unconsciously, just as all of us "have" a journeyer and live within our journeyer without realizing it. Only by divesting himself of his journeyer and descending into the land of forgetting and remembering does Everyman acquire the schema he needs to gain a differentiated understanding of his luminous egg. Before his descent, he stood rapt in *gnosis*, one-pointed contemplation of the One. But, having nothing with which to compare it, he was unable to recognize his *gnosis* for what it was. After his descent into Egypt and subsequent return, he *sees* that his heavenly robes are covered with images of the King of kings (the One) and the faculty for knowing the One (*gnosis*). At this point, he has come to *understand* his heavenly existence as he never had before.

To "see" something means to understand it, to grasp it according to a schema that makes sense of it. In this sense, Brennan's progress in learning to *see* and manipulate auras—from her earliest stage of *seeing* a vague glow around her psychotherapy patients to her present stage of moving deliberately through seven different layers of the aura—involves the acquisition of a complex set of schemata. She has descended into the "Egypt" of ancient wisdom, working diligently with her fleshly ego in libraries and training programs, and then returning to her journeyer with the schemata she has acquired.

In doing all this, she has gradually changed her internal monolog. In her childhood, when she was able to *see* the animals in the woods, her rudimentary internal monolog included aspects of cosmic consciousness, with its *imaginal* access to a realm generally believed to be impossible and unimaginable. She failed to appreciate the extraordinary nature of her talent, because she had no worldly experience with which to compare it. At this time, she resembled Everyman before his descent into the fleshly forgetting of Egypt.

In the second stage of her development, she forgot her heavenly home of cosmic consciousness entirely, as she ate and drank from the fleshly table of reading, writing, and arithmetic, the excitement of social involvements, clothing fads, television programs, and everything else that comprises our public world. She developed her intellect, acquiring a masters degree in physics and another in psychotherapy. There was no great "wisdom" involved in these pursuits. She had entered the Egypt of Alexandria, with its libraries and cultural excellence, the world of Isidore before he retired to the desert, a world that carries with it the dangers of arrogance in fleshly learning and the cruelty that turns the world and the human being into a clockwork without a soul.

The third stage of Brennan's development was heralded by noticing the auric glow about her psychotherapy patients. This corresponds to the heavenly message Everyman received in a *dream* from his family still residing in the greater cosmos of light. Brennan realized there was a "pearl" to be acquired. But to find it, she could not bask in the glow of her *imaginal* message. She had to retire to the Egyptian desert and sit at the feet of the ancient priests and masters of forgotten wisdom to dig out the schemata by which this wisdom could be understood.

In doing so, she was remembering the cosmic consciousness she had once taken for granted—but remembering with a difference. She was expanding her internal monolog, learning to talk to herself about the *imaginal* realities of cosmic-consciousness encounters between her own journeyer and the journeyer of her patient. At this point, she has learned to *see* the raiment of light out of which she unconsciously slipped during her childhood. If she does not *see* the King of kings and the flickering of the *gnosis* in that luminous egg, she *sees* many other things that are presently of greater value to her and her patients.

Edgar Cayce also *saw* auras—colors gently pouring from the head and shoulders of his patients. He lacked a word to name them until he met Arthur Lammers and was introduced to some of the metaphysical questions inspired by Theosophy. But he had noticed that the auras changed as individuals became ill, depressed, fell in love, or found fulfillment. Apparently, he did not need to know more about auras, as he had his own schemata for diagnosing and healing his patients.

There is evidently a limitless variety of schematic systems for making sense of what *imaginal seeing* reveals. Each brings certain realities to light and leaves others in the dark. The simplest schema for healing through cosmic consciousness has been proposed by psychologist Lawrence LeShan (*The Medium, the Mystic, and the Physicist,* 1975). LeShan's scientist's curiosity was aroused by the claims of psychic healers and their patients that this radical alternative to mainstream medicine actually seemed to work. Believing there had to be a rational explanation behind the confusing plethora of methods and mystical claims, he set out to find what they all had in common. He found that psychic healers all spoke of "shifting" their awareness. The central piece was that the healers entered an altered state of consciousness in which they achieved a oneness with their patients. It was apparently not necessary that the patients be aware of what the healers were doing or that they cooperate with them by trying to achieve an altered state themselves.

LeShan thought that, if he was right about this, he ought to be able to become a psychic healer himself, and began by practicing meditation. Once he had learned to achieve a meditative state in which he felt he was one with the cosmos, he *imaginally* brought a series of patients into his state of oneness. It worked rather consistently. Subsequently, he found that he could teach others to meditate and achieve the same results, even when the patient was hundreds of miles away.

Since learning of LeShan's work in the mid-70s, I have employed the technique several times. I never claimed to be a healer, never asked for the patient's cooperation, and never inquired afterward to see what results, if any, had been achieved. On one occasion, however, my intended beneficiary did seem to respond, and I tentatively chose to accept the response as a confirmation that something helpful had occurred.

The incident took place in the midst of a psychodrama session, where the young woman who was the evening's "protagonist" was called upon to make some kind of decision about how the psychodrama should be structured. She fell into an inner conflict complicated by embarrassment. There seemed no way out for her, and the tension in the room increased unbearably. I closed my eyes and imagined the two of us rising through the roof of the house and above the trees and roads on the steep slope of Herrliberg. The Lake of Zurich curved below us to our left in a long, rough arc down to the lights of the Bellevue Bridge and the Kongresshaus. Zurich became a spattering of lights, as we continued to rise. Then, all of Europe lay in darkness, and I had to guess where the Atlantic lapped. We stopped and held our position, as the whole planet glowed like a blue marble below us. The vision lasted a few moments until a change in the atmosphere of the psychodrama session called me back to Earth.

Somehow, the woman's confusion had dissipated and the evening's work went on. When the session ended, she singled me out and thanked me with notable intensity "for all my help." Nothing was specified; I asked no questions. I felt confusion over why she was thanking me, and warmth and gratitude of my own. Had I helped resolve her confusion; did she know I had? How had she known it was me? Was it her journeyer who was thanking me?

There was only a single schematizing idea behind what I had done, that her confusion stemmed from an inner conflict and that, if I could bring her into a state of oneness, the conflict would be resolved and she would know what she wanted to do. There were no aura levels, no hypotheses over what was bothering her, just the idea that she needed to feel united within herself and with the cosmos.

THE JOURNEYER'S STATE OF HEALTH

Novelist Michael Crichton has written an autobiography (*Travels,* 1988) organized around his pursuit of unusual experiences, from mountain-climbing and scuba diving with sharks, to New Age workshops. In 1982, he spent two weeks in the Lucerne Valley desert of California at a conference run by Los Angeles physician Brugh Joy. At one point, the forty participants had their chakras balanced by Joy and his assistants.

Crichton had plenty of time to observe the balancing process on the earlier recipients and was unimpressed. People lay on massage tables under blankets while soft music played. First, the assistants touched the participant's bodies in various places to activate their chakras. Then Joy spent about five minutes with each person, holding his hands over different parts of their bodies. Several minutes after the balancing, each person got up and silently left the room. "The only thing I noticed was that the atmosphere in the room got thick . . . like sitting at the bottom of a jar of honey" (Crichton, 1988, p. 271).

When his own turn came, Crichton felt a sensation of warmth from the assistant's hands where they rested on his body. Joy's hands, held a few inches above his body, seemed to radiate heat like a hot iron; but Crichton found he was too relaxed and dreamy to be able to pay attention. He fell asleep and missed the rest of the procedure. He was awakened by a hand on his shoulder, got up, and walked out into the desert, where he found everything "glowing, alive, and vivid." He got lost on the way to the dining room and was not hungry when he got there, but enjoyed looking at the food.

> I could stare at a cut strawberry for an hour, noticing the patterns, the colors. Or bread—a slice of bread was fascinating to look at. Everybody looked wonderful, too, even though I didn't want to talk. My sensations were too immediate, too compelling, to be reduced to conversation (Crichton, 1988, p. 278).

He was aware of having a psychedelic experience without having taken a drug. People began to speak of mystical visions and *seeing* one another's aura. Crichton was jealous.

A woman named Judith was describing Sarah's yellow and pink aura. Crichton asked how far out the aura extended, holding his hand above Sarah's head. Judith directed his hand until it coincided with the edge of what she was *seeing*, and Crichton was astonished to feel a distinct "contour of warmth." Following it, he discovered a bump on the left side of the body, which Judith confirmed. He and Judith repeated the experiment with several other people, Crichton trying in vain to mislead her and prove the whole thing a hoax (Crichton, 1988, pp. 280–281).

A couple of days later, Crichton had his aura "fluffed" by Eileen, who first "combed" through its invisible "fur" with her fingers, stopping to shake off invisible debris from time to time. Finally, she pushed up with her palms against the grain of his invisible "fur." "It was like taking a bath. I felt cleaned up, spruced up." Eventually Crichton had to agree that "energy findings are objective."

The extraordinary sensations continued after the conference, leaving him feeling "wonderfully alive," but they gradually faded after a few days and were gone.

> The energy work was real, the meditations were real, but what good was it if you couldn't maintain the high and apply it to your daily life? What had it all amounted to in the end? Just another illusion. Summer camp for adults. A lot of New Age mumbo-jumbo.

> It wasn't until much later that I looked back and saw that, within eight months of returning from the desert, I had changed my relationships, my residence, my work, my diet, my habits, my interests, my exercises, my goals—in fact, just about everything in my life that could be changed. These changes were so sweeping that I couldn't see what was happening while I was in the midst of them (Crichton, 1988, pp. 285–286).

The upshot of the experiences described in his book was that Crichton developed a healthy suspicion of his internal monolog. He says that, when he found himself rejecting an idea or an opportunity as fine for someone else but not for himself, he seized upon this automatic and unthinking rejection as indicating precisely what he *should* be doing. He began to recognize the flat certainties of the monolog as plugging a gap, and realized that life would be more satisfying and enjoyable if he could find a way to open the gap rather than sticking with his habits and leaving it closed.

Crichton's doubting, foot-dragging account of his two weeks with Brugh Joy leaves us in little doubt that a kind of "consciousness raising" had been going on during that conference. People who had perhaps gone to the California desert somewhat in the spirit of Isidore's retirement to the foot of Mount Sinai found fragmentary evidence that they were indeed soul people. They were awakened to the reality of their own journeyer and could use that knowledge to *see* what lay invisibly beyond the reach of their sensory existence. The energy work not only opened them to what lay outside their gaps, it also changed the way they lived. Some kind of realignment had occurred.

Crichton's experience with auras seems to verify the central principle of Barbara Brennan's work, namely that the aura is the larger reality of our bodily existence—which is precisely why we have taken the aura to be an image of the journeyer. Brennan's first corollary to this principle is also familiar to us. She says the aura's energy "supports us, nourishes us, gives us life." When it is in balance, we are healthy and vitally engaged in our lives. This claim agrees very well with what we have concluded from Crichton, Monroe, Brinkley, and Eadie. When the journeyer and our fleshly ego have achieved a balance, we live more essentially and with a satisfying sense of meaningfulness. But Brennan has a second corollary to her principle that the aura is our larger reality: When out of balance, the aura transmits its disharmony to the body, causing physical disease and psychological dysfunctions like depression and compulsions.

This last point may seem plausible enough, but it raises a problem. The problem does not lie with the priority of the luminous egg over the fleshly ego, for we are familiar with this idea from the Gnostics, Monroe, and Brinkley, all of whom "know" that the journeyer has come from the Cosmos of Light and donned a garment of flesh. The problem lies with the aura-manipulators' claim that the journeyer's imbalances enflesh themselves as our diseases and discomforts. We have not considered the possibility that there could be something wrong with the journeyer. Indeed, when we followed Brinkley and Eadie on their near-death sojourns, it appeared that the journeyer was the very image of health, balance, wholeness, and wisdom. The journeyer had the whole picture of the individual's life. We can imagine Brinkley's journeyer protesting the assassin's life that his fleshly ego was living, but not able to get his cosmic message through.

If the journeyer is this greater self, what is the aura? What gets distorted and out of balance? If luminous eggs can be distorted, they must resemble more the fleshly life we live than the wholeness of the journeyer. Evidently, the luminous egg the aura-readers *see* is not the journeyer itself, but the point where journeyer and flesh meet. To apprehend someone's aura is to consider an image of how the subject's life fails to live up to the journeyer's standards. *Seeing* an aura must be something like contemplating a life-review in a snapshot. To have our auras read must be something like taking a vicarious near-death journey. For, without actually facing the prospect of dying, we are obtaining a "read out" on how our fleshly lives have been incomplete and distorted versions of our journeyers' best intentions.

Aura reading resembles the dream of the Gnostic Everyman. Our fleshly life was supposed to have been a cosmic mission, but we have forgotten it. Having our auras read is a reminder, a message from the "home" of our cosmic origins. The distortions and imbalances in our auras may be said to "cause" our fleshly diseases and discomforts in the sense that our distorted fleshly lives of forgetting have caused them. To have our auras balanced and realigned is to have our fleshly selves reminded of the potential wholeness that resides in the eternal journeyer.

Suppose Brennan had been present at the monastery of St. Catherine around A.D. 700, during Isidore's seven years in the desert. If she had read his aura at the beginning of his residence there, she would have *seen* the distortions of arrogance and cruelty in his luminous egg—the results of the fleshly monolog he was carrying from his high-level career in Alexandria. If she had taken a second reading ten days before his death, at the point when the Abbott invited Isidore to join the community of monks, we have little doubt she would have *seen* an aura in beautiful balance. For, by that time, he had truly become a soul person. He was living his journeyer without distortion. His humble *koan* of begging at the gate had opened his gaps and reminded him of the life of soul he had forgotten. His *koan* had realigned his aura, brought his fleshly existence into harmony with the larger reality of his journeyer.

Now let us suppose further that the Abbott was a New Age man who had invited Brennan to the desert to assist him in the job of spiritually transforming his monks. In such a case, he would surely have wanted Brennan to manipulate Isidore's aura and bring it into balance. Very possibly, with an assistant like Brennan, the Abbott might have forgone the *koan* of begging at the gate and assigned the Alexandrian the task of having his aura manipulated—perhaps as often as once a week, for this seems to be rather more intensive a regimen than Brennan generally expects of her patients. Would this have been a more effective *koan* for Isidore? Would he have achieved balance in less than seven years?

I am inclined to doubt it, on the grounds of two independent sets of data. First, there is the story of Brinkley. Surely a near-death experience is a dramatic and profoundly moving monumental shock in which the nearly dead individual is confronted directly with the wholeness and balance of his eternal journeyer. While on his near-death sojourn, Brinkley's aura was fully balanced. Indeed, it is this wholeness and balance that enabled Brinkley to *see* his fleshly past for the distortion it was. Brinkley was reminded in no uncertain terms; and painful as it was, he loved it. He had a hard time leaving the Crystal City of his visions during the months of his physical rehabilitation.

When he resumed his fleshly existence, he had tremendous difficulty integrating that transcendent vision. He had been reminded well enough, but he did not know what to do with the reminder. He changed his life insofar as he avoided cruelty, but he had not yet gotten the full impact of his life-review or aura realignment. He required a second near-death experience fourteen years later. And he is still working on his *koan*: how to live compassionately.

Brinkley's experience makes it clear that an aura balancing functions as a reminder, not a metaphysical restructuring. This, too, is why Carlos Castaneda's apprenticeship to Don Juan has lasted so many years. Every one of his sojourns into the world of the *nagual* was a reminder; but, as he begins to learn in his sixth book, *The Second Ring of Power* (1977), he has forgotten those reminders. In the years since Don Juan has passed over forever into the realm of the *nagual*, Castaneda's task has been to struggle to recall what he had learned in his altered states of consciousness, and find a way to incorporate the lessons into his conscious life.

The second source of evidence leads to the same conclusion. I refer to my own experience as a Jungian analyst, working with people on a week-to-week basis to help them discover their essential identity and to realign their lives with it. Not a few of my patients have been to aura-manipulators like Brennan. They have been moved by the experience, and speak of how it has energized them, given new hope and vitality. Often I can see the change in them. But I also see that it does not last. They fall back into their old monolog and habits, and our work goes on in very much the same way it always had. They have been reminded, but they do not know how to utilize that reminder. The work of refashioning the monolog is still the essential piece in transforming their fleshly existence.

Those who have embarked on sojourns in the greater cosmos have fully experienced a unity that comprises—but extends unimaginably beyond—our planet of space and time. Those who have *seen* angels and auras or have experienced the profound connection they have with other humans have glimpsed a fragment of this same cosmic unity breaking through into their everyday lives. Their glimpse of the greatness that surrounds us has been a *hint* of cosmic oneness, something that might be followed up. For temporal and fleshly beings like ourselves, such a hint always occurs as a monumental shock that breaks through the gaps in our awareness and leaves us with a task. How are we to live in this broom-closet now that the door is open? Unconsciously, most of us pull the door closed and go on about our narrow lives. During the latter half of the Age of Pisces, we have talked ourselves into discarding the glimpse as a momentary fancy, a mistaken illusion, or merely a dream—if we have not suspected ourselves of outright madness. The New Age draws our attention to the open door and sets us to wondering what we may do about it.

Chapter

6

THE COSMOS: UNIVERSE OR MULTIVERSE?

The Sufi observes forms of exquisite freshness and subtlety through direct communication with the celestial powers. This is the intermediate stage in the stages of the People of Love. In a state between wakefulness and sleep one hears horrible voices and strange cries, and in the unconscious state of the sakina [divinely sent peace of heart] one sees great lights. . . . Such events happen to masters, not to those who shut their eyes in solitude and let their imaginations take flight.

(SUHRAWARDI IN MERKUR, 1993, P. 224)

We fail to see these other time-worlds because our conscious life is nothing more than a social agreement.

(WOLF, 1991, P. 225)

The belief today among many theoretical physicists involved in superstring research is that the universe evolved from a ten-dimensional string that was unstable. . . . Six dimensions have curled up, leaving our four-dimensional universe intact.

(VALLEE, 1988, P. 254)

Myth, says a Church Father, is "what is believed always, everywhere, and by everybody"; hence the man who thinks he can live without a myth, or outside it, is an exception. He is like one uprooted, having no true link either with the past, or with the ancestral life which continues within him, or yet with contemporary human society. He does not live in a house like other men, does not eat and drink like other men, but lives a life of his own, sunk in a subjective mania of his own devising, which he believes to be the newly discovered truth.

(JUNG, 1912, P. XXIV)

The universe is the sum of all the material beings in existence, holding together as an organized and interconnected whole. Myriads of galaxies moving in harmony, each comprised of countless suns, unimaginable in size and complexity, yet nevertheless One. Although we cannot see it all, even with telescopes, we can imagine boarding a spaceship to tour it.

The multiverse is something else. It is an assemblage of interrelated and mutually invisible universes. The discovery of black holes, for instance, raises the question of what happens to all the matter and light sucked in, never to return. Does it flow into other universes? Superstring theory requires ten dimensions to describe physical events. Our experience, however, knows only four (length, width, depth, and time). Where are the other six? Some say they are "curled" or "folded" up. Do they belong to other universes lying outside our experience? There is no way to tour the multiverse in a spaceship.

The journeying of people like Monroe, Castaneda, and Brinkley suggests a relativity of space and time much more "monumentally shocking" than the theories of Einstein. These people seem to have left time and space and entered a spirit world that gives them access, not only to the moment and locality where their bodies lie unconscious, but to a multitude of places and times both on this planet and elsewhere. Their unitary perspective outside of space and time implies that each of us may be living a multitude of simultaneous lives in parallel universes. Monroe's image of the luminous dome makes this mind-boggling alternative comprehensible.

Such journeying is not limited to the "higher" religious traditions of ancient Gnosticism, Christian mysticism, Jewish flights to the divine "throne" (merkabah), Sufi sojourns in the imaginal world, and the celestial ascent of shamans. The theme of journeys to alternate realms that cannot be located on any earthly map is to be found as well in folklore the world over. The entrance to the world of the fairies and other wee folk was said to be found at the base of small round hills, marked by circles of plants or stones, or in the roots of ancient oak trees. The jinn of Arabic legends can whisk the unsuspecting off to uncharted territory with promises of fabulous riches or supreme sexual delight. The greatest of King Arthur's knights, Lancelot and Galahad, owed their excellence of soul and prowess at arms to their mysterious underwater origins and rearing by the Ladies of the Lake. The few who found the Castle of the Holy Grail had to become unconscious and be carried by magic boats or steeds. Mermaids lure fishermen and lost explorers to a timeless realm beneath the sea or at the bottom of enchanted lakes. Many of these people never return, while others come back changed beyond recognition.

In a Japanese folktale (Cole, 1982, pp. 521–523), a boy named Urashima, who loves the sea like a brother, one day catches a turtle on his fishing line and, out of kindness, lets it go. A beautiful girl arises from the spray of the turtle's splash and reveals that she is the being to whom, in the form of a turtle, he had shown kindness. As a reward, she invites him to visit her Dragon Palace at the bottom of the sea. He lives four years with her in a dream of happiness before remembering his home. The Dragon Princess knows his desire before he speaks of it and lets him go, giving him a small pearl box that he is to keep unopened so that he will be able to return to her. Back at his familiar bend in the bay, Urashima finds 400 years have passed. It is no longer his home, but he does not know how to return to the Dragon Palace. In his confusion, he opens the box and a little white cloud rises from it, bearing the likeness of the Dragon Princess' face. As it floats away, he rapidly ages and melts. Under the light of the new moon, there remained only a small pearl box on the sandy rim of the shore, where the great green waves lifted white arms of foam.

Many of the themes in this tale are already familiar to us from the journeys of New Agers. Urashima has gone to a place that can be located neither by spaceship nor submarine, but by an *imaginal* process that lies outside of space and time—possibly in a "folded up" dimension of the cosmos. The sense of time passing there is so different from what we know here that four years or four days may correspond to four centuries or four millennia. The beings that inhabit that realm are more radiant, more clever, more beautiful, and more fascinating than any we may meet in our daily lives. They have no proper shape, but may assume any form: a beautiful woman, a turtle, or a sea dragon. They have their own way of life that is clearly happier and more fulfilling than ours. There appears to be a completeness to their lives that ours lack, and they know us intimately. There is nothing we can hide from them, for they know our every thought. Communication with them is instantaneous, fully accurate, and without words. They are guided by kindness and compassion.

To live in that realm is to enter a state of consciousness that is foreign to our waking lives, but by no means foreign to our larger selves. It resembles more our dreams than our sensory awareness. It satisfies in a different way. We move in that realm with an amazing swiftness, as though merely to think of a place is to be there; and we are guided by a compass whose dial we never see. Those who have been privileged

enough to visit such an alternate world have generally been unconsciously familiar with it all their lives. Urashima loves the sea like a
brother and spends every hour of daylight rowing about on its surface.
Eileen Freeman first saw her angel at age 5; Edgar Cayce at 13; Monroe
had his first encounter early in his teens and several more in the year he
spent as a hobo, after flunking out of Ohio State. In one version of "The
Little Mermaid," the prince has been enchanted by his aquatic lover hiding in the shape of foam long before he sees her human shape; and in
every version of the tale, the mermaid has loved him even longer.

An Irish variant of the tale of Urashima, "The Enchanted Lake"
(Stamer, 1987, pp. 93–96), provides a unique and humorous twist to the
story. The hero swims miraculously to the underwater palace and even
accepts a ring from the mermaid princess, but, refusing to marry her, he
returns to the shore, where he sells the ring for a few pennies and con-
gratulates himself on his cleverness. If we are not horrified at how
cheaply he values the privilege he has been granted, we are perhaps relieved that, at least in one instance, the story ends free of the tragedy and
nostalgia that saturate the general run of folktales dealing with sojourns
in the multiverse.

Two worlds meet in these tales, and somebody passes over; but in
the end we are faced with loss. Neither we nor the fabulous ones are ultimately satisfied with our respective existences. We long for their freedom from time and flesh, while they long for our entanglement, the
intensity of our emotions, the fatefulness of our Being-toward-death.

In the most hopeful variants on this theme, the protagonist is left
with a child. The baby-swapping tales of fairies generally leave the humans with a monstrous "changeling," a poor substitute for the lost son
or daughter. But in one Japanese tale, "Howori and Toyotama" (Time-
Life, [n.d.], pp. 87–95), the prince disobeys the rule his mermaid lays
down and loses her, but is left in this world with the offspring of his undersea marriage. Perhaps the lad will become an extraordinary person
and his father will be transformed in the process of raising him, but the
parents of exceptional children rarely acquit themselves well in fairy
tales. Their children generally succeed in spite of them.

Raising the child born of a love affair with a cosmic being corresponds to the task given near-death journeyers like Brinkley and Eadie,
the job of integrating the wisdom gained from a cosmic sojourn with the
everyday life of an earthly ego. The hybrid child is the symbol of that
union between temporal consciousness and eternal transcendence—a
living being comprised of both. But something is missing in the fairy

tales. There is no life-review, no higher unitive perspective gained. As dreamily wonderful as life in the undersea kingdom may be, it seems to be lived in a kind of daze. The earthly protagonists forget themselves, as though they have slipped into a coma. If, after four days or four years, they remember they had a personal life of their own, a home with family and friends, it is too late to get it back. The old life has been dead for centuries. If they succeed in returning from their liaison in an invisible dimension of the multiverse, they are left with an obsessive pining and nostalgia over what has been lost forever.

The New Agers we have considered have had their eyes opened. Their lives have become more fulfilling and meaningful, open to a transcendent realm they barely guessed before they sojourned in the greater cosmos, encountered an angel, or learned to *see* and live the journeyer implied in their aura. The heroes and heroines of folktales, in contrast, have become fixated—stuck between the dreamy marvels of the other world and the flat matter-of-factness of this one. They are left in a state of arrested development. Reconciling the two domains of their experience is utterly beyond their powers, and the earthly life that remains for them reeks of tragic loss. Death is the only mercy left them. There is no "happily ever after" in this genre of folktale.

Folktales represent the fantasies of those who have *not* journeyed. Both the teller and the audience are fully immersed in this world. The stories reflect a social consensus rooted in the internal monologs of those who have spun them and those who sit on the edges of their seats while hearing them. They allude to the gaps. What happens to those who set out to sea or into the forest and never return? They must have been drawn by something monumental. It must have promised them unimaginable rewards. Perhaps they were satisfied beyond their wildest dreams. But they never came back. Or if they did, it was long after the world they had known had passed away. They were left without a home. Perhaps it is better, after all, to stay right where we are and leave these transcendent delights to the realm of fiction.

When the story-teller rises and the fire in the hearth settles down to expiring coals, we retire in a state of confused excitement. Maybe there really is something "out there," something fantastically satisfying. But there is a dreadful price to pay. If we envy Urashima his four hundred years of bliss, we remind ourselves that, for him, it passed as quickly as four days or four years. We are thankful that we were not left on that beach watching the ghostly face of our lover dissipating over the sea. We still have our comforting home. No matter that it leaves us dissatisfied.

Our internal monolog has been questioned, but in the end reassuringly re-established. We sigh with relief before falling asleep.

FRAGMENTS OF ONENESS

Throughout the Age of Pisces, the Gnostics of various traditions and various centuries have been awakened to a cosmic oneness unknown in folktales. Yet they were aware as well that the experience of divine union could be subverted. There is too much "out there" that is more powerful than we are; and one whose compass fails is in danger of a compulsive attachment to demonic lesser powers. Such a sojourner becomes trapped in a realm that is less than ultimate. *Gnosis* is subverted, the One remains unknown.

In the Gnosticism that flourished at the dawn of Pisces, these demonic powers were generally called Archons. The Earth was surrounded by concentric spheres of light beings, each ruled by an Archon more interested in its own self-aggrandizement than in worshiping the One who was its origin and destiny. The souls of the Gnostics who sojourned through those spheres were in constant danger of destruction by these demonic powers who had lost their compass of *gnosis*. They had to be tricky and devout to succeed in their sojourn to the One.

"The Gospel of Mary," a Christian Gnostic text dating from the early fifth century, but incorporating fragments datable to the third, bears witness to the dangers of getting lost in one of the lower spheres. As the Gospel opens, Peter and the other disciples are afraid to preach the Good News of the Kingdom lest they fall to the same fate as Jesus. Peter calls upon Mary—whom "the Savior loved more than the rest of women" and with whom He had shared more of the mysteries of *gnosis* than with anyone else—to tell them what she has learned. Her answer describes the journey she made through the spheres of the Archons.

> When the soul had overcome the third Archon, it went upwards and saw the fourth Archon, (which) took seven forms. The first form is darkness, the second desire, the third ignorance, the fourth is the excitement of death, the fifth is the kingdom of the flesh, the sixth is the foolish wisdom of the flesh, the seventh is the wrathful wisdom. These are the seven [Archons] of wrath. They ask the soul, "Whence do you come, slayer of men, or where are you going, conqueror of space?" The soul answered and said, "What binds me has been slain, and what turns me about has been overcome,

and my desire has been ended, and ignorance has died. In a [world] I was released from a world, [and] in a type from a heavenly type, and (from) the fetter of oblivion which is transient. From this time on will I attain to the rest of the time, of the season, of the aeon, in silence" (Robinson, 1977, p. 473).

If the "Mary" of this Gospel is—as seems likely—not the Mother of Jesus but the Magdalena, the woman whose sexual "sins were forgiven because she loved much," her journey through the lower spheres and her answer to the challenges of the Archons makes a great deal of sense. She journeys (is a "conqueror of space") because she has succeeded in slaying her fleshly ego with its desires and attachments ("slayer of men"). Her old "type" of being has been transformed. Her internal monolog now dwells upon the revelations of the One through *gnosis*, and has given up its fleshly attachments. And because these have been relinquished, she has an answer to the Archons who would sidetrack her heavenly ascent.

In Jewish mysticism from roughly the same time period, *gnosis* takes the accomplished rabbi through seven palaces or spheres before reaching the divine Throne (*merkabah*). The rabbis often liken it to a *ladder* of ascent. The danger stems from accepting the visions reached at each stage as though they are real, and not illusory traps. For example, at the Sixth Palace, the initiate may find himself threatened by "thousands and thousands of waves of water, yet there is not a single drop there." To take the illusory for the real is to be as misguided as the Israelites in the desert who worshipped the golden calf. Dan Merkur, in *Gnosis: An Esoteric Tradition of Mystical Visions and Unions*, says:

> The visionary's destruction by the angels of the sixth palace could be forestalled by means of an appropriate prayer. Reciting a prayer served to control the anxiety that would otherwise have led to an experience of ecstatic death (Merkur, 1993, p. 166).

Clearly, the danger in a visionary ascent through the lower spheres is that what is of lesser and peripheral importance may be taken for the central reality, trapping the mystic in an illusory realm—like the Undersea Palace of the mermaids. The prayer uttered by the journeying mystic remembers the difference between the One and its lower manifestations. By uttering a fervent prayer, the Gnostic reorients himself to the One. When he does so, the overwhelming waves of the Sixth Palace dissolve and he *sees* they are merely the tiles of its floor. Remembering his *gnosis* reorients the Gnostic rabbi, recovers his compass, and overcomes his danger of getting stuck in a demonic distraction that would pervert his ascent to the Throne.

Less than two decades before the birth of the Ladder Man and no more than 800 miles to the southeast of the Monastery of St. Catherine, the Prophet Muhammad ascended a ladder through the seven heavens to see God face to face. Actually, his journey had two sections. In the first part, he traveled through what he believed to be Monroe's "Locale I," to the earthly city of Jerusalem, where he entered the Temple of Yahweh, met with the prophets of Judaism, and led them in prayer.[1] After this, the angel Gabriel showed him a ladder that ascended through the spheres and provided him with a steed, named Buraq, to carry him on his journey through "Locale II," the spirit world. The earliest biography of the Prophet tells the story this way:

> A trustworthy person has reported to me from Abu Saʿid that he had heard Muhammad tell: "After I had done the necessary in Jerusalem I was brought a ladder (*miʿraj*), and I never saw a more beautiful one. It was the one upon which the dead turn their glances at the resurrection. My friend [Gabriel] made me climb until we reached one of the heavenly gates, which is called the Gate of the Guard. There twelve hundred angels were acting as guardians" (Schimmel, 1985, p. 160).

Muhammad's journey resembles Dante's *Divine Comedy*. He finds that each sphere is ruled by one of the seven prophets who preceded him. Adam is in the lowest heaven, presiding over the punishments of sinners. Jesus is in the fourth and Abraham in the seventh. Muhammad undergoes tests as he rises from sphere to sphere; and finally, in Paradise, he meets Allah.

Additional parallels can be found in the Sufism of Suhrawardi, Ibn al-ʿArabi, and others, the Jewish Kabballah, the later Christian mystics, Pure Land Buddhism, certain schools of Hinduism and Tantra, and most anciently in shamanism. For many millennia, shamans the world over have ascended through the heavenly spheres on a ladder whose rungs are sometimes the branches of the World Tree. In areas where horses were domesticated, they have often ridden a marvelous spiritual steed.

---

[1] In fact, the Temple of Israel had long lain in ruins by the seventh century of Pisces, so that Muhammad must have been journeying in Monroe's "Locale III." He was traveling through time as well as space, but still on this planet.

The legends of Muhammad's *mi'raj* disagree on whether he made that journey in his body or out of it—reminiscent of the Apostle Paul's testimony in 2 Corinthians 12:1–10:

> I know a man . . . , whether in the body, or out of the body I know not, who was caught up even to the third heaven . . . was caught up into Paradise, and heard unspeakable words, which it is not lawful for man to utter.

In one Islamic tradition, the Prophet's wife, 'Ai'sha, says that "his body was not missed"; and a cup of water overturned on his departure was not yet empty of its last drop at the moment of his return. In this tradition, Muhammad's sojourn was made out-of-body and in the twinkling of an eye by earthly time, although it seemed to last much longer in the other world (Schimmel, 1985, p. 161).

In another tradition, Muhammad is supposed to have journeyed *bodily* to Heaven. He was the "Perfect Man," a fact that distinguishes him from the saints who follow; for they must journey in a lesser manner, i.e., in a soul which has left its body. Catholicism has taken a similar view of Mary, the Mother of Jesus. She was the only human being "perfect" enough to have ascended to Heaven, body and soul. In shamanic cultures, it is universally said that, in the days of long ago, when shamans were truly powerful, they used to make the celestial ascent in bodily form. But today, now that shamanism has declined, shamans must leave their bodies to make that journey.

New Age journeyers like Monroe surely belong to these latter times and travel out-of-body. But the journeys they make also take them through spheres inhabited by beings of light, and every one of them has a demonic aspect that can result in entrapment. For Monroe, these lesser spheres are close enough to the Earth that what he calls "M-band noise"—the emotionally charged chatter resulting from the billions of internal monologs maintained by everyone still occupying a body— works like a kind of radio jamming that prevents the journeyer from opening the eyes of the soul. He finds, for instance, that the souls of the recently departed are easily trapped in a sphere that supports an old internal monolog and prevents them from knowing that they have died. Some are trapped by promises they have made ("I'll never leave you"; "I'll die before I give up"); and others are trapped by religious doctrine ("I must be still alive, because the Bible tells me Heaven and Hell are nothing like this").

The universal discovery of lesser spheres provides a convincing context for folkloric accounts of visits to underwater kingdoms of mer-people and underground fairy realms. It is clear that the marvelous "folded up" dimensions discovered by the protagonists of legend are the less-than-ultimate spheres of *imaginal* journeying. Folktales know only about the first stage of Gnostic journeying—the danger of entrapment. Knowing nothing of *gnosis* itself, they do not know how to escape the lower spheres and continue a sojourn that might potentially lead them to the One. Even Monroe has only the dimmest presentiment of what lies in store for his luminous dome at the point when its series of fleshly missions is complete and it returns "home."

THE UNIFORM STRUCTURE OF THE MULTIVERSE

Some physicists today, following the logic of their mathematical constructions, are inclined to wonder whether the universe we can see with our telescopes may only be one of many subuniverses. One line of speculation wonders what happens to all the matter and light sucked into "black holes," never to return. It is unthinkable that matter and energy may be destroyed. Furthermore, the evidence seems to show that the universe is expanding, requiring at least a constant sum of matter and energy, if not a growing quantity. Perhaps black holes are the portals through which matter and light are sucked out of the universe we know and sent into other universes, which may have an entirely different structure than ours. If so, there may perhaps be other, as yet undiscovered, portals through which matter and energy are brought in from other subuniverses. If we were able to construct a spaceship that could travel fast enough to reach a black hole before its inhabitants had lived out their years, it would tell us nothing. For, not only would its radioed messages not be able to escape from the black hole and return to us, but the ship and its inhabitants would be crushed in the transit—compacted into subatomic fragments.

Another line of speculation bases itself on "string theory." According to Steven Weinberg (*Dreams of a Final Theory,* 1993), a "string" is a rent in the fabric of space-time that is so narrow as to have "no width." These strings vibrate in multiple dimensions, generating, it would seem, the particles and fields studied in quantum mechanics. Because their vibrations occur in so many dimensions (some say ten) that lie outside our four-dimensional universe of space and time, it is possible to speculate that other subuniverses lie "folded up" in those invisible dimensions. Any spaceship we might construct in space and time would belong to the four dimensions we inhabit (length, width, depth, and time). It would be trapped in the universe that includes our Milky Way galaxy and planet Earth, the universe we can see through our telescopes. There would be no way to have that ship "change dimensions" and enter one of the other subuniverses of the supposed multiverse.

Some theorists, like astronomer Jacques Vallee (1988), are inclined to believe that we might be able to gain access to the "folded up" dimensions of the multiverse through out-of-body travel. Surely out-of-body journeyers are traveling "somewhere" outside of space and time, in "other dimensions." But the *imaginal* realm of out-of-body sojourns does not seem to be made up of any matter at all. It is surely not filling up with the matter and light drawn through a black hole. It is another kind of "place" altogether. Furthermore, if the other subuniverses comprising the multiverse are supposed by physicists to be multiple and varied, it may be that the cosmos of the Gnostics is only *one* of them. For all sojourners report encountering the same structure of spheres nested inside of spheres. Even more problematically, they find it to be an *ultimate* experience, *the* "place" outside of space and time, from whose perspective the realm of the senses is merely the broom-closet. Possibly there are other broom-closets; but the Gnostics of the Age of Pisces, including the New Agers, have not yet discovered them—unless they are those less-than-ultimate spheres in which we may become trapped.

Leaving aside the mathematical speculations of the physicists, we have a problem of our own to consider. How is it that these out-of-body journeyers have all encountered a greater cosmos with a similar structure? Have they discovered what is objectively "out there"? Or have their *imaginal* journeys been unconsciously structured by a schema passed down from shamanism through yoga, Gnosticism, Jewish and Islamic mysticism, alchemy, Rosicrucianism, and Theosophy to the New Age? Have we encountered the latest form of an historical transmission of mystical ideas? If so, how did Monroe, Brinkley, and Eadie learn of it? They seem to have been unexposed to the history of religious ideas when they entered the *imaginal* realm that has been visited for millennia by people of all races.

When the naive reach the same conclusions as the learned, we are inclined to accept that something "real" must be involved. Either the greater cosmos is really structured as nested spheres of light, or else the soul's faculties of *imaginal* knowing are so structured that the cosmos has to be *seen* as nested spheres.

When Immanuel Kant demonstrated that our sensory knowing is structured by space and time, he could appeal to what everybody knows. There is no instance of *sensory* knowing that is not spatial and temporal. Once he pointed it out, the world wondered how this simple fact could have been overlooked for so long. In the case of *imaginal* knowing, the issue is not so simple. We are talking about the experience of an elite, rather than everybody's experience. What they report is by no means obvious to us. Nevertheless it is reasonable to guess that *imaginal* knowing may have its limitations and rules, just like sensory knowing.

British psychic, Eileen Garrett, reports: "I asked these spirit figures if I was seeing *them* or if I was seeing what was in my own brain. They answered, 'Both'" (Garrett, 1967, p. 5). Christian mystic, Meister Eckhart, says, "The eye with which I see God is the same as that with which He sees me" (Happold, 1970, p. 67). Ibn al-'Arabi, titled the Greatest Sufi Master, warns, "Whoever imagines that he sees the Reality Himself has no *gnosis*; he has *gnosis* who knows that it is his own essential self that he sees" (Merkur, 1993, p. 226). In the greater cosmos, we *see* with the eyes of the journeyer; we *see* the journeyer's reality. Dan Merkur describes the "other world" of Suhrawardi, one of the seminal mystic philosophers of Islam this way:

> Suhrawardi's otherworld was also not a spatial extension of this world. It was not an upper world, high in the sky, as is heaven in Judaism, Christianity, Mandaeism, and Islam. Suhrawardi's otherworld was a different dimension or order of existence, whose mystery defied logical description and explanation. It was spatially both within a person's earthbound body and a distinct region of the cosmos. It was not simply upper, or nether, or invisible. It was distinctly other (Merkur, 1993, p. 224).

Testimonies like these suggest that we have three modes of knowing. The first and most obvious is what we call "reality-testing." Based on the sensory knowledge Kant defined, it is characterized by discrimination: Yes, A is true; no, B is false. In its purest form, it designs experiments to prove and disprove its own hypotheses.

Somewhat in conflict with this first, highly conscious mode of knowing, are the less conscious themes of our internal monolog. Because we are incapable of knowing the whole sensory world and our entire lifetime of memories in a single act of consciousness, our internal monolog tirelessly repeats simple and misleading summaries ("My boss is just like all the rest"; "If you want something, you must pay the price";

"If I let people see who I am, they'll reject me"). We each maintain a variety of these monologs, every one of which unconsciously gathers around itself a selection of personal memories that supports it. Each monological theme represents a cluster or "complex" of memories and aspirations, united by a single emotional tone.

If *my boss is just like all the rest* is spoken with a tone of self-pity, we may expect to hear a whole catalog of events in our friend's life in which sincerity and good intentions were misunderstood and devalued. If spoken with a tone of self-righteous rage, we may instead be subjected to a series of battles and arguments fighting for what is right and just, demolishing opponents with moral superiority—only to suffer a martyr's fate of losing with honor. Internal monologs are supported both by fragments of social consensus (minority rights and their suppression, modern society's loss of integrity and compassion) as well as by elements of personal experience (parents who were too preoccupied with their own problems to pay sufficient attention, colleagues who dismissed one's ideas without listening).

Our ordinary nocturnal dreams are assembled entirely by the associative way of thinking that makes up internal monologs. We find ourselves fighting again and again with authority figures, for example, or chased by threatening figures lurking in the shadows. If we look carefully at these scenes, we may discover that our battles with our bosses frequently take place in a building that reminds us of our parental home or the halls of our high school. We may take these repeating facts as hints about where and when the themes of our monolog were established and ask ourselves whether they are adequate to our present-day experience. In this manner, we may learn to expand and update our monologs, bringing them into better harmony with the individuals we really are.

Our "big dreams," in contrast, present us with larger perspectives that contradict the themes of our internal monolog. For example, a 20-year-old woman reports a repeating dream in which she is attending a wake. Her brother, who had been killed five years earlier in an automobile accident, walks into the room and stands beside her. "How does it feel to be dead?" she asks. He answers with another question, "How does it feel to be alive?" She has been pondering this *koan* for five years: "What does it mean to be *alive*, and not just living?" Clearly her brother's death has been a monumental fact for her, whose significance she is still trying to digest. Possibly an old internal monolog presents life as a process of learning to conform to expectations, a kind of dreary plodding that is not fully "alive." Her brother's death has opened a gap in the world constituted by that monolog. Is this plodding life really much different from death? If I were truly *alive*, what would I do with my life?

Our soul—that is to say, our journeyer—finds itself too restricted by the themes of our internal monolog. In our "big dreams" and in our cosmic journeying, we are presented with the much greater landscape of the soul. The near-death journeyers have *seen* clearly and unmistakably that their former lives were limited by an unconscionable internal monolog that has to be relinquished. When Monroe gave up his experiments in clairvoyance and let the *dream* take him where *it* wanted to go, he was presented with a series of myth-like images and narratives: the orgiastic pile of corpses, the story of the demiurge who lives on death, the image of the luminous dome.

C. G. Jung has taken note of these three dimensions of psychological life: ego consciousness, the complexes of ideas reiterated by our internal monologs, and the more comprehensive, generally human themes of the "collective unconscious." Just as the personal/social themes of the internal monolog structure our semi-conscious lives, so the larger themes of human existence are organized by what Jung calls the "archetypes." An archetype is an unconscious mode of apprehension. A cat responds to a twitching string as though it were a mouse's tail and turns a wine-bottle cork into a scuttling object of prey with a stroke of its paw. In similar fashion, our human souls apprehend the meaning of images and events in typically human fashion.

Jung criticized Freud for forcing all human unconscious life into the procrustean bed of a single archetypal form, that of the Oedipus story. Despite his intention of remaining open-minded to the great variety of mythic themes that can be found in the history of human cultures and religions, however, Jung himself favored another "monomyth," that of the Sun hero. Based on the universal human observation that the Sun descends into the western sea every night and rises out of the eastern sea every morning, most human societies have viewed the Sun's "night sea journey" from west to east as a process of renewal in which the celestial source of all earthly light has to fight the forces of darkness every night in order to be revitalized. Human heroes—that is, all of us—have to enter the dark, watery world of the unconscious and fight the forces that would keep us there in order to renew ourselves with new perspectives regarding who we are and what it means "to be alive and not just living."

Our study of the New Age has brought to light another mythic theme—the quest for *ultimate* meaning, the exploration of the greater cosmos. We have found that it has the same general structure as that reported by a great variety of shamanic and Gnostic out-of-body travelers throughout the Age of Pisces and extending far back beyond the Age of Taurus. We have had to conclude that this is the way our journeyer or larger self envisions the cosmos within which our fleshly, temporal existence is little more than a broom-closet. In every case, we find nested spheres of light, all emanating from an ineffable One who is pure light, love, and compassion.

We cannot say if there is some larger reality beyond those nested spheres, a reality which places the One in a greater context, somewhat as we now see the little Sun of our solar system within the galaxy of the Milky Way. If we could, we would likely be led upon another quest to find a greater One—much as our scientists are intrigued by the possibility of explaining the entire visible universe on the basis of a "Big Bang." All we can know for certain is that this is the way our journeyer understands itself. We have encountered the journeyer's way of knowing.

THE MYTH OF THE NEW AGE

Myth is a problematic word. In everyday language, it means that which only *seems* to be true, a deceptive untruth. Newspaper columnists, for example, may list the "myths" perpetuated in our uneasy race relations. They mean our stereotyped and inaccurate notions that will not stand up to reality-testing. These "myths" describe the ways we mislead ourselves into living in a delusional world of fear and paranoia. Myth, in this sense, belongs to what Don Juan Matus calls our internal monolog.

In its more essential meaning, *myth* refers to an *imaginal* way of knowing. Anthropologists and scholars of comparative religion use *myth* to describe a *cosmic narrative* that makes sense of life and gives it transcendent meaning. Preliterate agricultural communities, for example, generally tell a story whose setting is long, long ago, far earlier than the memories of the oldest inhabitants, before time began, when the divine Being who laid down the models for their way of life was tragically killed. Just before his death, he bade his companions to chop up his body and plant the pieces in the ground. In the spring, he came back to life as the corn or taro or potatoes that are that community's staff of life. Every year at planting season, the story is retold in a ritual context; and the fields are planted by individuals who are living simultaneously in two worlds: the world of space and time that hopes for a harvest, and the *imaginal* world that exists outside of space and time. The planters *imaginally* identify with the gods, and their planting is a sacred act that carries incomprehensibly more meaning than any secular act could ever muster.

In the Middle Ages, the story of the Christ still functioned as a myth. This means that the life and death of Jesus unquestionably expressed the deepest truth for the serfs, aristocrats, and clergy of the day. They lived in this fleshly world as the testing ground of their faith, the place where they proved their identity as soul people exiled in a temporal body. By consciously living according to the rules and imagery of the world of the soul, they were confident of enjoying eternal bliss after their death. Without leaving the secular world of space and time, they simultaneously lived in the eternal world of the greater cosmos. Although their everyday lives may seem dreary to us, for them it was suffused with transcendent meaning.

To say that Christianity is a "myth" is to invite the indignation of believing Christians. They will say, "No, it's not a myth; it's the truth; it's the way things really are, even though the evidence for this truth is invisible." This is the way people speak who are *really* living a myth. They do not see it *as* a myth; they see it as the fundamental and deepest truth of their lives. For them, Jesus of Nazareth was wholly a man, but simultaneously he is also the eternal Christ. Everything he did had a double meaning: his secular acts in space and time were at the same time the cosmic acts of God. As Christians, they, too, have a dual life, at once secular and sacred. Christianity is a myth for them because it gives their lives cosmic significance.

Today there are rather few people—even among churchgoers—for whom Christianity is still a myth. Indeed, the mythic reality of Christianity has been a problem for us over the entire second half of the Age of Pisces. As the effectiveness of our sensory way of knowing has produced ever more amazing technological wonders and our philosophies have tried to rearticulate the metaphysics of a Heaven and God in a manner that does not conflict with what we see to be the matter-of-fact realities of our everyday lives, the greater cosmos has become more and more a problem for us. From Descartes to Nietzsche, we have talked ourselves out of a belief in another world that makes sense of this one, and the substance of myth has become a deceptive untruth.

If the New Age has any importance at all, it is that the greater Cosmos is being rediscovered. For New Agers, this larger cosmic reality is not a matter of mere belief—something we try hard to accept despite its absurdity. For them, the evidence of a greater cosmos is too abundant to be overlooked. Some, like Monroe, have been sojourning through it for decades. The near-death journeyers have gained an incontrovertible perspective that has placed their fleshly lives in a meaning-giving context. Those like Freeman and Burnham, who have encountered angels, have had their eyes opened to rents in the fabric of space-time that have revolutionized their internal monologs. Readers of auras *know*, rather than believe, that our fleshly reality is contained within a luminous egg of transcendent significance.

For the New Age, in short, the world of the soul is no longer a matter of hopeful speculation supported by intricate metaphysical argument. It is a matter of experience. New Agers have rediscovered the cosmic consciousness that has always been an option for human beings—even though it has been neglected and forgotten by the majority of Westerners over the course of the last few centuries. They have gone beyond sensory knowledge and entered the *imaginal* realm that is its larger context. They have shut off, for moments or hours at a time, the internal monolog which maintains the fleshly world and gained access to a meaning-giving mythic reality. In this greater cosmos, their knowing is not structured by space and time, but by the more fundamental *imaginal* mode of apprehension that Jung calls "archetypal."

The New Age is surely moved by a myth, even though it has not yet been told as a narrative. No doubt few New Agers have asked themselves whether there is a sacred story lurking behind their viewpoints and activities. But if we put together what we have learned about the New Age at this point, we can tell a pretty interesting tale.

In the beginning was the One, a being of ineffable pure light. Having nothing outside itself to serve as a point of comparison, the One did not truly know itself. Wanting to know, the One emanated from itself spheres of light in a progressive series, each less pure than the last. These spheres were not inanimate realms, like the circles on the surface of a pond, but were filled with living, intelligent beings of light. From the very beginning they all knew, through *gnosis*, their origin and destiny lay in the One. They were riveted by the One in their *gnosis* and did not know themselves.

Just as they were created to reflect the One and enable it to know itself, so they needed something other than pure light by which to know themselves. Inspired by their memories of the creation of the cosmos of light, therefore, they created for themselves lesser worlds from the most impure substance of all, matter.

With the creation of worlds of material life, time began. Time is the measure of change and growth. This is the one feature that had been missing from the static nested spheres of the cosmos of light. Material beings are characterized by growth. Each one is born, develops to its maturity of optimal independence and autonomy, and then declines toward death. Material, temporal existence is always a Being-toward-death. In death, living beings decompose into their elements; and these, in turn, comprise the fleshly bodies of the beings who live at a later time. On account of this cyclical process of life giving way to death and death supporting life, every material world, every growing world, is itself engaged in a process of evolution. Higher, more complex, forms of material life evolve out of simpler forms.

All material beings live by changing, are in fact nothing but the series of changes that constitutes growing, temporal, material existence. Fleshly life in time supplies the change and opportunity for learning that is missing in the static cosmos of light. Recognizing this, the beings of light *saw* that their chance to gain self-knowledge would best be realized, not simply by observing material existence from afar, but by choosing to enter it themselves. They entered it in the only way they could, as the souls of newly conceived human bodies. In doing so, they had to accept the biological conditions of human life: birth, growth, the struggle for existence, and death. They entered on a temporal basis, in each instance only for the lifetime of a single human being. But because, from the viewpoint of the greater cosmos, all time is simultaneous, each being of light was able to enter many lives.

We are those beings of light as they have become enfleshed in the last centuries of Pisces. The beings of light are our more complete reality, our soul, our journeyer, which becomes visible as the luminous egg of our aura, and which has been incarnated many times before and will likely undergo many more incarnations in the future. Human existence is a forgetting in order to learn. We have had to forget the being of light who is our journeyer in order to immerse ourselves in this world of emotions and thoughts. The evolution of human consciousness represents a collective learning process—learning what it means to be alive, what it means to feel, what it means to know. Above all, it is a process of learning who we are.

Ages ago, before the rising Sun in spring had entered the Sign of Taurus, we had cosmic consciousness, but little else. Our human existence was a fight for survival, but we had not yet entered that fight in earnest. We relied on our cosmic consciousness to help us find the food, shelter, warmth, and companionship we needed to survive on Earth. But we also remained detached. Our cosmic consciousness lent us a knowledge of being one with the Earth and all its creatures. We had a vague mystical awareness, but we had not yet come really to *know* the planet or ourselves.

In the Age of Aries, the beings of light immersed themselves more deeply in their human flesh. The ambitious and talented used their newly developed sensory knowledge to overpower and control others in order to increase their own wealth, fame, and comfort. They were the kings, traders, and military officers. Everyone else had to become cunning to survive. Cunning guided a thirst for the knowledge of techniques and strategies. We largely forgot our cosmic consciousness, mourning it vaguely, establishing religions to try to rekindle it.

In the Age of Pisces, we developed stable egos for the first time, began to know ourselves and to appreciate one another. We developed highly diverse literatures, histories, philosophies, and science. We mastered the physical world with our machines. We completed a phase in our immersion in the world of time and flesh, but paid a rather high price. We have come to distrust cosmic consciousness. For most of us, it has become an unthinkable impossibility. We have been marshaling arguments for centuries to prove that it does not exist.

The New Age of Aquarius represents a monumental change, something like the reversal of millennia of suppression. People are spontaneously encountering fragments of cosmic consciousness—excitedly talking about the auras they have been *seeing*, and the beings of light that have appeared as angels and other entities alien to our bodily experience as fleshly egos. We are again enthusiastic about the possibility of reincarnation and other amazing wonders. People who have nearly died are returning from their experience with reports of the nested spheres of light they have seen, and the suggestion that we ourselves are the beings of light that live in that greater cosmos. Many are beginning to challenge ideas that have dominated the Age of Pisces: the separateness of individual egos and the mastery of the planet. We hear talk of a Global Village and Spaceship Earth. Beings of light who had largely forgotten their essential identity over the last two astrological ages are beginning to remember who they are. Their cosmic consciousness is making a bid for equal consideration alongside the sensory and conceptual knowledge of fleshly egos. The plan of the One to know itself is making a huge leap forward. The "One Pearl" has been *sighted* in the land of forgetting and remembering.

Like every myth, the sacred narrative of the New Age functions as a moral exhortation. Having discovered how things "really" are, we are called to change our lives. But this time there is no Code of Hammurabi or Ten Commandments, no imperial decrees regarding which specific acts must be done and which avoided. Still, the New Age is hardly a call for licentiousness and moral chaos. A larger principle has been discovered—something akin, perhaps, to what Nietzsche called "Beyond Good and Evil."

Each of us is faced with the discrepancy between our larger, essential identity as a being of light and our more limited habitual persona as a fleshly ego. We catch *sight* of our life-review in the snapshot that is the luminous egg of our aura. It calls us to a wider perspective, not one that can be encoded in general rules of right and wrong. Instead, we are each presented with our own individual task to balance our aura by bringing our fleshly life-course into alignment with our journeyer. What does it mean to be *alive* and not just living? What do I say to the One, as I sit every day in meditation? Why am I standing here at the gate of the New Age, begging the prayers of those who pass in and out? What is knocking at the gaps in my internal monolog? Why do I imprison myself in a broom-closet, now that the door is open?

The morality of the New Age eschews simple generalities. In each case, it formulates itself as a mysterious *koan*. The being of light incarnated in each life-course has its own lesson to learn. We distract ourselves by developing self-righteous internal monologs that condemn other beings of light for following their own *koan* instead of ours. We close our gaps and abandon our own holy obligation when we look about and condemn ourselves for our stupidity and inadequacy at not having made the achievements that others seem to have made.

In each case, our moral task is our individual life's work and may not be exchanged for anyone else's. At the same time, however, each individual task is the work of a being of light who is coming to know itself, thereby revealing another facet of the ineffable One. In each case, therefore, our individual task is a small piece in the monumental work of the One's quest to know itself. Each is a contribution to reconciling *gnosis* with sensory knowledge and a self-conscious way of life. Each is an attempt to *see* for the first time the image of the King of kings and the flickering of the *gnosis* that adorns the raiment of light that clothes our journeyer.

OUT IN INNER SPACE

We can, perhaps, reconcile this vision of the aura as a journeying being of light with the "new physics." We can imagine that those nonphysical light beings are energic realities vibrating in multiple dimensions. Perhaps they restrict themselves to four dimensions in order to enter this biological world of growth and change. If so, the luminous egg that glows around our physical body may emanate from those "folded up" vibratory dimensions spoken of in "string theory." These would be the dimensions that cannot be confined within space and time. Possibly the seven different auric layers that Barbara Brennan negotiates when she performs an "energy healing" correspond to seven discrete vibratory dimensions. If so, we can imagine that the seven spheres of light surrounding the Earth represent the Earth's "aura" and are constituted by the same vibratory dimensions.

This line of thought will only take us so far. How do we account for those who find three layers in the aura or ten spheres of light? Furthermore, if the spheres through which Monroe travels represent the aura of the Earth, how do we reconcile this with the more fundamental structure of the New Age myth—the claim that the spheres were generated by the One and that the Earth is a late arrival in the cosmos of light?

Most significantly of all, the cosmos of light exists outside of space and time, yet the myth speaks of a linear process (time) that precedes the creation of a temporal world, and its image of nested spheres is a spatial metaphor. Outside of space and time, Monroe *sees* the *spatial* image of his luminous dome, and knows that the dome is waiting for the *time* when it will have learned enough to return to the One.

The myth of the New Age, like every myth, does not bear literal-minded scrutiny. If I were to leave my body this evening and sojourn in a greater cosmos, I would be surprised to come upon Planet KT-95, the home of Monroe's friend and alter ego, "inspec BB." It would be as improbable as discovering Urashima's Dragon Palace. I would be somewhat less surprised to find nested spheres, as this seems to be a pretty universal feature. But if I were to note the character of the various spheres, I doubt very much that I would find each one ruled by a Jewish or Christian prophet, as Muhammad did.

It was probably a tendency to literal-mindedness in his disciples that moved Ibn al-'Arabi to say, "He has *gnosis* who knows that it is his own essential self that he sees." For Ibn al-'Arabi, every body has a soul, which is its more essential meaning; every soul has an angel; every angel has a lord; and that lord is one of the Names of the unknowable One. This Gnostic metaphysics of the soul is very much the same as that which we have determined by following the reports of New Agers. We have said: every body has a journeying soul that is its larger self; every journeyer has a compass-bearer (the "angel") whose *gnosis* points to the One. But the evidence shows that the spaceless-timeless greater cosmos journeyed with a compass always has a distinctly *personal* character. It is a *facet* (or "Name") of the One that each journeyer contemplates; and the "lordship" of that facet gives meaning to our own individual lives. This is the reason that the morality of the New Age is in every case a private

affair between the fleshly ego and its journeyer. Because of this unique-
ness, the One comes to know a new facet of itself through each individual created being.

There is a common structure to the greater cosmos, shared by all
journeyers, because *imaginal* knowing is structured by the archetypes of
imaginal apprehension. We all journey through a similar greater cosmos.
But we all *see* that cosmos from the unique and distinctive perspective of
our journeyer. This idiosyncrasy is not a fault. It is precisely what the
One designed for the sake of its own self-knowledge. The One prizes
that idiosyncrasy. If the One had been sufficiently mirrored by nested
spheres of light, there would have been no reason for the generation of a
material, fleshly world. It is a limitation, but a fortuitous and intended
limitation: *it is our own essential journeyer that our gnosis sees.*

This is why the journey outward into the greater cosmos is also a
journey inward into our essential self. We become literalists when we
think that our own journey has provided us with a "gospel" to preach to
others. Our journeyer discovers only its own "good news." By learning
of others' experience, we ought to be inspired to discover our own, not
to imitate theirs. Some have the gift of journeying out-of-body. Some
have the gift of contemplating a near-death life-review. Some have the
gift of *seeing* auras. Some have the gift of encountering angels. The gifts
are diverse, but the spirit who inspires them is the One; and they all lead
to the cosmic reward of the One's self-knowledge.

To take the imagery of the journeyer's *sight* in a literal manner, is to
get stuck in another broom-closet. It is to mistake one of the Archons
for the ultimate, ineffable One. It is to be trapped in the Palace of the Sea
Dragons, or to drown in the waves of illusory water in the rabbis' Sixth
Palace. In the words of Don Juan Matus, it is to become a shaman who
has given up this world for the world of the *nagual* and to have gained
nothing.

The imagery of each sojourn constitutes an opportunity which is
also a dangerous challenge. The opportunity lies in escaping from the
broom-closet of our internal monolog in order to contemplate the facet
of the One that each of us essentially is. The danger lies in taking that
facet for the complete and literal truth about the One. The challenge lies
in developing a *discernment* which takes the images as symbols that point
beyond themselves in two directions. On the one hand, they point to
the One who lives beyond all imagery. On the other hand, they point
back to ourselves, to the unique journeyer that each of us is. When we
lose sight of this dual dimension of what we *see*, we become trapped in

another broom-closet—no matter that it is a glorious undersea palace or a Crystal City of light.

We have misunderstood the myth and cosmic meaning of the New Age if we become dazzled by what we have *seen* and take it for a final statement of what is. In such a case, we are no more enlightened than the Israelites who carved a golden calf in the desert at the foot of Mount Sinai. They allowed the internal monolog of their Egyptian slavery to subvert their relationship with the One. *Whoever imagines that he sees the Reality Himself has no gnosis.*

Transcendental experience, that is to say, *gnosis*, consists in knowing that we are participating, each in our own unique way, in the contemplation of the cosmos as the One's self-reflection. Each of us is a facet of the One. Restricted to our fleshly existence, we forget this. But through its *gnosis*, our journeyer implicitly knows our role in the mythic purpose of the cosmos. The danger of *gnosis* is that it can be perverted by being turned into a confirmation of our literal-minded monolog and not *seen through*. We lose sight of our essential calling and our essential self. The One requires nothing more than that we come to know who *we* are, for the substance of our journeyer is but one of the infinite Names by which the One comes to know itself.

Chapter 7

LITTLE GRAY MEN AND THE TECHNOLOGIZING OF THE SPIRIT

In 1560 west of Ceylon some fishermen caught several mermaids in a net, which were taken ashore and dissected with great interest by a learned physician. He reported that internally and externally they were constructed like human beings.

(LEACH & FRIED, 1984, P. 710)

Legends are not only "out there" in the shared culture. They are also "in us" psychologically. They are the models by which we live. They provide ready-made exemplars of goodness and evil, scenarios for working toward ideals, and explanations of tragedies.

(VICTOR, 1993, P. 72)

Often the last thing these abductees want to do is look in the Being's eyes. They know if they look, they will have to acknowledge the presence . . . that is completely inconsistent with the construction of reality they've maintained. It's as if it shatters their reality.

(MACK IN BRYAN, 1995, P. 272)

Some of this stuff ain't real! Help me sort it out!

("ALICE," AN ABDUCTEE IN BRYAN, 1995, P. 229)

In the last twenty-five years, more than 10,000 reports of UFO sightings have been filed away unexplained by competent investigators (Vallee, 1988, p. 153). One conservative extrapolation from the available data estimates that at least three *million* flying saucers must have landed somewhere on the globe during the last two decades (Vallee, 1988, p. 231). This is a phenomenon of monumental proportions that has generated intense debate. Deniers of UFOs say the reports of witnesses and abductees are unimportant details of contemporary life. In doing so, they assert the absolute value and dependability of our everyday Piscean worldview. Believers in UFO sightings and abductions claim these experiences are of crucial importance and that they call for a radical revision of our picture of the world and of ourselves.

I agree with the second group. Any phenomenon of this size must be of crucial importance—but to what end? Do UFO sightings alert us to an immanent invasion? Are they evidence of governmental manipulation and cover-up, or the preliminary stages of an intergalactic plan to assist humans in downloading cosmic wisdom and love? Is it a warning to stop hating and killing one another and destroying our planet's ecology? Or is the UFO craze important because the experiencers' lives have been transformed by a brush with cosmic consciousness? C. G. Jung's *Flying Saucers: A Modern Myth of Things Seen in the Skies* interprets these events as our longing to rediscover the "self," the "knower" of cosmic consciousness.

On the western coast of Normandy, about twenty-five miles south of Cherbourg, two fishermen, a father and son, saw an intense yellow "window" in the air above their nets at 5:30 A.M. on December 2, 1973 (Vallee, 1988, pp. 212–214). It was about eight feet wide and five feet high and cast a cone-shaped beam of light toward the ground. The light grew more intense as they drew nearer, and they were very much afraid. But as the nets had to be retrieved at low tide, they felt they had no option but to ignore the object. At about 6:05, the light "turned off," and they saw in place of the "window" a blue-green sphere about the size of a soccer ball that disappeared to the north. At 6:10, the radar installation near Cherbourg picked up an unidentified object flying north. That same morning, the French trawler *Archipel* ran aground just north of Cherbourg, apparently because its magnetic navigation system had given erroneous readings. A ham radio operator near the beach where the fishermen had seen the "window" reported that his receiver was blocked for several minutes. A few days later, astronomer and UFO investigator Jacques Vallee interviewed the younger fisherman, who reported that he had seen three spheres flying in staggered formation over the same beach two months earlier. After the second sighting, his father locked himself in his house and gave up fishing. Vallee considers the case "unexplained," despite implausible attempts by the French government to account for the reports.

This story is a particularly intriguing "close encounter." It has certain typical features. A seemingly absurd and impossible event has caused boundless fear on the part of the older fisherman, leaving us in no doubt that, in his mind at least, something monumentally unthinkable has occurred. The government, too, has reacted to the "unthinkable" by hurrying to cover it up with a series of contradictory explanations, none of which is satisfying. Are the officials trying to protect us from ourselves? Do they know something we do not? Or are they just as frightened as the older fisherman?

It is typical, as well, of UFO sightings that the object seen has the ability to change shape, color, and activity in a manner that defies all of our habitual expectations. Furthermore, this was not the first time a UFO had been seen by the younger fisherman. Frequently, those who see or have been abducted by a UFO have had a history of such encounters—often in the same general location, and sometimes stretching far back into childhood.

This first set of facts, dealing with the details of what was seen and the emotional reactions they inspired, might well support a suspicion that the UFO sighting was merely a subjective illusion. Indeed, many alleged sightings have been dismissed precisely on this ground. But the Normandy event has a number of features that render the subjective-illusion hypothesis untenable. In the first place, *two* men saw it and agree upon what they saw. More tellingly, however, there appear to be some electromagnetic data that are not easily dismissed. Three separate and unrelated reports verify that an event of at least quasi-materiality occurred. The radar sighting agrees with the fishermen's observation of the trajectory of the blue-green sphere. That trajectory carries it over the course of the trawler that subsequently ran aground due to an electromagnetic disturbance, and the ham radio's malfunction occurred just at the time the UFO was alleged to be in the area.

Apart from contradictory, unverified, but nevertheless intriguing rumors, there is no undisputed *physical* evidence for the visitation of the Earth by extraterrestrial vehicles and persons—no nuts and bolts or fragments of metal and rubber such as we find strewn along our highways by passing automobiles; no personal objects like cigarette lighters, buttons, or goggles that might have been dropped by the hundreds of thousands of alien visitors that are said to have disembarked from those craft;

no clear and convincing photographs or video recordings by an earthly population well supplied with auto-focus cameras and camcorders.

On the whole, our physical understanding of the universe seems pretty much to prove the impossibility of extraterrestrial visitation. Space travel, as our physicists and engineers conceive of it, would require 33,000 years to reach the nearest star (Proxima Centauri) and fifteen billion years to reach the nearest galaxy (Andromeda). The acrobatic feats flying saucers are reported to have performed would destroy any craft we can imagine, or kill the inhabitants, even if appropriate construction materials could be found. We cannot conceive how the aliens and their human abductees can pass through walls, levitate on beams of light, or communicate complex messages telepathically.

Nevertheless, scientifically trained people—pilots, astronomers, and physicists—have reported seeing UFOs and surely know how to distinguish them from unusual natural phenomena. Furthermore, UFOs have been picked up by radar, meteor-detecting devices, and satellite-tracking cameras. Thus, the "best" evidence seems to be electromagnetic: for instance, radar reception, televisions and radios being turned on and off or blocked with interference, automobile ignitions failing, and street lights shutting off.

But electromagnetic disturbances may also imply a psychic component. Journalist Douchan Gersi (*Faces in the Smoke,* 1991, e.g., pp. 161–168) has reported in detail his repeated attempts to record shamanic healings and other "paranormal" activities, only to have his recording devices fail. Repairmen have informed him that the destruction of his equipment can only be explained by high charges of electricity capable of overloading and burning out the components. As Gersi was very careful to use appropriate energy supplies, the only source for such high charges of electromagnetic energy must have been the psychically gifted performers he was trying to record. Other explorers have reported the same phenomenon in their books and articles, and I have heard personal accounts from individuals who have not written about them. Furthermore, some alien abductees have reported bodily/psychic states in which they felt charged with electricity and which seemed to cause the appliances in their homes to go haywire. In short, it seems that exceptional states of consciousness in ordinary human beings may be accompanied by powerful electromagnetic fields.

Even if we imagine, however, that the "window" in the sky was a kind of "psychic materialization," an electromagnetically-charged illusion, caused perhaps by the spooked fishermen, how do we account for the trajectory of that illusion and the fact that it brought about disturbances at other locations while the fishermen continued to work on their local beach? Could it have been someone traveling out-of-body?

Again and again, we come back to the fundamental question: Are the alleged aliens and their vehicles real or not? The most vocal of UFO researchers look to national governments for answers, as these authorities have immense data-collecting agencies at their disposal. Those who have looked most carefully, however, have found that government information and disinformation leads us into a "hall of mirrors" (Vallee) or a "minefield" (Strieber), in which official press releases are contradicted by self-described dissidents who have left governmental service to protest the "cover-up." Unfortunately, however, these reports only lead us back into the maze, where hoax cannot be distinguished from genuine information. Indeed, it is not infrequent that the so-called dissident has publicly relinquished one governmental post, only to secretly take up another.

In the end, there seems to be no alternative but to return to the eyewitness reports themselves. In the Normandy sighting, for instance, something evidently happened. We have two frightened fishermen, one who has locked himself in his home and abandoned his livelihood and another who is baffled but continues fishing because the alternative is death by starvation. We also have a wrecked trawler, a frustrated ham operator, and an official radar recording. Alongside all this, we have the improbable image of a "window" in the sky, a symbolic statement that there may be something to see, if we will only take the trouble to look. There is also a cone of light cast upon the Earth, as though there is someone on the other side of the "window" looking down at us. Finally, the "window" transmogrifies into an aquamarine sphere the size of a soccer ball and speeds off in the direction of England. Did the visitors acquire enough information from the French fishing nets to conclude it was time to study the English art of angling, or were they as fearful of the fishermen as the humans were of them? What size would these beings have to be, if they could fit inside a soccer ball? We are left with a mystery wrapped in an enigma.

UFOS AND FOLKLORE

Folktales universally describe a realm that exists on the border between the familiar physical world and the mysterious domain of nonmaterial beings and landscapes. The human protagonists often find or are given an object in the other world which disappears upon their return to space and time. Alternatively, it may change into something ordinary. A jewel may turn out to be a common stone, or a gold necklace may mutate upon return into a plaited loop of grass. The same phenomenon occurs in abduction accounts. In the fall of 1987, aliens transported Whitley Strieber through "Locale I" from his home in Westchester County, New York, to the house of a friend in Boulder, Colorado, where he placed some stones from the driveway in his mouth. Upon his return home, the stones were gone (Strieber, 1995, pp. 40–49).

Similar mysterious disappearances occur with the so-called "implants" that aliens are believed to have inserted in the noses, brains, and other body parts of their abductees. Thousands of these people have undergone careful medical examinations in which scratches may have been found, but no object of any kind. In a single case, a tiny object was retrieved, but microscopic analysis revealed it was comprised of normal human cells.

In Eagle River, Wisconsin, April 18, 1961, Joe Simonton, a 60-year-old chicken farmer, found a silvery flying saucer hovering about five feet above his front yard. A hatch opened and he was greeted by three "Italian-looking men" in turtlenecks and knit helmets. They handed him an empty jug to fill with water, which he did, and rewarded him with three crispy pancakes they had been "frying in a flameless grill of some sort." He ate one and found it "tasted like cardboard." He handed another over to the U. S. Department of Health, Education, and Welfare for analysis. The scientists found it to be "an ordinary pancake of terrestrial origin," composed of buckwheat hulls, soya bean hulls, and wheat bran (Vallee, 1988, p. 43). Jacques Vallee has found parallels to this story in Evans-Wentz's 1909 study, *The Fairy Faith in Celtic Countries*.

Fairy rings, marking the entrance to the realm of that fabulous race, also have parallels in UFO stories. In Delphos, Kansas, November 2, 1971, a mushroom-shaped vehicle was seen to hover above the Earth and then take off, leaving behind a white circle on the ground that resisted wetting by rain and snow. In a similar case in New Zealand, Vallee managed to obtain a sample of the white material of the ring and have it subjected to analysis. "The fibers were vegetal in nature and belonged to an organism of the order of Actinomycetales, which is an intermediate organism between bacteria and fungus" (Vallee, 1988, pp. 164–165).

In 1691, the Reverend Kirk of Scotland wrote *The Secret Commonwealth of Elves, Fauns, and Fairies*. Vallee has extracted sixteen characteristics of these wee folk, all of which bear a strong resemblance to what we have recently been hearing about extraterrestrial aliens (Vallee, 1988, pp. 192–195). They have light and fluid bodies that can appear and vanish at will or change into other shapes. They appear most frequently at twilight, evidently a universal "time of power." They "swim" through the air, changing domicile frequently. They are divided into tribes, have a hierarchy of leaders, and live in wonderfully large and beautiful houses equipped with lamps that burn forever and fires that need no fuel. They communicate with one another in a kind of whistling sound, but can speak the local languages of humans. They can be made to appear before us through magic. Vallee also finds seventeen parallels between Catholic miracle stories, including the appearances of the Blessed Virgin Mary, and UFO reports.

There is a considerable literature on the folkloric dimension of UFO reports, and the morning of the fourth day of the 1991 Abduction Study Conference, held at the Massachusetts Institute of Technology, was devoted to the subject. C. D. B. Bryan reports that the discussion was interrupted by an angry John Mack, one of the organizers of the conference: "John Mack says heatedly, 'I'm surprised nobody in this group has gotten up to say what we are dealing with here is radically different and has no connection with folklore'" (Bryan, 1995, p. 144).

Mack is a well-respected psychiatrist and professor at Harvard who has published the results of his hypnotic regression work with self-described abductees (*Abduction,* 1994), a book that has occasioned a great deal of controversy. His work will be discussed later in this chapter. What is important for us in the present context is Mack's deep misunderstanding of Vallee's folklore thesis.

Evidently for Mack, folktales are whimsical works of fiction, suitable as bedtime reading for children, but having no relevance for serious-minded adults—particularly the patients with whom he has worked. His abductees have undergone horribly traumatic experiences which, while unexplained, leave no doubt in the mind of a sympathetic listener that something real and undeniable has happened to them. They have suffered grievously, and their lives have been changed. He finds the folklore parallels to be trivializing coincidences, and believes that those who take up this line of thought are trying to ridicule and deny the disturbing reality of what the abductees have experienced.

Nothing could be further from Vallee's intentions. To understand what the French-born astronomer and UFO investigator is trying to say, we have to turn the whole argument around. It is not that abduction reports are being relegated to whimsy. Rather, the content of folklore is being revalorized. For Vallee, folktales are the literary residue of real encounters between humans and unthinkable beings of an entirely different order. Although these old-time encounters are sometimes humorous—as, indeed, is Joe Simonton's pancake story—they are also deeply disturbing.

People abducted to the realm of the fairies or mermaids have been changed forever. There is an unspeakable tragedy in the story of Urashima; and, although Howori is left with the offspring of his marriage with the Sea Dragon Princess, the loss of his scaly bride leaves him heartbroken and alone with the task of raising a hybrid child amidst a misunderstanding and probably hostile human community.

Fairytale abductions are filled with wonder and ecstasy, but are also deeply disturbing. Pining and loss are essential. The protagonists end up isolated from both worlds. Unable to return to an uneasy bliss in the fabulous realm, they are equally unable to return to the human society they have left. They are isolated and alone and no longer know who they are. The world of space and time has lost its former self-evident sufficiency. It has become treacherously shot through with gaps and devoid of any semblance of security.

Parallels between folktales and UFO reports take us back to the lower Gnostic spheres, where human journeyers run the risk of being trapped by the Archons. To encounter an Archon is dangerous business. It does not simply pervert the celestial ascent of *gnosis*, it entangles us in demonic obsessions, alienates us from ourselves, undermines our old way of life, and supplants it with an overwhelming emotionality that clouds our vision, leaving us gripped by rage, lust, fear, or victimization.

The Archons are "powers," as their name implies. They are far more powerful than we are, and cannot be subdued with the meager resources available to our everyday egos. The Gnostic Mary Magdalen and the rabbis of the Jewish *merkabah* required a transcendental consciousness to slip past the Archons and remain on their mystical course. Only an intimation of the One, through *gnosis*, kept them oriented to the center and prevented their falling victim to the distractions of the lower spheres.

To attend to the parallels between folktales and UFO reports is to suspect that the sightings of UFOs and the encounters with their inhabitants belong to the *imaginal* world. Because the human imaginal faculty is structured by the archetypes in the same way that the sensory faculty is structured by space and time, sojourns in the *imaginal* world always display certain typical themes. Folktales and celestial ascents seem to be variations of an archetypal theme wherein the meaning of our fleshly existence is found in some parallel universe that pervades our planet and extends far beyond it into a greater cosmos.

To know this truth and to find a way to live it, is the most meaningful and satisfying thing we can do. But it is fraught with perils. Everywhere we look, there are powerful beings and enticing realms, and every one of them is a trap. In some, we may be abused, in others, filled with our sense of chosenness and self-importance. We need a compass for a journey like this; and the folktales, by and large, know nothing of a compass. This is another reason UFO reports resemble folktales: most people who encounter the fabulous ones have no idea what they are up against and no way to get oriented.

If some of the folktale encounters seem trivial, like that of the Irish fool who sold the mermaid's ring for a few pennies and went back to his cronies in the pub, so may some of the UFO visitations. The overall-clad Joe Simonton seems to have met beings no more foreign to his rural WASP background than a group of Italians in turtlenecks. He is the kind of man Ibn al-'Arabi might describe as "able to pass through walls but does not do so, or even wish to" (Ibn al-'Arabi, 1980, p. xv). Others, like Urashima, have passed through and been horrified.

Folktales and UFO reports, therefore, appear to be variants on an ancient human theme. What formerly were beings of light, living in supercelestial spheres, more akin to angels than to humans, now seem to have become the "small grays" of UFO lore: three-and-a-half-foot tall, spindly-limbed, huge-headed humanoids with large, liquid, black eyes, and apparently clad in silvery gray suits of lycra. The Archons of 2000 years ago were frankly described as "spirits." But we live in a world that has no place for spirits. Our Archons have become technologically advanced denizens of unknown planets, somewhere "out there" in the trackless universe. It is tempting to conclude that the fairies, brownies, gnomes, and mermaids of earlier centuries represent intermediate forms of what were once Archons, but have become "small grays."

Nevertheless, UFOs are not unique to the 20th century. Vallee makes a strong case for the similarity of UFO visions and the art of the ancient Near East and Japan of 3000 B.C. Furthermore, he has uncovered nine incidents of UFO sightings in Japan between 1180 and 1749. Around A.D. 800, only a century after the death of Climacus, Archbishop Agobard of Lyons inveighed against a widely popular belief in the physical reality of cloud ships from the celestial land of "Magonia" that were sending alien beings down to farm lands to steal and destroy crops (Vallee, 1988, pp. 9–15).

Jerome Cardan, in 15th century Milan, witnessed seven men composed of air, mortal, but able to live for three or four centuries. A hundred years later, the Swiss physician and alchemist, Paracelsus, wrote a treatise on *Why These Beings Appear to Us*. In the 18th century, the German literary giant, Goethe, observed moving lights that seemed to resemble living creatures more than will-o'-the-wisps.

In 1896 and 1897, there were many sightings in the USA of an airship that sailed a leisurely course over large urban areas. It was said to steal cattle by means of a large anchor the inhabitants let down on a rope.

Various witnesses disagreed on the details of the ship, but it often seemed to be a kind of celestial steam engine that chuffed and groaned like a locomotive.

If the UFO accounts of the past forty years, constitute a "folklore in the making," this means that local and temporal variants are being applied to a central mythic theme. Vallee reports the changing appearance of the extraterrestrials according to national temperament:

> In the United States, they appear as science fiction monsters. In South America, they are sanguinary and quick to get into a fight. In France, they behave like rational, Cartesian, peace-loving tourists. The Irish Gentry, if we believe its spokesmen, was an aristocratic race organized somewhat like a religious-military order. The airship pilots were strongly individualistic characters with all the features of the American farmer (Vallee, 1988, p. 141).

We can surmise that Americans are prone to technologize the beings of light, if that is what they are, because the outer space of countless galaxies is the only place left us that remains sufficiently unknown. It is the last gasp in our attempt to hold onto a conception of these spirits that can be fudged as an unexplored habitation within the realm of space and time. Several centuries ago, there were still accommodatingly unexplored reaches of the planet, and maps represented those lands and seas as the dwelling places of fabulous beasts.

The folktales we now have on our shelves were frozen in time by collectors like the brothers Grimm. When those tales were still part of a living oral tradition, their locations were always uncivilized places on the Earth—enchanted lakes and forests. The people who spun those tales, as well as their audiences, were very much aware of how uncanny and dangerous it felt to come near such unexplored domains, particularly in "times of power" like the twilight of evening or the dark of night.

There may have been bears, wolves, and snakes in those forests. But wild animals, as dangerous as they might be, were well enough known to inspire a merely *rational* fear. The wee folk and the mermaids inspired something else, the *dread* of encountering something radically other, beings that had no proper shape, but were able to assume whatever form would be enticing or threatening. They could be more intelligent, beautiful, and luminous than we, but were always monstrous. They had an animal component, an instinctual simplicity and freedom from moral restraint that made their intentions inscrutable. Although they might sometimes reward us or promise us our heart's desire, they were intrinsically treacherous. They could lead us into uncharted realms we might never escape. They could bring us face to face with fears and compulsions that had lurked inside us all along and that were better left alone.

When the uncharted lakes had been ringed with cottages and weekend anglers had learned the deeps and sandbars beneath their surfaces— when the favorite haunts of bass and pike and bluegill had been discovered—the fabulous ones had already moved on. Perhaps there was a lake far back in the mountains, where roads had not yet been built, or a tangled no-man's land where the sprites might still sport among the tree roots. Today there are almost none of these places left. Even the seas and the air have been conquered by our machines. No place remains for them to hide but the airless outer reaches of dark space, where countless stars and planets remain unnoticed by even our most powerful telescopes.

The uncanny ones have always had a technology superior to ours— whether this took the form of fairy fires that needed no fuel or flying saucers that defy the law of gravity. The cloud ships that cruised above the countryside of eighth-century France resembled the sea-going craft that berthed at French wharves, with the obvious difference that they had managed to conquer the air rather than the sea. Nevertheless, those cloud ships still depended upon the wind to fill their sails. Similarly, the airship that stole cattle from American farmers a hundred years ago employed the advanced technology of the day, that of the steam engine, but adapted for voyaging through the air. Today, rumor has it that some of the flying saucers presumably responsible for cattle mutilations in the American countryside have crashed—at Roswell, New Mexico, and perhaps elsewhere—and that these have been studied by the American military. Many believe that these alleged wrecks have been "back engineered"—possibly at locations under the deserts of our western states— and that the Pentagon is preparing a secret fleet under the code-name Aurora.

Such speculations can be as trivializing as the stories of Joe Simonton and the Irish fool. They are attempts to demonstrate the physicality of these beings and their vehicles, so that we can fit them into our everyday world. We want to see them as fundamentally no more different from us than the Spanish Conquistadors were from the Aztecs, or the English from the Polynesians. We want to find a place for them. It may be over the horizon, but you can get there in a sailing ship or a "back-engineered" flying saucer. Anything else is unthinkable.

RUMORS OF DEMONS

John Mack's book, *Abduction* (1994), is a work of considerable dedication. It reveals an author genuinely concerned with and affected by the unthinkable experiences his self-described abductee patients have undergone. Mack has a reputation as a most careful investigator, who uses hypnosis intelligently to allow his subjects to discover their own stories without leading questions or suggestive images. We gather the impression of a man of integrity who cares about his patients and has allowed them to affect *him*, as any really *human* therapist must. In the tradition of the best luminaries of his field—people like Pierre Janet, Eugen Bleuler, and C. G. Jung—he *believes* what his patients tell him. Not literally, surely, in every detail, but with human empathy. Best of all, he has no answers, no doctrine to impose upon and distort their experiences.

The theme of his book is that people who have experienced what they remember as abductions tell internally consistent stories with appropriate emotional reactions. They are immensely believable. Furthermore, there are so many points of agreement between the various personal accounts, so much commonality, that he is unable to avoid the conclusion that some common human experience must be involved. They have come face to face with a monumental exception to the rules of reality we all take for granted. It has thrust them into an existential panic. Most of them would like nothing better than to be convinced that their awful recollections are nothing but bad dreams. But the experiences are too real. They cannot be denied. If accepted, however, they imply the world is radically and disturbingly different from what we all believe.

Sheila N. is the second abductee Mack describes, a 44-year-old social worker who first fell into a crisis of meaning and terror upon the death of her mother, eight years before consulting him (Mack, 1994, pp. 69–90). She felt the doctors had been "abrupt and uncaring" toward her mother and that they needlessly "robbed her of her dignity" by maintaining life-supports when hope was gone. Her mother's coffin was left exposed in the grave for three days before the vault was covered and the soil replaced. Her husband had given her no support in her time of anger and grief, because "he has to be happy." She became emotionally estranged from him and began to sleep in another room.

Around this time, she began to have "electric dreams," in which she vibrated like Monroe and felt that her body was being controlled by someone or something—possibly she was "possessed by demons." In most of these dreams, she recalled intense light coming in through all the windows of her house and small silvery beings with big heads and thin arms and legs. There seemed to be evidence that her young daughter was experiencing something similar, and Sheila felt terrified and impotent to protect the girl. The psychiatrists she consulted prescribed drugs to control her anxiety, but invalidated her experiences with their lack of belief. She felt oppressed and "tied down," witnessing inexplicable images that inspired overwhelming fear. She wanted to know why she fell asleep during these terrifying dreams, when ordinary nightmares would wake her up. Why did the "dreams" take place in her bedroom? Was it a real experience? If so, what had happened that was so painful for her to remember?

Before consulting Mack in 1992, Sheila had already recalled incidents from ages 6, 8, and 13, one confirmed by a brother and another by a sister. She had three hypnotic regressions under Mack's direction. She recalled surgical-like procedures in which a square or rectangular instrument was pressed through her abdominal wall; needles were inserted into her forehead, thigh, and hip bone. An electric-shaver-like instrument was drawn across her abdomen, causing her to feel cold. Another instrument was "suckin' stuff out from inside of my body." She felt embarrassed and violated to have to lie naked on a table with a crowd of beings standing around her, staring.

On one occasion, she found herself inside a towering, cone-shaped dome comprised of red stained-glass windows, "so awesome . . . that it scares me to death to look at it." It seemed to be a powerful statement that "my body is not my own." Most disturbing of all, however, were the large black eyes of the beings: "There's power in those eyes"—particularly those of the "leader," who controlled her and the other beings with his eyes. "Everyone respects him." When she looked into the eyes, "They take control and then you don't have the energy to fight." Nevertheless, she felt she had to gaze into those large, black, liquid orbs "to figure out how they got there." The sight plunged her terrifyingly into "the black." One moment there was intense, bright light, and the next moment "it was real black." It shows "how insignificant we are as human beings." Still, the eyes made her feel more relaxed. The contradictions between these two eye-inspired experiences made her fear she could be psychotic, "like you're not in touch with reality."

Sheila's regular therapist, Dr. Waterman, reports that, as a result of her three apparently inconclusive hypnotic regressions with Mack, she has done a great deal of work in integrating her experiences. She seems to have become "a different person." "She seemed more energetic, with a bright, direct look in her eyes, and said she felt more hopeful."

Sheila and her fellow abductees are suspended between two worlds. One place feels like it ought to be "home." But it is too insecure, too shot full of disquieting gaps, to be "home" in the old sense ever again. The other world is totally unthinkable, absurdly unpredictable, and terrifyingly assaultive. Abductees feel invaded, violated, in the grip of powers they could never have dreamed up. Despite all this, however, these people are changing. There is a progressive structure to *Abduction*. If the abductees described in the first chapters feel mostly violated and abused, those at the end have begun to find a compelling transcendent meaning for their lives. They find they have a kinship with the aliens; perhaps they are part alien themselves. The rift in the fabric of reality has been a monumental opportunity for these individuals, though not without the dreadful *koan* of existential panic.

Despite Mack's responsible, sympathetic, and even hopeful thesis, several people have told me that they have not been able to read his book. They found the stories of Sheila and Ed (the first two cases discussed) too disturbing, too evil. Perhaps these scenes of abduction, bodily probes, and sexual abuse could happen to them. Perhaps they *had* happened. One woman was afraid to let her dogs out at night and afraid to go to sleep unless the dogs were in her bedroom. Another reported nightmares.

Sexual abuse, bodily and psychological intrusions, falling into the hands of inscrutable beings of apparently limitless power, the stealing of babies, the propagation of unwanted hybrids for mysterious purposes— much of this material from abduction reports seems "satanic." Every thoughtful person who has not been abducted surely has reason to wonder about these things. How is it that the abduction reports retrieved by hypnotists very often recapitulate the themes of our daily newspapers, supermarket tabloids, and the most sensational of our daily television programs? We are told more than half of the women in our society have been subjected to sexual abuse as children, and the most horrific stories come from people who, with the help of hypnosis, have recalled scenes of "satanic ritual abuse," involving not only rape but cold, calculating seductions, the intrusion of foreign objects into bodily orifices, the propagation of unwanted babies for sacrifice, the theft and violation of infants, and even cannibalism.

Furthermore, the hypnotists who are retrieving these stories from adults believe their patients on the same grounds that Mack asserts. They tell internally consistent stories and report them with appropriate emotional reactions—horror, repugnance, anger, and cringing terror.

Hypnotists who have assisted their patients in retrieving these accounts invariably respond to their critics by saying: "I wish you could hear these people. If you were there while they were reliving their stories, you would have to believe. This stuff is too *real*."

Dozens of people are in prison across America for having practiced "satanic ritual abuse" in child-care centers and elementary schools, although there is not a shred of physical evidence in any one of the cases that anything of the kind ever took place. Physicians' "expert testimony" on the basis of supposed abnormalities in the hymen membrane of little girls or observed "winking" (involuntary opening) of the anal sphincters of boys and girls have been proven spurious. These things had never been studied before. There were no data on what a normal girl's hymen would look like and no studies of anal "winking."

Extensive data collection on normal children has shown that there is no such thing as a typical hymen. The frills, flaps, and tears that seemed to be evidence of abuse are in fact normally occurring structures. Anal "winking"—mistakenly taken as evidence of sodomy—turns out to be a normal response in a squatting human being when the anus is stroked with a cotton swab. Furthermore, there are no dead bodies, infant or otherwise, no blood, no bones, no ritual paraphernalia, and no meeting places. Just as in the case of alien abduction, there is no physical evidence; or what *seemed* to be physical evidence has turned out to be normally occurring, everyday objects and processes. We seem to be faced with rumors rather than facts.

Jeffrey S. Victor's exhaustive study of the ritual abuse craze that swept over Jamestown, New York, where he is a SUNY professor of sociology, makes an overwhelmingly convincing case for the causes and dynamics of what he calls a "rumor panic" (*Satanic Panic,* 1993). He has identified sixty-two such outbreaks in the contiguous forty-eight states, all but one occurring in rural, blue-collar areas where economic dislocation has brought on financial and job insecurity, forcing both parents to work full-time, causing family tensions, and making traditional-minded parents rely guiltily on day-care centers for their children.

These people are facing deep insecurity, loss of traditional family roles and identity. Not knowing whom or what to blame for their troubles, they are on the lookout for scapegoats. Furthermore, the rural regions where rumor panics of satanic abuse have erupted are also highly religious areas, where Protestant fundamentalism has dominated for generations. In these districts, Satan has long been the metaphysical source of all evil. Furthermore, apparent evidence of Satan's doings serves as an indirect proof for the existence of God. Victor found even psychiatrists, social workers, and judges who defended their views about satanic abuse in the absence of "hard data" by appeals to the Bible.

Nathan and Snedeker (*Satan's Silence,* 1995) have documented the process of leading questions, disturbing pressure techniques, and use of dolls with breasts, penises, vaginas, and pubic hair to extract the internally *inconsistent* reports from children that have sent their parents, teachers, and care-givers to prison. The reader cannot avoid the conclusion that the interrogation process itself was abusive.

Victor's sociological study defines the conditions for the development of a rumor panic (Victor, 1993, p. 8). First, local rumors "need to find a channel to reach a broad mass audience." This is provided by local newspaper and television reports, and spreads through national exposure on programs like "Geraldo!" Second, "carrier" groups have to disseminate these stories over many years and in the face of strong skepticism. This is accomplished by national organizations like Believe the Children and traveling "experts" from the clergy, police, and psychological disciplines holding seminars to warn and explain. The second condition thus blends into the third: "It is necessary for some kind of authority figures to legitimize the rumor stories, by publicly endorsing them as being true, or at least plausible." We live in a world where these horrendous possibilities have a context: cult scares, "deprogramming," the Manson murders, the Jonestown mass suicides, rumors of cattle mutilation, and Procter and Gamble's alleged "satanic" logo.

What strikes *me* in all of this is that the same complex of ideas and images keeps coming up: sexual abuse, the stealing of babies, and the dismemberment and cannibalization of infants in the context of demon worship. The ancient Romans persecuted the early Christians for these things; European Christian societies instituted pogroms in the Jewish ghettos to exterminate the same rumored complex of abuses. The witch hunts of Europe and Salem, Massachusetts, were also driven by demon-haunted fears of sexual abuse and the sacrifice of infants. In the last dozen years, this panic has broken out sixty-two times in our supposedly advanced country. Throughout the Age of Pisces, human societies threatened with profound insecurity have again and again produced the same ghastly images of evil and found scapegoats to prosecute for indulging in them.

All of this suggests that the sexual abuse/infant cannibalism theme emerges as a way to schematize radical insecurity. No doubt Jeffrey Victor is right about the financial conditions and social unheaval generated by the economic dislocations of our changing society. It is surely terrifying to face the breakdown of the family and one's impotence as a provider for one's dependents. Surely the children are the most defenseless victims of these social crises. But I think the predicament must be deeper still. Beneath the everyday privations, loss of prestige, and impotence to control our destiny must lurk something even more hair-raising. The loss of every kind of security in our daily lives exposes us to an *existential* crisis.

When we find that all our assumptions about our lives, about the world, about the very nature of reality, have been wrong, we no longer know who we are. We do not know how to live. There is nothing to fall back upon. We find ourselves standing at the edge of an abyss of meaninglessness. Absurdity laughs at us and mocks our best intentions. The future lacks all hope and becomes an inscrutable threat. In a situation like this, we grasp at anything that seems to explain the nature of the evil that is overcoming us. Unable to *think* our way out of such an impasse, our imagination conjures up the worst evils we can imagine. Invariably, these are sexual abuse and the stealing, mutilation, and cannibalism of infants. People reach for Satan and send people to prison for being his minions only when they are facing existential panic.

No one is facing existential panic more directly than the people who understand themselves to have been abducted by aliens. These beings who dwell invisibly among us, or who visit us from outer space, can "materialize" at any moment. They are not subject to the laws of the physical universe as we know them, and they seem to be able to do with us as they will. We have no idea what that will is. They are completely unfathomable and leave us no dependable refuge. Having invaded our home world, they leave their abductees essentially homeless. Their visitations bring us face to face with the fundamental questions: Who am I? What are they? What kind of place is this world?

In such a context, is it any wonder that the monumental shock to which they expose us drives us to resurrect the archetypal image of evil: sexual abuse, the stealing of babies, the propagation of hybrids—possibly for dismemberment and cannibalization? I think we are mistaken to stop at these almost stereotyped images—either to reject the abduction experience as a hoax or to embrace a new satanic terror. We have known since Freud's first observations that, in the face of "free floating anxiety," people are prone to conjure an horrific image in order to convert an unknown dread into a known fear. No doubt the abductees are facing the monumentally unthinkable.

Let us maintain Mack's attitude of not knowing. Perhaps their bodies have not been sexually abused. Perhaps it is their reality that has been abused, dismembered, and devoured. That, after all, is a far more frightening possibility. Let us suspend judgment about the literal truth of their recollections in order to see what these experiences are doing to them.

There is one, last, terrifying possibility. Perhaps we all are familiar with these unearthly beings. Perhaps we all have periods of "missing time." Perhaps, like Sheila, we do not notice these gaps unless something truly disturbing occurs within the domain of public reality—something like the inattention and disrespect shown to a dying mother and to her corpse, and the estrangement experienced when a husband is unable to share grief and frustration. Without a "real world" set-back of this kind, perhaps our internal monolog will not be sufficiently challenged in its tireless repetitions and will retain its ability to gloss over the most obvious of contradictions. If we all live through non-ordinary states of consciousness and then forget them—as Castaneda managed to forget the vast majority of his sojourns in the *nagual*—then perhaps the abductees are simply more courageous than the rest of us. For they, above all, know the door of the broom-closet is open and can never be closed again.

PETER'S DOUBLE LIFE

Mack employs "Peter" a 34-year-old former hotel manager and recent acupuncture school graduate, as a central figure in his argument in *Abduction* (Mack, 1994, pp. 293-334). To forestall his readers' possible suspicions that the story represents nothing more than the ravings of a madman, Mack makes a point of personally vouching for Peter's high-functioning, good psychological health. He also refers him for a battery of psychological tests that fully confirm his own impressions.

Before undergoing his first hypnotic regression, Peter was aware that he had always known that there are angels, that he could commune with God, and that "there are UFOs and extraterrestrials." He knew that he had been having frequent encounters with them, that they had a laser beam they shot into the center of his forehead, that after one encounter he had small red lesions behind his ears, and that "there is some destiny for me . . . in this alien thing, something for me to do" (Mack, 1994, p. 294). He felt he had gotten as far as he could go on his own, was "stuck," and needed to explore his experiences in greater depth through hypnosis. His terror about the experiences was, he thought, the problem. He would have been delighted to learn that the beings were not real, that it was merely "in his imagination."

His first regression took him to the Caribbean, where he was managing a hotel in 1988, four years before his meeting with Mack. He found himself naked, humiliated, and paralyzed by the beings, whom he was enraged enough to kill. One of them hit him over the head with what looked like a flashlight ("shut me down") and made him feel more peaceful. The nakedness, humiliation, and fear were gone. As he floated through the house and up above the island to a spaceship, he felt it was an "adventure," and that he was "honored" and "special."

Inside the ship, he was strapped down to a form-fitting table that was "extremely comfortable," where his abdomen was probed through the groin and something was implanted in his rectum. He was enraged and crying as he relived the experience: "I'm stuck for life"; "I feel like one of those polar bears with a collar on" (Mack, 1994, p. 300). He believed the experience "indoctrinated" him and made him "one of theirs." Despite feeling violated and traumatized, however, he also felt he was a "willing participant" in the process, that it had to do with evolving to a higher consciousness.

In his second regression, something was extracted from his brain. He thought it was a little black chip the aliens had implanted earlier and that they would read it to know what is recorded inside his brain. He was enraged: "I'm just a piece of meat to them. I hate it. I just hate this" (Mack, 1994, p. 303). But he also spoke sympathetically of their intentions saying, "They've got a plan for me," that had something to do with expanding consciousness and a "spiritual plane."

In his third session, Peter stole a page from Monroe. Instead of choosing a specific memory to explore, he allowed his "inner radar" to take him where *it* wanted him to go. He hopped about through several different scenes, from childhood to the recent past. His dominant emotions were terror, rage, and impotence. Sperm was taken. But at the end, he announced that his terror was the problem: "It has more to do with having an experience that goes beyond my accepted perception of reality" (Mack, 1994, p. 308). The experiences were, "no question about it," designed to expand consciousness. He was certain humanity is headed for a cataclysm, and the aliens are preparing us for it.

Before being hypnotized for his fourth session, Peter announced that re-experiencing the agony had already changed him. He felt "happy to be alive" and no longer isolated and disconnected from other people. He felt part of a "continuum." The session began with screams of fear and pain, but many insights unfolded for him. He learned that the aliens know us deeply and want us to like them. He felt he had to overcome his involuntary fear and hatred of them. He observed that they are afraid of our anger, but want to learn love, care, and compassion from us. They are willing to share their intellectual growth, if we will share our emotions. He felt an overpowering sadness for the longing he saw in an alien's eyes.

Just before the fifth regression, Peter recalled a Jehovah's Witness door-to-door preacher, a woman, who had looked at him as though she knew him. Her eyes reminded him of an abduction experience he could not recall in detail. Exploring it through hypnosis, he found himself rocking on his haunches on his bed in the house of a friend on Nantucket Island. The aliens wanted him to step *through* the roof of the house. He was being asked to willingly pass out of this world into the other dimension. He vacillated in the terror that if he did step through, there would be nothing on the other side.

Finally, he screwed up his courage and did it, as though in four earthly strides. "One, two, three," and he was face to face with the steeply canted ceiling wall; *four* and he was through. His journey took him to a flying saucer where he was introduced to a female alien whom he perceived to be his guide and instructress. Then, suddenly, he realized something unthinkable. The aliens expected him to "breed" with her—"It's not even about making love or sex, but breeding with her." Looking into her penetrating eyes, he *sees* that they belong to the Jehovah's Witness woman. He does not know whether she is a human in alien form on the ship or an alien in human form on Earth. He realizes with horror that this woman is his wife, and that all the hybrid children he has seen are his offspring with her. He is afraid of losing connection with the Earth and with his earthly wife.

Peter saw this experience as a turning point. Having willingly, and under his own power, passed through the wall into the other world, he had gone "from a victim role to a participant role." He had lost some of his habitual identity and learned that he is "part alien." In his next two sessions, he experienced this more deeply and witnessed scenes of the destruction of the Earth. He came to realize that the "breeding program" was a design to evolve the human species and repopulate the planet for a "Golden Age of learning and openness and opportunity." "I'm connecting with the beings, and I have a sense that they are connected with God, whatever God is . . . [a]s intermediaries" (Mack, 1994, p. 329).

This case illustrates clearly that we have little reason to suspect John Mack of leading his patients with suggestions in order to extract a story to justify his own favorite theories about abductions. In every instance, Peter arrived at his session with definite fragments of knowledge about what he had been through. He used hypnotic regression to re-enter those scenes and experience them more deeply and in greater detail, to immerse himself in the emotional values that lay behind his dim conscious recollections. Furthermore, apart from realizing his own part in the "breeding program," he already knew before beginning the hypnotic process that he was trying to discover his *destiny in this alien thing,* something he *had to do.* By the second session, he was aware that it had to do with expanding his own consciousness; by the third he knew that it had something to do with expanding human consciousness generally, in order to face an earthly "cataclysm."

There is not a single change in direction. There is only a deepening of his appreciation of what is taking place. It has to do with learning, accepting, and willing participation with those beings from the greater cosmos. Peter immersed himself in the rudiments of everything we have observed about cosmic consciousness. The beings knew him thoroughly, better than he knew himself. Their intentions turned out to be the best he could imagine for himself—a role of transcendent meaning that reached far beyond the themes of his old internal monolog and provided him a sense of himself, making him "happy to be alive" and connecting him, not only with those unthinkable beings, but with humanity at large. He no longer felt isolated and lonely. He was part of a "continuum."

To get to this point Peter had to go through an agony of terror and pain. In the beginning, this torment was schematized as bodily abuse. He was forced to go with them and impotent to resist. The most horrifying aspect, however, was that he had to accept what was happening to him. He had to understand and embrace their cosmic perspective. The terror and the pain, he realized, stemmed from his own resistance, the fact that, if he accepted what was happening, his old certainties, the secure-seeming illusions of his internal monolog, would be destroyed. He would lose every security he—and everyone of us—had taken for granted. He faced an existential panic.

Despite the psychological tests and Mack's informed impressions attesting to Peter's sanity, we may wonder at the bizarre imagery of his having to mate with an alien woman. If we think this must surely be a piece of psychosis, we need to recall how the *imaginal* world is structured by mythic themes. Evidently, Peter had stepped through the ceiling wall into the realm where folktale heroes mated with mermaids and fairies. Indeed, this theme goes far back beyond what the Grimm brothers collected—back to the ancient mythology of Greece, where the greatest heroes and heroines were the off-spring of humans mating with the gods. Back beyond even that to the cosmic consciousness of our pre-Taurean ancestors. Eliade, has collected the following first-person story from a shaman of the Goldi people of Siberia:

> Once I was asleep on my sick-bed, when a spirit approached me. It was a very beautiful woman. Her figure was very slight, she was not more than half an arshin (71 cm.) tall. Her face and attire were quite as those of our Goldi women. . . . She said: "I am the 'ayami' of your ancestors the Shamans. I taught them shamaning. Now I am going to teach you. The old shamans have died off, and there is no one to heal the people. You are to become a shaman." . . .
>
> She has been coming to me ever since, and I sleep with her as with my own wife, but we have no children. She lives quite by herself without any relatives in a hut, on a mountain, but she often changes her abode. Sometimes she comes under the aspect of an old woman, and sometimes under that of a wolf, so that she is terrible to look at. Sometimes she comes as a winged tiger. I mount it and she takes me to show me different countries. . . .
>
> Now my "ayami" does not come to me as frequently as before. Formerly, when teaching me, she used to come every night. She has given me three assistants—[panther, bear, and tiger]. They come to me in my dreams, and appear whenever I summon them while shamaning. If one of them refuses to come, the "ayami" makes them obey. . . . When I am shamaning, the "ayami" and the assistant spirits are possessing me: whether big or small, they penetrate me as smoke or vapour would. When the "ayami" is within me, it is she who speaks through my mouth, and she does everything herself. . . . (Eliade, 1964, p. 172).

Not unlike our own period at the end of the Age of Pisces, the Goldi people of Siberia had lost their connection with cosmic consciousness when this man's "ayami" first appeared to him and announced that she was going to restore that connection by teaching him to shamanize. The ancient *imaginal* knowledge of the old shamans was to be restored, and the means to accomplish this lay in the dual life Eliade's protagonist was called to lead. Like Peter, he was to have two wives, one in the world of flesh, who maintained his connection to space and time, and another from the greater cosmos, a bright, tiny woman, who appears to him in his sleep or in his shamanic trance. The "ayami" does not come from outer space, for evidently there were still uncivilized locales in the Siberian mountains where she could set up her hut. She personifies the entire domain of cosmic consciousness, commanding the lesser spirits to obey and to serve the fleshly human community through her earthly husband, a man who passes back and forth through the veil that stands between the worlds.

The bond of sexual love, where "two become one flesh," is one of the most fundamental structures of human imagination. It represents the ultimate enduring connection. The Goldi shaman and Peter are asked to embrace, to love, and to intermingle with that which is wholly other than the fleshly world. Far from being passive conduits for the spiritual powers of the greater cosmos, these human heroes must actively engage with, willingly participate in, and be attached by erotic desire to the domain of cosmic consciousness. They truly live a double life, having a family in each world. The Goldi shaman is resigned to having no children in the other world, while Peter is resigned to having no children here (for his loving and supportive wife, Jamy, the eldest of nine children who had to raise her siblings, feels she has spent enough years in motherhood).

The *truth* of Peter's encounters with the little gray men and women lies in his parallel lives—simultaneously fully engaged, through Jamy, in space and time and fully engaged, through his alien wife, in the greater cosmos. We might wish to withhold judgment on his visions of worldwide destruction of the planet—he saw ecological disasters involving the movement of tectonic plates and the inundation of the eastern half of the North American continent from the Atlantic Ocean and the Gulf of Mexico. We do not know whether he has seen the actual future of the planet as it will be experienced in space and time or whether this was a symbolic representation of the destruction of human consciousness through its loss of connection with the world of soul. In the same way, we do not know how to evaluate all those hybrid children he has fathered. Are they literally the future flesh-and-blood inhabitants of the Earth, or do they symbolize the potential of a life lived simultaneously on two planes?

COSMIC AMBIVALENCE

The most transformative event in Peter's story is his out-of-body stride through the steeply canted ceiling wall of the house on Nantucket. In that moment, he conquered the major portion of his fear and entered the greater cosmos of his own free will. Perhaps he would have been taken there against his will if he had not chosen to do so on his own. But the point is that he did *choose*, and from that instant onward his life in both worlds was changed. He left behind all the Joe Simontons who have encountered the world of UFOs and have the ability to pass through walls *but do not do so, or even want to*. He gave up his victimhood and became a participant. Mack tells us Peter became a leader within the abductee community and was able to go public with his experiences. Evidently, his encounters were no longer something to be ashamed of. He found he could accept his double life, that it added cosmic meaning to his earthly existence. In very large measure, the conflict between the public realities of this world and the *imaginal* realities of the greater cosmos were—if not resolved—at least eased.

On the other side of that fateful wall, some rather monumental shocks awaited him. He found that, with his alien wife and hybrid children, he had been working willingly, but unknowingly, for some considerable time toward bringing together the fleshly world and the world of soul. Above all, he stumbled across the missing piece—what we have been looking for in vain in the folktales and UFO rumors. He found the cosmic compass: *I'm connected with the beings, and I have a sense that they are connected with God, as intermediaries.* On the other side of his daring step through the wall, the Archons who overpower, distract, and trap the gnostically innocent have become his mediators. They point to the One. Freely to choose the greater cosmos and accept his cosmic wife in love brings him to the brink *gnosis*.

All is not roses, however. In an unexpected final regression, which Mack tacks on as a postscript to his account, Peter lives through a recent abduction. Evidently he is still neglecting his ability to pass through walls, since the aliens are still catching him unawares, still coming to get him. But this last adventure is the encounter we have been waiting for: "a deeply emotional and sexually exciting connection with his alien partner, who had assumed a kind of appealing hybrid form":

> It was an enjoyable union, awkward in some ways, between a fully embodied human being and another obviously unversed in the densities of sexual love. Yet Peter felt disgust and revulsion after the experience ended, at the time it occurred, and once again when he was coming out of the trance state in which the experience was remembered (Mack, 1994, p. 334).

When he speaks of what he has learned, Peter sounds like a man of wisdom. He is on the brink of *gnosis*. He talks a good game. But when he gets out on the playing field, ambivalence tears him asunder. From the very beginning, he has felt "abused" and "just a piece of meat to them." He is terrified to realize that his mind may be under their control, even while he is in an ordinary waking state of awareness. Immediately after his talk of expanding consciousness, he screams: "I'm suspended!!! They've got me!!!" "This little being, I'd rip his head off"; and, "Those eyes. Those eyes" (Mack, 1994, p. 307). They remind him of the eyes of an animal, like a raccoon.

In the sixth session, when he finds himself on a table with the being he had already come to know as his human/alien partner standing beside it, he begins to scream and hyperventilate. In the seventh, he has the mistaken sense that he will never see his alien wife again, and says: "I don't want to leave her. I don't want to leave. I'm starting to be afraid now. It's all new." Yet, when Mack observes that they are treating him with cruelty, Peter says, "That which you feel is cruel is just the human mind trying to understand" (Mack, 1994, pp. 326–327). Mack comments to the reader that he was "not altogether convinced" by Peter's declaration of faith.

It seems that, when the aliens are safely far away, Peter longs for them and speaks primarily of their wisdom and benevolence, of how his encounters with them are expanding him, making him a happier and more complete person. But as soon as the unthinkable beings appear, he is filled with terror and feels himself at the point of obliteration. Peter is by no means alone in his violent ambivalence. It appears, in fact, that abductees may be divided into two types: those who view the entire experience one-dimensionally, as purely destructive abuse, and those who, like Peter, experience two dimensions and are suspended between horrified revulsion and transcendent promise.

It may seem strange that someone who has caught a whiff of the divine in those beings, as Peter has, should suffer from such extreme ambivalence. But we encounter this same duality in ourselves—somewhat attenuated, to be sure—every time we come face to face with the unique soul of another human being. It rarely happens in casual, task-oriented meetings, but only when the unique otherness of a fellow human strikes us disturbingly and attractively—somewhat as the eyes of the Jehovah's Witness woman seemed to penetrate into and *know* Peter intimately, so that he felt he had been connected with her for a very long time.

In such a moment, our separateness from our partner is overshadowed by the sense of a marvelous *we* that promises to dissolve us into a fascinating unity. We do not simply wonder if we can resist this dissolution, we *want* to dissolve. Enlargement, opportunity, and a wonderful sense of *becoming* are offered in this *we*. In a situation like this, it even seems to us that this promise of transcendent *we-ness* is our partner's doing. For each of us has been "just myself" all our lives; but now through our partner, amazing new possibilities are offered. She or he seems to hold a momentously compelling fate for us—a luminous oneness in which all meaning and vitality seem to dwell.

No sooner do we recognize this, however, than, deep in our conservative and habitual sense of being our own unique selves, we react in horror to the prospect of losing irreplaceably everything we have known of ourselves. We find ourselves on the brink of disaster, our balance deeply compromised, an instant away from the death of our individuality. All our instincts for self-preservation are mobilized. We try to flee the threat of dissolving into oneness; but, as soon as we do, we are confronted with the loss of that transcendent unity. As we oscillate between the forward urge to dissolve and the panic to retreat, our anxiety becomes overwhelming.

This passionate ambivalence lies at the heart of our most compelling novels, plays, and films. It is the fundamental structure of erotic interaction. It manifests itself starkly in any relationship that vacillates violently between rage and lust. In lust, we want to give ourselves over completely to the draw of oneness. In rage, we desperately try to re-establish distance.

If such ambivalence can occur between two ordinary human beings—and precisely when a meaningful transformation is offered to us—how much more powerful may we expect it to be when a Peter looks into the eyes of his alien wife? These aliens seem to know us more fully and see more deeply into our souls than anyone who belongs to our own material species. They evidently know us as intimately as Brinkley's journeyer knew his fleshly ego. When we recognize this, it mobilizes our latent desire to be *seen* and to be known thoroughly. And yet it leaves us *exposed* as no merely human interaction could ever do. The oneness that is glimpsed in the black, liquid eyes of an alien is both more far-reaching and more threatening than anything we can encounter in ordinary consciousness. The promise and the threat are elevated to monumental proportions.

Furthermore, nearly all of the abductees speak of an *animal* quality in those eyes—a disturbing and uncontrollable instinctuality far more powerful than the forces our ego seems to have mastered in our everyday lives. Abductees encounter something at least as unsettling and fragmenting as Monroe's "animal panic," when he confronted the totality of his instincts upon leaving his body. In our everyday lives, we believe we have tamed these powerful drives. But the moment we step through the veil into the other world, we face the instincts on *their* terms. It is tempting to think that the Archons and the aliens *are* those instincts in personified form.

If all of this is true, as it surely seems to be, there may be a way that we can prepare ourselves for an encounter with the monumentally other. Perhaps those who have more experience in erotic interactions—those who have repeatedly and consciously borne the tension between a longing to dissolve into a human oneness and a terror of losing themselves—can meet the aliens with greater equanimity. To my knowledge, no study has been done on this question. But Mack presents one promising instance along these lines.

Arthur, the subject of the last chapter in *Abduction*, is a kind of St. Francis. Growing up on a large country estate, he learned to communicate with porcupines, skunks, woodchucks, rabbits, birds, and even trout. He speaks of "zuzzing" rabbits. He would lie still with his chin on the ground until a rabbit approached close enough that he could scratch its head. He learned to rub a muscle behind the rabbit's ear, until "they get so trusting they put their chin on the ground and it's a state of zuz . . . In this euphoria the rabbits will lick your nose, and if you continue to zuz their heads, they just get totally zuzzed and it creates that bond" (Mack, 1994, pp. 369–386).

He describes his encounters with aliens in a somewhat similar way. In the initial portion of his meetings with them, he "plays" with them telepathically. The aliens tend to "huddle like rabbits," he says; and he and they loosen one another up by "throwing blobs of [telepathic] color" back and forth (Mack, 1994, pp. 378–379). Then the aliens get serious and send him "information" that is truly overwhelming. He insists that it is the sheer quantity and unimaginability of the information that frightens him. Although he has a limit to the amount of information he can accept at any one time, he works at eliminating his fear so that he can remain open to the information.

Clearly he and the aliens "zuzzed" one another with their initial playfulness, so that they could communicate across species much the way Arthur related to wild animals. No doubt he would have frightened and overwhelmed the rabbits if he had found a way to send them human "information." It had never occurred to him to try. But it has occurred to the aliens. They want to tell us we are destroying the Earth. They sent Arthur an image of a great "blob of darkness" falling over the planet like "a massive water flood" that suffocated every form of life. He has learned that we can avoid this disaster if we learn to communicate. "The most beautiful thing is between people who can communicate with one another like you can with these little guys" (Mack, 1994, p. 380).

There is ambivalence and fear in Arthur, but they are nowhere near as devastating as with Peter or Sheila. It is hard to avoid the conclusion that Arthur's relative ease in interacting with the aliens is something he learned from the rabbits. His form of cosmic consciousness suggests the cross-species harmony of the Garden of Eden, surely the prototype of cosmic oneness for all of us in the West, whose greater cosmos has been schematized by the stories of the Old and New Testaments and the Qur'ān.

Arthur's experience gives us the hope that there may be an approach to the monumentally unthinkable that avoids or minimizes the shock that will drive us into panic. In the moment we receive a blast of cosmic "information," there is no point in trying to *think* the unthinkable or to grasp the unimaginable. These realities are too much for any human mind accustomed to the simplicities of an internal monolog. The unthinkable confronts our habits of thought like a nuclear explosion. We find ourselves with little option other than to schematize it as destruction and abuse.

Instead of trying to master the greater cosmos with our intellects—in place of struggling to reduce it to the structures of sensory knowledge—we might open ourselves at a more primitive level and allow ourselves to be "zuzzed." In the euphoria of "zuz," genuine communication of a non-intellectual sort can take place. Perhaps this is how sex functions between humans engaged in an erotic interaction. Possibly we use our sexual organs to "zuz" ourselves into accepting an ecstatic dissolution in the *we*. If so, our human interpersonal life with one another is already being lived in two separate, but related, domains. Our deepest connections with one another always take place in the cosmic consciousness of "zuz" and in the ordinary consciousness of our fleshly egos.

By familiarizing ourselves with the animal euphoria of "zuz," we might open a channel that by-passes the "animal panic" inspired by the unthinkability of the greater alien cosmos. In Arthur's experience, "zuzzing" is the channel for that "most beautiful thing," communicating with one another the way the aliens communicate with us.

Chapter

8

OUT
BEYOND THE
QUASARS

*The most interesting thing about all this [UFO] material, the most impor-
tant, haunting thing, is that in the past half-century it has slowly stripped itself of all the illusion, the armies in the sky, the fairies, the incubi, the glorious
creatures of old, and come down to what it really is: a difficult experience, ter-
ribly enigmatic, the very existence of which implies that we very well may be
something different from what we believe ourselves to be, on this earth for reasons that may not yet be known to us, the understanding of which will be an
immense challenge.*

(STRIEBER, 1987. P. 250)

*If we really use a different metaphysical system (and not just think or talk
about it), we are in an altered state of consciousness. An altered state of consciousness means that we are perceiving and reacting to the universe as if it
were run on a different set of laws and principles than those which we "normally" believe to be operating.*

(LeSHAN, 1975, P. 153)

*You are the total consciousness which you seek, but bound by life's many ex-
periences. One thing must be clear to you: there is no interruption; the experiences and you are the same.*

(GARRETT, 1967, P. 7)

*There's a Starman waiting in the sky. He'd like to come to meet us. But he
thinks he'd blow our minds.*

(BOWIE, 1993)

A few years ago, I took my son, Lukas, who was 12 or 13 at the time, for a week of "hanging out" together on a little lake in the Green Mountains of Vermont. We played a lot of board games and tried to watch the baseball All Star game on a snow-filled black-and-white television. But the central event of every day was a fishing expedition in which we generally caught a number of disappointingly small perch and rock bass. Nothing that came over the gunwales of the boat was worth keeping, but it was fun and kept us hoping for bigger game.

As we rowed out onto the lake, it was possible to be swept up in admiration for the beauty of the rounded, tree-covered mountain-tops surrounding us. But I rarely looked at them, being enchanted with the lake itself. Our silent skiff glided over a strange and marvelous world. The water was crystal clear. When the light was right, we could see all the way down to the seaweed's deep, loosely-woven pile, as green as the trees above us and undulating over hills and down into valleys. Between *us*, awestruck on the silvery surface, and the emerald floor of our vision, browsed the dark, intent forms of northern pike. Flirting with the surface, bluegill and perch glinted. On a lake like this, you can hardly doubt the presence and activity of spirit in nature.

One morning when the wind was still, we allowed the boat to drift upon a wild-seeming corner of the lake and cast our plastic and metal spinning lures toward the shore, where trees were leaning precariously in our direction, as though to catch sight of the visionary world that had so entranced us. It was contrary to our lazy habits to get up early enough to fish in the morning; but it was late in the week, and we thought our luck might change if we tried to take advantage of the "time of power" that attends the rising Sun, rather than that more convenient dusk that comes before the night.

For about an hour, it seemed we had violated the self-indulgent spirit of our week for nothing. The Sun was up, and we had worked our way through just about every lure in our baitbox without success, when I decided to tempt fate with a metal spoon that was sure to sink right down into the weeds and entangle itself, causing us some needless bother in trying to extract it. But the morning seemed a loss anyway. It would be one last frustration before returning to the cottage for breakfast.

No sooner, however, did the gleaming silver lure strike the surface on my first cast, than it was grabbed by a sizable bass—an order of reward and excitement we had begun to think lay beyond the reaches of our good fortune. The fish leapt and dove and pulled our little boat slowly toward the shore. Eventually, we drifted directly over the location of its last dive, and I could see my fishline, straight and taut, all the way down to where it disappeared in the rug of seaweed. I was dumbfounded. Where was the fish? It could not be that I had just hooked into some tenacious weed at the bottom.

Lukas reminds me that I was angry. I was. I felt cheated by fate. I was sure I had not been mistaken, that I had actually *seen* the silver of that bass's side, slightly yellowed from a weedy diet, when it had broken the surface. I knew I had not let my line grow slack, despite my wily opponent's clever maneuvers. Not being able to imagine how the fish could have tangled my line around something and gotten away, I began to doubt what I had seen. Had I imagined those leaps? Was I losing my grasp on reality? Had my angling frustrations been so deep that I had had to cook up the *illusion* of a bass? I did not know whether I was angry at the thing on the end of my line or at myself.

I cautiously pulled harder on the weight challenging my tackle, and explosive resistance informed me I still had my fish. So I was no fool after all! But I had to reel in several feet of line before I could *see* it again. And when it broke through the weeds, it was as though I had pulled it up through the floor of the lake from some alien dimension. I shuddered with horror and wonder as I realized the lake was much bigger and more terrible than I had assumed. The weeds I saw constituted not so much a carpet on the floor of the lake as the leafy roof of a submarine rainforest. Beneath the crystalline, fairy world that had so inspired us with awe, lurked a dark and dangerous realm of aggression and stealth. Another whole world! Demons and cannibals dwelt down there, moving to wild and ruthless laws.

When that fish tore its savage way through the weeds below me, it broke through a false bottom in my soul. Although I had the presence of mind to land it, I had been deeply unsettled and remained so for the rest of the week. Ringed with cottages though it may have been, the lake now inspired an uncanny dread. Our vacation was no longer a bucolic idyll. It teetered on the edge of a horrible abyss. I could no longer look at the lake without shuddering. The tame had become the enchanted. Decades of comfortable internal monologs about the joys of fishing had been torn asunder by a water sprite in the form of a largemouth bass.

The world's "certainties" had been placed in an unsettling context, and I began to recall boyhood dreams—the ones I had for weeks every summer after returning home to the city from the family's lake cottage in Michigan. Exotic, impossible fish in angelic shapes and colors glided uncannily through those dreams, telling me that I had missed something at the lake. Something far more marvelous and ghastly than I could guess. Those fish, real and fantastical, embodied something "other," some pure viscerality, moved by cold, impersonal, and demonic forces.

From the leafy upholstery of the mountaintops to the weedy rug of the visible lake, Nature sang and splashed in joy and harmony, feeding the soul with bliss, freedom, and an expansiveness unknown in the city, drawing me into a tame and illusory sense of oneness, gratifying me with the feeling that I was part of this innocent kingdom. In this realm, fish were the most exotic and wonderful of Nature's population, gliding with ease through deeps and shallows in their pure fishiness. When they swam, they simply *became* their swimming, swinging their powerful tails from side to side without a thought, cherishing the smooth, cool rush of water over their heads, shoulders, breasts, and backs; wanting nothing; relishing everything.

Now I saw them differently. Their blood running as cold as the water through which they moved, I caught sight of their isolation and shuddered. Even when they roam about in great schools, each individual is fluttering frantically hither and thither, apparently oblivious of its neighbors. Moving in great togetherness, as though dancing to the design of an invisible choreographer, each is utterly alone, hoping only—if hope were possible—that someone else will fall victim to the predator constantly lurking out of sight, just beneath the floor. Violence, intrusion, cannibalism, enemies of formidable power poised at every gap. Gaps too numerous to comprehend. A cold, impersonal world of death and the struggle for survival.

I began to wonder about that fascination that had drawn me all my life. Like Urashima, I was never bored rowing about on the surfaces of lakes, my eyes searching the watery world below, on the lookout for something marvelous. Had I, like the abductees, courted the uncanny and horrendously other from earliest childhood? Had I, as they, blotted out my encounters and forgotten them utterly? Does a yearning from the very bottom of our human souls scan our world in search of some wider scope, some taste of transcendent wholeness, some hint that a greater cosmos lurks beneath the floor and above the ceiling of what we know? Because our yearning scans *silently*, do we go on for years without becoming aware of its secret quest? Do we remain oblivious until the day some Loch Ness monster blips across our sonar screen, much deeper than we would have thought possible? Surely the kingdom of the water sprites is always to be found in the deepest recesses of our souls, beneath the false bottom that grounds the illusory, warm-blooded security of our everyday. When we encounter those alien beings, our false bottom is broken through, and we are exposed to wild and primitive terrors and longings we would not otherwise have guessed.

WHITLEY STRIEBER'S COSMIC VISITORS

Whitley Strieber is the Robert Monroe of UFO encounters. Once he realized that unusual experiences had been happening to him, he consulted with artist and retrieval expert Budd Hopkins and had four hypnotic regressions with a psychiatrist who had not yet been exposed to abduction phenomena. After this brief search for assistance, he chose to deal with his unsettling adventures on his own. He correctly perceived that hypnosis is ultimately a method for tapping into the human imagination and that gaps in one's memories are bound to be filled in with dream-like images which may be emotionally accurate, but of dubious factuality.

Strieber has written up the memories of his experiences in three books that present no final answers: *Communion* (1987), *Transformation* (1988), and *Breakthrough* (1995). No speculations, either of the romanticizing or of the catastrophic variety, get in the way of his conscientious reportage. He is frank about his own failings and mistakes and chronicles his hypotheses, showing in detail how subsequent experiences have forced him to change them. He presents a very human, intelligent, and critical account of his meetings with the "visitors." Like Monroe, he includes appendices containing the results of psychological testing that demonstrate his sanity and earnest sincerity.

Before his encounters reached consciousness and became a consuming problem for him, he had already written a series of "imaginative thrillers" or "horror novels," as he himself describes them, that had made him a wealthy man, giving him the freedom to pursue his nonordinary experiences quite single-mindedly. In the two years before his memories of unthinkable events emerged, he wrote "more serious fiction about peace and the environment—more firmly grounded in fact" (Strieber, 1987, p. 10). After beginning to take his encounters seriously, it dawned on him that all those books were probably based on forgotten memories of incidents that had been occurring to him over the course of some thirty years—at least since he was 12 years old.

Most of Strieber's encounters took place at his cabin in the woods in Westchester County, New York, an area he eventually learned was witness to an extraordinary series of UFO sightings. The events of December 26, 1985 broke through his wall of denial and forced him to question why he had had such an elaborate burglar-detection system installed in his cabin and why he slept with a loaded gun beside his bed. He remembered being floated out of his bedroom, finding himself sitting naked in a depression in the ground in the woods, and then being transported above the trees to a messy round room, where he felt no longer himself, but "an animal," and where a needle was inserted in his brain, a cage-shaped contraption sent up his rectum, and an incision made in his forefinger (Strieber, 1987, pp. 69-84). He awoke in his bed with a memory of having seen an owl outside his window. Owls, he learned, were a common "screen memory" for abductees (Strieber, 1987, p. 117).

Physical symptoms persisted after this December encounter, an infection in the finger, rectal pain, and an ache behind his ear. Later, he recalled the smell of the beings. When he tried to ease his mind by writing a short story, he found that it contained the themes of his early horror novels. This convinced him that there was something that required investigation. Yet he also thought: "Nobody must ever, ever know about this, not even Anne" (his wife).

The hypnotic regression opened a flood-gate of memories about December 26 and the previous October 4, as well as an incident from childhood in which he was traveling on a train from Wisconsin to Texas with his sister and father. He saw the beings as insect-like and wondered if they did not have a "hive mentality," as though a single intelligence governed the whole lot of them, none of whom, individually, had a distinct consciousness. He thought the beings were interested in us because of our capacity for independent action (Strieber, 1987, pp. 90–91). Nevertheless, there was one female being who was ghastly, compassionate, very old, and who had a special relationship with him. "Nobody in the world could know another human soul so well" as she knew him (Strieber, 1987, p. 68). He was so impressed with her that he commissioned an artist to paint her face and used the painting as the cover design for *Communion*.

It was humiliating to be mastered by beings who exercised the same kind of powers over us "that we easily assume over an animal." They sent him "a glut of symbolic material that hurt my brain and body" (Strieber, 1987, p. 119) and made him think that his entire conscious life may have been "nothing more than a disguise for another reality" (Strieber, 1987, p. 109). He recalled months of lost time in 1967, when he had left the University of Texas at Austin and traveled with unexplained urgency to London and then left that city for Italy and finally turned up in England again to find that the possessions he had left in his apartment had been put in storage. There was another series of unexplained but urgent changes of residence that he and his wife had made a few years before, all of which had been hidden behind implausible explanations. Evidently he had been running from something for a very long time (Strieber, 1987, pp. 131–139).

Strieber met with other abductees through Budd Hopkins and found that they, too, spoke of an "animal terror" they experienced in the presence of the beings. But they also felt love for the beings, as he did. His wife and son knew about the beings. Anne felt excluded, as though she had been ordered not to remember anything in order to be supportive of Whitley and to re-establish his security in the world of space and time (Strieber, 1987, p. 208). His son, Andrew, had clearly had some frightening experiences, but was also remarkably philosophical about the whole thing. At the age of 7, when he was sharing haiku poetry with his father, Andrew said quite out of the blue, "Dad, the thin ones *are* the haiku. Inside, they are haiku." On another occasion he said, "Reality is God's dream"; and, "The unconscious mind is like the universe out beyond the quasars. It's a place we want to find out what's there" (Strieber, 1987, p. 277).

Strieber refers to the beings as "visitors" rather than "aliens" because they "know us so well" and "are like family." When months passed without an encounter, he felt lonely for them; but when they appeared he invariably fell into another panic. Nevertheless, he kept changing. He cites a couple of events that were particularly transformative. The first was a series of attempts to walk in the woods at night in order to approach them and make deliberate contact. It took him a month of trying before he could step off his porch, walk across the yard, and enter the woods. "Stepping outside at night I became like an animal, listening, peering around, sniffing the air, feeling as if every shadow concealed some terrible being with great, black eyes" (Strieber, 1988, p. 169). He realized that the important part of this exercise was not facing the visitors themselves, but facing his own fear.

The second test was facing his own death (Strieber, 1988, pp. 170–182). He had been told by them that he was to take two airline trips to visit his mother in Texas and that on one of them he would die. His mother did subsequently become critically ill, and he made the trip. There was no physical mishap; but he was so convinced that he would die that it changed his mind about death. He came to accept that his wife and son had their own fates and that he had his. Death was "precise and correct." It gave him a new sense of freedom and enabled him to see the world with new eyes. Afterward, he was able to take his midnight walks in the woods regularly. He was no longer afraid of dying, but now could not shake the idea that the visitors were predators who would devour his soul.

His relationship with the beings seems to be a classic case of erotic ambivalence raised to monumental proportions. He built a stone bench in the depression in the woods where he had found himself naked on the night of December 26, 1985, and went there regularly to meditate and call to the beings, asking for a deeper communion with them. But when a visitor appeared in his bedroom and seemed to rush toward him in a manner that suggests Monroe's description of the atom-for-atom interpenetration of sexual encounters in "Locale II," Strieber "felt like the devil himself was about to leap right down my throat." He picked up a chair and threw it at the visitor, who then stayed away for months. When the little being was gone, "I felt loved, I felt there was something good and decent there, and I found myself wanting it to come back . . . longing for a way to open myself to surrender to this . . . gentleness." He decided that they wanted a deeper and more intimate union with us than we are able to have with one another (Strieber, 1995, p. 131).

Eventually, the being came back, and Strieber awoke one night to find it at the foot of his bed, looking scared. Whitley crept closer, and they shook hands. He felt he wanted to hug the visitor, and immediately the being withdrew his hand "like a shot." Strieber apologized, and the being seemed to enter him through his eyes. "I felt him come down inside me, felt something starting to bloom—a flower opening, a fire starting." Then an "unconscious fear reflex" threw them apart and Strieber sank deep into sleep (Strieber, 1995, p. 199).

After this, the being took up residence in the Strieber cabin, much like the brownies of Scottish folklore. He slept in the guest bed and would wake Whitley at midnight, 3 A.M., and 6 A.M., for three hours of joint meditation every night. Strieber also began to find half-sucked pieces of candy left on his bookshelves before the bindings of books the being apparently wanted him to read. The family was very cautious concerning their visitor, rarely spoke with one another about him, and never mentioned him to people outside the family. When Strieber lost some of his caution and tried to photograph the being asleep in the guest bed, the visitor stopped sleeping there. The unearthly boarder was finally driven out the night Strieber awoke to hear newspapers rustling downstairs and fell into a panic. He heard a low voice say, "It's me"; this terrified him so much that he grabbed his gun and searched the house (Strieber, 1995, pp. 197–207).

This lengthy episode raises a disquieting question—not so much about what the visitor might be, but about who is the real Whitley

Strieber. Clearly our conscientious author is living in two worlds. The Strieber who lives in the space-and-time world of public reality has undergone some major changes in his internal monolog. Before he became fully conscious of their reality, he talked to himself about fleshly burglars and intruders and had light-sensitive detection devices installed. Later, when he began to appreciate that the intruders were real in a different sense, he became afraid of abduction, abuse, and death. After his confrontation with his own death on the airliner, he gave up his fear of dying and began to talk to himself about the devouring of souls.

On another plane entirely, Strieber was conscious of their love, gentleness, and wisdom. He longed to have them around, wanted to "hang out" with them as a friend, learned that he was communicating with them soul-to-soul. When he lived in this world of longing and spiritual promise, he was subject to hair-trigger changes of mood in which his fear made *him* the dangerous party. Should we say that he was "asleep" in a cosmic dream when he felt intimately connected with the visitors, and that his nightmarish fear woke him up to reality? Or should we conclude that his fearful stance as a rational human being was the real "sleep," and that what he calls "communion" with the visitors was the real awakening? Is it his journeyer, his larger self, that interacts wisely with the visitors? Has he faced the same disjunction between the journeyer and the fleshly ego that plagued Monroe for twenty years before his cosmic consciousness fell into place and he began to see that the broom-closet of survival panic looked quite different from the perspective of the luminous dome? Or is the greater cosmos the seductive nightmare?

By the end of his second book, Strieber had come to answer some of these questions for himself. He believes that the visitors are physical beings, although they are able to operate "on a non-physical level" which may in fact be their primary form of existence. They have been living with us humans for a very long time, and have been perceived differently by us according to our cultural conditioning. They are, in fact, the mermaids, brownies, fairies, and gnomes of previous centuries, as well as the angels, spirits, and gods of earlier millennia. "They can enter our minds and affect our thoughts," and even draw the souls out of our bodies (Strieber, 1988, pp. 256–258).

Strieber had experiences that he recognized as out-of-body journeys and concluded that it is not the journeying outside of the body that is essential. Rather the fact that we can leave our bodies demonstrates that we, in a very real sense, *are* our souls. We are "integrated beings with marvelous capabilities that have not yet been tapped," largely because we have identified with our bodily existence and have come to consider our souls as quaint, abstract notions rather than our larger reality.

The reality of the soul is not only experienced directly through journeying, but appears to the journeying eyes as a being of light. In his "Locale I" trips about this Earth, Strieber recognized the brilliant lights of cities, but knew he was *seeing* the luminous "living souls" of the citizens rather than street lamps. During a sojourn in the greater cosmos, he saw "star clusters" unmapped on any astronomical chart of the heavens that were caused by the glow of ensouled beings living on other worlds (Strieber, 1995, p. 192).

Fully to encounter the reality of the soul throws us into panic. The seeming solidity and security of the world of public consensus dissolves. The bottom drops out of the tame lake of our bucolic idyll in space and time, and we are confronted with realities of overwhelming power. The terror this generates in us cannot be denied or suppressed. We have to learn to accept it and not be surprised by it. "We must learn to walk the razor's edge between fear and ecstasy" (Strieber, 1988, p. 257).

When viewed from the out-of-body perspective of the journeying soul, human beings in their ordinary, everyday consciousness appear to be functioning as robots—as though we are keeping ourselves in a kind of trance. The sight is "weird and frightening" and suggests that "human society functions like a giant machine" in which each individual is no more than a cog (Strieber, 1988, p. 220). We awaken to our greater reality only when we fall into a physical sleep. When he encountered sleeping human beings in his out-of-body state, Strieber felt an "aching, anguishing love" for them. Generally only when we are asleep are we open to truths that extend far beyond our conscious viewpoints. Very likely this is why the visitors usually approach us at night while we lie abed.

Strieber speculates that the Garden of Eden was probably a real place, a kind of tropical paradise in which our needs were supplied in abundance and we lived constantly in a state of cosmic consciousness. Our expulsion from this sublime state of being was probably accomplished by profound changes in climate which forced us to struggle for our survival. The struggle enabled us to discover ourselves. Hardship "compelled us to evolve." The determined efforts of the visitors to contact us are forcing another evolutionary change, a reintegration of the realities of soul with those of the body, a bringing together of mystical consciousness and critical scientific knowledge (Strieber, 1995, pp. 195–196).

Strieber bemoans the fact that governments seem to be concealing what they know of the reality of UFOs and believes that it would be valuable for us to know that encountering these visitors is not a sign of madness or of an intergalactic invasion by a hostile species. Beyond this, however, there is little governments can do, for it is clear that the visitors are contacting us individually. Each of us has to take up the individual challenge they provide us, and use it to grow. When they come near us, "the meaning of the world itself changes." They want us to "regain the ability to surrender, to live with open, innocent eyes, to be as guileless as an animal" (Strieber, 1995, pp. 279–280).

Encountering the visitors is like being presented with a life-review. "Those eyes take you to your conscience, those brilliant eyes." They do not bring forgiveness, but teach us a lesson in the consequences of guilt (Strieber, 1995, p. 189). Their message is that we must "live with our sins, taste them, face what we have done and what we are, for that is the direction of freedom." When we learn to pass beyond our guilt, we can accept our mistakes as opportunities, "valuable gifts." To accept our greater reality is to "journey into our sins," an experience of profound education that enables us to become compassionate with ourselves and to "embrace our own fractured soul" (Strieber, 1995, p. 195).

The experience reconnects us with God. Strieber rediscovered the meaning of his childhood prayers, which were now "reforged into spiritual arguments of unexpected potency." His fragmentary encounters with the greater cosmos brought him back to the world of everyday existence with new eyes, so that he could see "the divine in the commonplace" and "taste at last of the sacred light that floods the universe" (Strieber, 1995, p. 279).

THE MYTHIC UNDERGROUND

Whitley Strieber's visitors introduced him to the full reality of the myth of the New Age. Every element is there: a history that presents the human adventure as beginning in cosmic consciousness, from which we have been distracted for millennia by the struggle for survival and which we are now about to regain; a description of human being as comprised of a body limited to a space-and-time sensory world and inhabited by a soul which is a being of light capable of sojourning in a greater cosmos and which is our greater identity; an heroic quest in which the individual can expect to encounter frightful, "soul-devouring" beings who will awaken powerful instinctual reactions that can tear us asunder, but which, if we manage them well enough, will bring us to wisdom; a life-review which reinterprets our fleshly biography from the perspective of a greater cosmos; a supremely individual moral task which amounts to bringing one's fleshly existence into harmony with the luminous egg of the journeyer; and a *gnosis,* a direct and unassailable knowledge of the One as the ground and origin of all that is and which is perceptible in other human beings, in nature, indeed in any physical thing as a "sacred light."

The fact that critically thoughtful individuals like Monroe and Strieber have separately arrived at the same mythic viewpoint impresses us far more than the agreement of any number of aura readers and psychic healers. For the more traditional New Agers, the ones who give and attend weekend workshops, may be suspected of having picked up a widely promulgated doctrine. But Monroe and Strieber come across as skeptical individuals, people who avoid every sort of pack mentality. Their conscientious examination of the data and frank self-doubts reveal that the myth of the New Age emerged for them as the only way to make sense of their experience. Their testimony leads us to suspect that the myth has a real inevitability. It suggests that, when the bottom drops out of our conscious public consensus, another collective agreement—albeit a deeply unconscious one—lies ready to receive us.

We might contrast the New Age myth with another widely accepted structure of meaning. The so-called American dream has played an important role in the way Americans have understood themselves for nearly four centuries. It, too, takes the form of an organizing belief system. Regardless of our financial, religious, or racial origins, each of us has a "reasonable expectation" of improving our lives and providing a better starting point for our children than our parents afforded us. All we have to do is to take charge of our own destinies, earnestly follow our opportunities, and "play by the rules." If we succeed, we are not only better off in a material sense, but have proven our virtue. There is a history behind the American dream in which the Pilgrims' City on a Hill, the revolution against King George, and the moral battle of the War Between the States play central roles. There is also the heroic quest of the rugged individual, the moral task of self-discipline and hard work, and a faith in the perfectibility of every human being.

As we saw in connection with satanic rumor panics, however, the American dream is vulnerable to economic upheavals such as we are presently undergoing. As big corporations have become international in their search for labor pools and markets and computerized production has rendered whole categories of employment obsolete, job security is in question and family structure is changing. Hard-working men and women are losing hope. Even apparently successful women and African

Americans complain of coming up against a "glass ceiling" that limits their upward mobility and denies our rugged individualist ideal.

The American dream describes how things ought to proceed on the tame lake of "life, liberty, and the pursuit of happiness." As our "civil religion," it structures our public consensus by shaping the internal monologs of our citizens. We hear its echoes in every politician's speech, every news broadcast, every man-on-the-street interview, and every product advertisement. The successful loftily insinuate that those living "below the poverty line" are victims of their own moral turpitude. For them, failure implies laziness and thereby proves the validity of the dream. In contrast, the frustrated angrily assert the high virtue of their own hard work and cast about for the villains responsible for the unfairness they have experienced in our social structure. They, too, believe in the American dream, for they are on the lookout for what blocks their access to it.

Ultimately, the American dream is a strategy for negotiating the world of survival. It is a consciously articulated faith which describes how things *ought* to be, rather than how they are. No doubt it has worked for many. We hold before ourselves the fabulous success stories of sports stars, rock personalities, actors and actresses, business moguls, and "log-cabin" presidents. They are the impossible few who demonstrate, either that the American dream is still alive and functional, or that we who belong to the ordinary run of Americans have been excluded.

When the bottom falls out of our predictable lake, we are exposed to ruthless demons who abuse and cannibalize us for their own advancement. We find ourselves in Monroe's dreadful survival world ruled by the Lord of Death. When the American dream fails, as it does often enough, we are exposed to gaps in our internal monolog, the fact that what we tell ourselves about the world does not accurately describe the whole of our experience. Because it leaves so much out of account and makes no attempt to provide a comprehensive description of human existence, the American dream lacks the ultimacy of myth. It is a fragmentary narrative which speaks only of the tame and says nothing of the wild. It poses as a myth, but speaks only of the fleshly world. We ought to call it a pseudo-myth.

Its narrow scope leaves us with two uncomfortable options. The first is to cling to the American dream and try to force it to work for us by demonizing those we can identify as the sources of its failure: unwed mothers, illegal immigrants, the trading practices of foreign nations, the drug trade, declining morality. Perhaps we can restore the dream by passing a set of laws that will reinsure fairness. As impossible as this may seem—given the diversity of our population and the wide variety of our demons—it is surely more comfortable than our second option, which is to face up to the limitations of the pseudo-myth and carefully examine the frightful evidence that appears in its gaps.

Those like Monroe and Strieber, who have been dragged out of the fleshly world kicking and screaming, have been forced to examine the unthinkable, to face the terror and dread that the public pseudo-myth strives to tame. They have confronted the Being-toward-death that structures our fleshly existence far more ultimately than any tame pursuit of happiness. Those who understand themselves to be abductees have been thrust into a no-man's land where the stories we tell ourselves publicly have been rendered meaningless. Unless they seriously grapple with monumental shocks of radical otherness, they will remain suspended between the chimeras enshrined in our public consensus and the madness of the unthinkable.

Our compatriots by the tens of thousands who have been snatched unceremoniously out of their bodies have lost the two most common sources of certainty: the reality-testing that undergirds our science, philosophy, and history, and the publicly accepted platitudes that structure our everyday dealings with one another. We can hardly blame them for wishing it would all go away and resolve itself into a bad dream. But unfortunately it does not. Their predicament leaves them no alternative but to fall back upon the one way of knowing that our public consensus denies and ridicules, the *imaginal*.

When they do so, they recover their kinship with our pre-Taurean ancestors. More than 6000 years ago, people had not yet developed the dogmas that have been structuring our religious life for the past 4000 years, or the philosophies, histories, and sciences that have been shaping and changing our public consensus during the Age of Pisces. Our contemporaries who struggle with the unthinkable are becoming reacquainted with the cosmic consciousness we have been suppressing as far back as humans can remember. They are finding that it is no escape hatch into fuzzy-minded romanticism. It has a hard, demanding structure that sets us moral challenges of a very high order.

Because aura manipulators, near-death experiencers, out-of-body journeyers, and abductees have all arrived at the same picture of a greater eternal cosmos that suffuses and surrounds the broom-closet of space and time and claims our journeying soul as our forgotten wholeness, we are prompted to wonder whether they may not have uncovered some ultimate truth. Perhaps beneath the comforting rug that constitutes the false bottom of our domesticated lake, there really lurks a greater cosmos with dependable features.

As long as we can avoid the dreadful enchanted world beneath our everyday lake, we surely will. For the evidence is unmistakable. When they come oozing or rushing through the gaps, the first representatives of the greater cosmos appear abusive, humiliating, even satanic. Our terror schematizes them as Archons, "small grays," and demons. As long as the water sprite is nothing more than a largemouth bass, everything is in its place. We recover our old monolog—"I don't know what came over me. I thought for a minute it wasn't a fish at all"—and settle back to our rod and reel. But the more we accept the possibility that that silvery being bashing through the rug of seaweed down below us might very well be *more* than a fish, anything can happen. The world is suddenly devoid of dependable rules. We know not where we stand.

Mack's abductees, Whitley Strieber, Dannion Brinkley, and Robert Monroe have all found their way past those guardians at the gate of the greater cosmos. They walk the *razor's edge between fear and ecstasy*. Their old internal monologs have been dismembered. They have *seen* the fleshly strategies of the public world from the perspective of the journeyer. And they pretty much agree upon what they have *seen*. It is hard to avoid the conclusion that, if our everyday certainties were snatched away and we had the courage and persistence to find the compass of orientation in a greater cosmos, we might *all* agree. If so, this may be the myth we are living right now without knowing it, the proper domain of our undiscovered journeyer.

In the preliterate societies Western explorers have discovered, the means to enter cosmic consciousness have not been forgotten. They may dance or chant, meditate or ingest consciousness-altering drugs. But invariably they also have a sacred story which maps the greater cosmos and reinterprets fleshly existence from the perspective of soul. At the end of the Age of Pisces, we have forgotten our sacred story. We think our fleshly existence is all there is. We have limited our attention to strategizing space and time with our American dreams. The possibility of something wholly other is unthinkable.

The greater cosmos is unthinkable only according to our conscious assumptions. If the New Agers are right, each of us is already living in that "Locale II." We who stand at the gate of the New Age, begging the prayers of those who pass in and out, have begun to recognize a characteristic light in the eyes of those New Age monks. They all seem to have discovered the same thing. Perhaps there really *is* a world of soul.

THE DREADFUL JOLT OF THE REAL THING

Strieber's struggle with the reality of the visitors closely resembles Monroe's compulsive spasms of reality-testing. In his first book, there is no doubt in Strieber's mind that something "real" is happening, but he vacillates between seeing the events as psychological (taking place inside his own mind) and physical (caused by material agents, the visitors). He puzzles over his wife's opinion that "Whitley is not a down-to-Earth guy"; and yet she does not think he should see a psychiatrist because, "I think he can deal with these problems." Strieber concludes, "Perhaps she knew that there would be no point, because on the level she would not directly address, she was aware that these are the side effects of real experience" (Strieber, 1987, p. 197).

Evidently people see psychiatrists when they are convinced that unreal things are real. They relinquish the world of public consensus in favor of what is merely delusional. In contrast, the Striebers, Whitley and Anne, *know* in some unconscious but incontrovertible manner that the encounters with the visitors are neither delusional nor in agreement with public reality. The experience is both absurd *and* real.

By the end of his second book, Strieber asserts categorically: "The visitors are physically real." Their materiality, however, does not exhaust their realness, for, "they also function on a non-physical level, and this may be their primary reality" (Strieber, 1988, p. 257). Although he was not able to bring back the stones he placed in his mouth during an out-of-body journey to his friend's home in Boulder, Colorado, he did manage to grab one of his cats and take it along with him on an abduction to a flying saucer. The visitors put the cat to sleep temporarily by applying an instrument to its thigh. It slept for a full day after returning from the spaceship and limped for months afterward, seeming to have a stiffness in the leg that received the knock-out blow. It was even longer before it stopped acting spooked and resumed its former feline placidity (Strieber, 1988, pp. 220–223).

His cats played an important role, too, in the pair of events which Strieber takes as undeniable proof of the visitors' physicality. At 11 P.M. on August 27, 1986, he was reading in the living room of his cabin in a perfectly ordinary state of consciousness while his wife and son slept, when he heard three groups of three knocks on the wall of the cabin just beneath the roof. The cats reacted with terror, as did Strieber. The windows were open, yet no sound was heard on the gravel driveway beneath the location of the knocks, and the motion detectors installed outside the house did not respond. Strieber determined that the knocks could only have been made by someone standing at the top of a twelve-foot ladder and holding a long pole. In experiments to duplicate the sounds, he found there was no way for a purely physical being to get to that location without being detected. Furthermore, human-generated knocks had no effect upon the cats. Not only were they not spooked, they paid no attention at all (Strieber, 1988, pp. 130–143).

After he had described this event in the manuscript of *Transformation*, but before the book was published, there was a very strange incident in Glenrock, Wyoming, in which several people in different houses reported nine knocks in groups of three. Strieber reacted to the reports of the Glenrock incident by shouting, "They've just proved it!" (Strieber, 1995, p. 30). He meant that, as there was no way for his book to have influenced the people of Glenrock, the occurrence had to have been staged by the visitors to prove their physical reality by manifesting to others just as they had done to him.

On reading of the Glenrock "proof" in Strieber's third volume, *Breakthrough*, I have to confess some bewilderment. If it had happened to me as it had to Strieber, I am sure I, too, would have been excited. I would surely have taken it as an unusual communication of singular significance for me. But I can also not help but recall Monroe's statement about life after death: "If you want to prove—to yourself and no one else—that we survive physical death, you can learn to move in the out-of-body state and seek out a friend, relative, or someone close to you who has recently died" (Monroe, 1994, p. 11). I find it hard to believe that anyone else could be as convinced by these events as Strieber was. It was a proof for *him*, and perhaps no one else.

Nevertheless, these events do raise a very important question. Why is it that the abductees insist so strongly on the *physical* reality of the aliens? Their own reports make it clear that the psychic component far outweighs any physical dimension that an encounter might have. The visitors nearly always approach when their abductees are asleep or in some other state of consciousness that differs from the ordinary waking state. They and the aliens pass through walls, levitate on beams of light, cover immense distances in moments, frequently recognize in themselves hypnagogic states of consciousness and catalepsy (the inability to move the body or limbs despite attempts of the will). Everything points to events occurring to them while they are out-of-body or at least in a similar state of consciousness. They even report the same feeling of being charged with electricity and vibrating that Monroe reports when he was in the process of leaving his body.

True enough, there are sometimes marks on the bodies of abductees —bruises, cuts, and the like—that Mack affirms follow no known psychosomatic pattern. But the absence of established patterns does not rule out psychosomatic effects. Indeed, researches into bodily "stigmata" were a common element in the dissociation studies of a century ago. It is clear that powerful psychological experiences can leave somatic effects.

None of this explains the Glenrock incident, which was accompanied by a dense fog hovering ten feet off the ground and about fifty prowler calls made to the Glenrock police department in the space of fifteen minutes. Some said they saw a UFO. There was an unverified rumor that someone got a photograph of it. And the knocks, three sets of three, were heard all over town on the sides of houses, roofs, and gates. If it was a psychic event, it was a collective one, analogous to the story of Castaneda and the four apprentices.

It may have been physical. It may have been the material "proof" that Strieber takes it to be. But it may also have been a collective psychological event that was *perceived* as physical. Poltergeist phenomena, for instance, when objects fly across the room and impossible knockings are heard, are generally attributed to the unintegrated and repressed sexual energy of adolescents. Surely those who encounter the visitors are filled with unmanageable psychic energy which might also have physical effects. If this were the case when Strieber first heard the knocks, his claim to have been in an ordinary state of consciousness only implies that whatever excitement he contained had been repressed.

But why is it so important that he demonstrate the materiality of the visitors? He himself would be the first to claim that the most significant effect they have had upon him, upon his friend in Boulder, Colorado, and upon everyone else he knows who has been "visited," is the change that has been brought about in their lives. These people have taken up their lives with greater conviction, live them with a sense of transcendent meaning that was formerly unknown to them. They find, very frequently in retrospect, that they have made changes in every aspect of their lives: occupations, friendships, domicile, habits, and interests. If these things are of prime importance, why so much attention to proving the materiality of the visitors?

There seems to be an implication that, unless the aliens are solidly material, they are not fully real. Strieber has convinced me they are real, but he has not stilled my doubts about their materiality. What does it mean that *they are physical beings even though they live primarily on a nonmaterial plane*? Would it not make more sense to put it the other way around? They are nonmaterial beings, even though they can manifest themselves to us with such a jolt that we cannot doubt their materiality.

It is fundamental to everyone's way of thinking that a thing is real if you crack your shin on it. If you can walk right through it, it isn't there.

Those things are real that need to be fed and clothed, watered and mowed. What is real beyond question is the fleshly world. We *know* that exists. It is the world of soul that we wonder about. We will surely not take the world of soul seriously unless it is as real as our bodies. The physical world is our prime model for what is real. It is so real for us that we think nothing immaterial deserves equality with what is solid.

Strieber needs to touch and smell the visitors. In his first remembered encounter, he tells us his "animal panic" was out of control. He saw them as brutal and evil and wanted nothing more than to escape. At this point, the female being whom he sometimes saw as his guide and ally asked him what she could do to reassure him and calm him down. He answered, "You can let me smell you" (Strieber, 1987, p. 19). He called upon the most primitive of the sensory functions, recalling not only the woodland mammals who orient themselves by sniffing the air, but also the lower animals whose olfactory lobes are the most developed portion of their brain. It is as though he said: "Show me that you belong to nature. Still the terror caused by your absurdity and unthinkability. Let me know you are real."

A being is real for us only when it has equal status with the physical world. In the literal-mindedness of our fleshly ego, a thing is real only when it is physical. The monumental jolt of encountering the visitors stems from *seeing* that the absurdly unreal can crack us in the shin, probe our intimate orifices, implant tracking devices the way we put radio collars on polar bears. Only a real being can grab us by the scruff of the neck and take us where we think we do not wish to go. The beings are real because they can do these things to us.

Strieber's insistence on the physicality of the visitors *could* be a rhetorical device. Surely he knows that his readers are so stuck in the broom-closet that nothing but brooms and mops are real for us. He might have chosen to insist on their physicality, not for his own sake, but for ours. But he does not. *He* needs to know that the visitors are physical, because he is still struggling with a reality that *lives primarily on a nonmaterial plane*. What has jolted him is real because it has jolted him. He knows very well that his perceptions of this absurd reality are "culturally conditioned." That is why they look like spacemen in lycra suits rather than water sprites in scales or diaphanous fairies.

Faced with the choice of viewing the visitors as immaterial as brownies or claiming the wee folk of yesterday are as material as spacemen, he recalls the jolt. Because the physical remains his criterion for the real, he searches for proof that they are not truly other than his own fleshly self. They smell unwashed and distinctly musty. They do not contradict in an ultimate manner the physical world that cannot be denied. Perhaps the door to the broom-closet has come unlatched, but it opens only onto the pantry. There is more space than we ever thought possible, but it is filled up with pots and pans and dinner plates which are, after all, not so different from brooms and mops.

If all of this seems amazing in a man who claims he has finally discovered the living reality of the soul and reconnected to God, we might recall the three stages of relating to power according to Don Juan Matus. Certainly power has begun to manifest *uncontrollably* in Strieber's life. He has no option but to *take it seriously* and has begun to *understand what it is all about*. He even knows it *controls his actions*, or at least some of them. However, he does not yet know that it *lives within him but obeys his commands*. Evidently, Strieber has some distance to go; he has had a fairly conscious relationship with the visitors for only ten years. It was twice that long before Monroe was able to let his journeyer take him where *it* wanted to go, and there is some question whether Castaneda has reached that point after thirty years.

WHERE ARE THE ALIENS?

There seem to be three theories regarding the proper domain of the visitors. The most popular suspicion is that they are spacemen from some planet outside our solar system. Mars was a favorite option before our telescopes and space probes "tamed" it as an uninhabitable rock. Now the enchanted planet rotates beyond our technological reach, around some unknown star. The problem with this theory—leaving science aside—is that the visitors have only been seen as spacemen for the past few decades. Centuries ago, before the visitors had the technology to travel through outer space, their characteristics were found in mermaids and fairies. Thousands of years earlier they were angels and Chaldean gods. Such details suggest a second theory: the visitors dwell right here with us, probably not in caves or lakes, more likely in another dimension. We have been calling that other dimension the greater cosmos, and imagine that it interpenetrates and surrounds the Earth. According to the third theory, the visitors have all the earmarks of "unconscious projections." They appear when we are in altered states of consciousness; they do things with us that can only take place in dreams; and they know us better than we know ourselves.

The problem with the "unconscious projection" theory is that it seems to imply that, in the cluttered file cabinets in the basement of our psyche, we have an immense supply of holograms. We picture ourselves altering our consciousness as we descend the cellar stairs and begin to rummage. If each of us sees more or less the same things, it is because we have inherited a pretty standard set of files with our DNA. Indeed, the holograms in the basement of our psyche are so similar from individual to individual and across cultures that they deserve the name "collective unconscious."

This is the most popular *misreading* of C. G. Jung's psychology. Although his often careless language is responsible for the misunderstanding, Jung frequently tries to combat the misconception by insisting that it is not archetypal *images* that we inherit, but the structure-giving forms of *imaginal* perception. Just as space and time structure our sensory experience, so our *imaginal* experience is structured by the archetypes.

While the file-cabinet model implies that we never leave the basement of our psyche, except when we climb the stairs and go out the door into the fleshly world of space and time, Jung's actual thinking makes no such claim. We do not have to fold up the greater cosmos and shove its hologram into a file drawer in order to accept the theory of the archetypes. Rather, the greater cosmos is the *domain* of the collective unconscious. It is the realm we enter when we *see imaginally*. It is really "out there" in the sense that it is an objective reality that can grab us by the scruff of the neck and take us where we think we do not wish to go. It regularly cracks the shins of our fleshly ego. Our conscious will is at least as puny in the face of the greater cosmos of *imaginal* perception as it is in the indomitable space-time world of sensory perception.

According to this more accurate reading of Jung, there is no difference between the second theory about the habitation of the visitors and the third. The aliens are really "out there" in the *imaginal* dimension, prepared to visit us on their own terms, more powerful and wise than we are. But we cannot know what they are *in themselves*. We see them as they appear to our *imaginal* apparatus for *seeing*—just as the trees, mountains, and lakes of the Earth appear to the space-time apparatus of sensation. Neither the Earth nor the greater cosmos is folded up in a psychic library. But when either of them appears to us, what we see is mediated through one of psyche's three modes of knowing: sensory reality testing, internal monolog, and the archetypes of the *imagination*.

We do ourselves an injustice when we picture the *imaging* psyche as a kind of movie theater inside the brain. That 7-year-old sage, Andrew Strieber, had it right when he said, "The unconscious mind is like the universe out beyond the quasars." Little Andrew has grasped that the greater cosmos is that monumental domain which is organized and given shape by the unconsciously operating archetypes of *imaginal* knowing.

Unless the domain of cosmic consciousness be "out there," we tend to think it is nothing but a private delusion—something our unconscious mind has devilishly concocted to lead us astray, pulling holograms out of file cabinets at random. Strieber and the other New Age pioneers will not let us get away with such a distorted view. They have no doubt it is as much "out there" as the material world. The domain of cosmic consciousness is so incontrovertibly real that they are driven to insist the aliens are physical beings, despite all indications to the contrary—which they do not deny.

There is another reason to accept the domain of cosmic consciousness as objectively "out there." Those who have journeyed all agree on the general structure of the greater cosmos and the unsettling nature of the beings they have encountered there. Nested spheres of light, emanation from the One, a journeyer who knows our bodily life better than we have known it ourselves, the overwhelming power of the beings who take us where *they* want us to go, and the cultural variants whereby Archons became mermaids and extraterrestrials: all these things belong as much to the journeyer's knowing as the space/time world belongs to the knowing of our sensory ego.

Even if we have not made the trip ourselves, the fact that those who have agree about what they have *seen* convinces us that the domain of cosmic consciousness is no private delusion. Still, there are differences in the details. Sometimes the luminous dome looks like the top half of a human aura, sometimes like a glowing "mother ship." Sometimes the beings are angels, sometimes invaders from outerspace, sometimes "Cartesian tourists." All these details imply that the domain of cosmic consciousness is schematized by cultural and personal presuppositions. It is *seen* by the subjective act of each individual journeyer. Furthermore, what is most subjective about cosmic consciousness is that journeying always issues an individual "call," and the work of bringing one's fleshly ego into balance with the journeyer is always an individual struggle. In each case there is a somewhat different set of internal monologs to refashion.

The process of realigning ego and journeyer, as idiosyncratic as it may be, nevertheless has a common structure. It recapitulates the three stages Jung has identified as the process of "individuation," or coming to terms with the collective unconscious: the encounter with the shadow, the encounter with the anima or animus, and the encounter with the self.

:aks of "shadow," he means our dark, unconscious
e left out when we constructed our lifeworld. To en-
he shadow, therefore, is a devastating experience. We
thing that seems demonic and destructive. It is as
ion has shifted and, instead of seeing the leaves and
that is our lifeworld, we see the shadows and gaps. Everything taken for granted is called into question. The domain
of the shadow and the beings that dwell there are inevitably experienced
as satanic and abusive, for they pose a monumental challenge to our old
world and way of life.

Whether pictured as the universe out beyond the quasars or as
Freud's id of uncontrollable drives lurking in our psychic basement, the
shadow is what lies beneath the false bottom of the tame lake of our
public consensus and our conscious identity. The greater cosmos and
the id represent the objective and subjective components of our encounter with a wholly other that would overpower us. It is "other" to everything we want to believe and think we have tamed. Its very existence
threatens us with annihilation. To accept it is to acknowledge that the
universe is dreadfully more than we have imagined. And so are we. It
constitutes the first stage of recognizing a reality that dwarfs all that we
thought we knew and reveals that we are not in control of our destiny as
we had believed.

The objective component of the shadow is the threat from "out
there," in the domain of darkness. It is as denizens of the shadow realm
that the aliens first appear—as demonic Archons or Nazi-like experi-
menters. It is the *objectivity* of the shadow that threatens us with torture
or the devouring of our soul. The shadow will not be conjured out of
existence by appeals to logic. It is the rest of what is "out there," the part
we have not begun to tame. In the first stage of our work at bringing our
fleshly ego into alignment with our journeyer, the greater cosmos is the
domain of the shadow.

But the shadow is also *ours*. Strieber says that the most terrifying image he ever encountered in connection with the aliens "was my own
face reflected in the eye of a visitor" (Strieber, 1988, p. 257). All the
abductees who have struggled with their plunges into the domain of the
shadow report that their biggest obstacle is their own "animal panic."
They perceive—at least in retrospect when the aliens have departed—
that their own subjective fear is what schematizes the visitors as aggressive and abusive. Because they cling in terror to reality as they have
always misconstrued it, the greater cosmos is seen as the ultimate
destroyer.

Those who pass beyond the first stage and begin to accept the reality of the shadow find themselves *walking that razor's edge between fear and ecstasy*. On one side stands fear, because they still feel the threat of annihilation. On the other stands ecstasy, because they have begun to attend to the thrill the greater cosmos inspires. This opens the second stage of the transformation process. The domain of cosmic consciousness fascinates us with the promise of experiences we do not want to miss. It is as though we fall in love with it. Indeed, it seems usually to be the case that a powerful figure of the opposite sex (anima for men, animus for women) emerges as a disturbing and attractive guide and partner in the realm of the greater cosmos. Mack's patient, Peter, has an alien wife who has borne him hybrid children. He loves this woman and panics when he believes he is losing her, but when she appears he generally has an attack of terror. He is walking that razor's edge. Strieber, too, was so impressed with the female figure who was his guide and mentor in the greater cosmos that he commissioned an artist to paint her portrait and used it as the cover design of *Communion*. This is the kind of behavior we encounter in men who are head-over-heels infatuated with a new lover. Nevertheless, statistical psychologist Kenneth Ring probably speaks for us all when he says he finds that Strieber's portait depicts a "horrid little alien" (Ring, 1992, p. 8).

In the language of Jung, anima and animus personify the disturbing attractiveness of another realm of experience. As members of the other sex, they represent what we are not, our other half. As objective realities, they offer us partnerhood, a wedding between our habitual, limited conscious identity, and the otherness of cosmic consciousness. To paraphrase Jung, if the encounter with the shadow is the apprentice piece of our personal transformation, reconciliation with the anima or animus is the master piece. It provides that erotic element whereby the abductees find they long for the aliens when they are absent, and speak of a profound love and intimacy much greater than they have experienced with human partners. Just as human partners rearrange our self-image and provide a sense that we are discovering ourselves in a new and deeper manner, so the visitor of the opposite sex who seems to be our mentor and lover reveals that we, too, are "part alien."

After accepting the complimentarity of our fleshly reality and our cosmic identity, we are prepared to enter the third stage of transformation, the recognition of the unifying principle which makes sense of our duality. For the ancient Gnostics, this meant perceiving that the demonic and compellingly attractive Archons were emanations from the One, merely aspects of a unified greater reality. The abductees, near-death experiencers, and out-of-body journeyers who have persisted courageously have eventually gained a sense that there is an order and a center to the greater cosmos. Jung calls this experience the encounter with our greater self, the sense that what lies beyond our conscious ego is not merely the roiling chaos it first seems to be, but a transcendent and spiritual source of all meaning.

The encounter with the self has both an objective and a subjective component. Its *objective* form is the One from whom everything in the greater cosmos and on the Earth proceeds. The One is the origin and destiny of the All and of every one of us. It is the center and balance point of the universe out beyond the quasars, and its light indwells everything and everyone. The *subjective* dimension of the self is the journeyer, our greater identity, the being of light which every one of us essentially is. It is *seen* as the luminous egg of the aura, and it is *lived* as the sojourner who is free of all space-time perspectival limitation. The journeyer is our whole self, knows our fleshly ego better than it knows itself, sojourns freely through the greater cosmos, and carries the compass of *gnosis*.

The nested spheres of light, Brinkley's Crystal City, Monroe's luminous dome, and Strieber's unmappable starscape are all images of what Jung has called the self. They are simultaneously a picture of the greater cosmos as an ordered whole and our own greater identity as far larger than our fleshly ego, structuring our lives with an intentionality that is monumental and cosmic. Only an understanding of the visitors which sees them both as denizens of the greater cosmos and as given form by the archetypal structures of *imaginal* knowing does justice to Ibn al-'Arabi's description of *gnosis*. "He who believes he sees the Reality Himself has no *gnosis*. He has *gnosis* who knows that it is his own essential self that he sees."

Chapter

9

CHANNELƧ
ⵕF ⵕLIEN
WIƧD⵰M

*The saucer's occupants told him they were the survivors of a great war be-
tween Atlantis and Lemuria, and that they had contacted him instead of
someone more highly placed because it would upset the "ego-balance" of the
Earth's civilizations if they were to reveal themselves.*

(BRYAN, 1995, P. 8)

*Dr. Andrija Puharich . . . gets messages on his tape recorder, coming from a
mysterious cosmic source. But the tape vanishes regularly. There is nothing he
can do to prevent it, and he is totally committed to the idea that he and Uri
Geller are now guided by a very high source of wisdom and that the only
course for mankind is to place its destiny in "their" hands.*

(VALLEE, 1988, P. 250)

*Whatever has loomed upon the world of his ordinary concerns as something
terrifying and baffling to the intellect; whatever among natural occurrences or
events in the human, animal, or vegetable kingdoms has set him astare in
wonder and astonishment—such things have ever aroused in man, and become endued with, the "daemonic dread" and numinous feeling, so as to become "portents," "prodigies," and "marvels." Thus and only thus is it that
"the miraculous" rose.*

(OTTO, 1958, P. 64)

*Therefore God destroys, crushes and overwhelms the soul in such a deep
darkness, that it feels as though melted and in its misery destroyed by a cruel
death of the spirit. Even as though it were to feel it had been swallowed by
some savage beast and buried in the darkness of his belly.*

(ST. JOHN OF THE CROSS, 1979, P. 337)

The "Woman Who Lived on the Moon" introduced C. G. Jung to one of the most important themes of his psychiatric career (Jung, 1961, pp. 128–130). He frequently told her story when called upon to explain his unique approach to dealing with the mentally ill. She taught him something so essential about the reality, richness, and vitality of an inner life that he insisted she really had *lived* on the Moon and not just believed she had.

When he first encountered her, she was locked in a mute, catatonic prison that rendered her utterly unresponsive to anything that happened around her. According to her hospital file, she "had been seduced by her brother and abused by a schoolmate" when she was 15. Within a year of these traumatic events, she had isolated herself from the human race and was able to find emotional connection only with a vicious neighborhood watchdog. As her behavior became more and more bizarre, she was taken to the Burghölzli asylum in Zurich. By the beginning of Jung's employment in that hospital, the 18-year-old incest victim had already been there a year and a half, hearing voices, refusing food, ignoring the staff and other patients, and maintaining an absolute silence.

The 26 year-old Jung sat with this woman for several weeks before she began to speak. Apparently the first words out of her mouth were devoted to her consuming interest, the nature of her life on the Moon. She said that only men were to be found living on the lunar surface, the women and children being hidden in an underground dwelling so as to keep them safe from a terrible vampire who lived on a mountaintop. She was outraged at this situation and determined to free the captives by destroying the vampire. She convinced the men to build her a tower with a platform at the top, where she stood night after night to attract the monster, a long knife concealed within her gown.

Finally, the fateful night arrived, and she saw the vampire winging his way toward her out of the far distance like a great black bird. The fiend alighted on her elevated platform in a rush of feathers, his multiple pairs of wings folded about him, hiding his face and figure. Filled with curiosity, she approached, knife in hand, hoping to see what he looked like before drawing blood. When she came within a pace of the vampire, he suddenly opened his wings, and she found herself spellbound by his unearthly beauty, immobilized by her awe of him. Seizing her in his iron talons, he carried her away.

Once the story was out, she was able to speak freely, and went on to inform Jung that this earthly world is a dreary and ugly place, whereas the Moon is beautiful and lunar life filled with meaning. She soon learned, however, that telling her story had betrayed the secret of her extraterrestrial existence, and that she was no longer able to return. When the enormity of this realization sank in, she fell back into her catatonia and became "violently insane" for a period of two months. By the time she had calmed down and was able to resume her meetings with Jung, she began to understand that life on Earth was unavoidable; and this precipitated another collapse into insanity. This time Jung did not wait for her to be released from the locked ward:

> Once I visited her in her cell and said to her, "All this won't do you any good; you cannot return to the moon!" She took this in silence and with an appearance of utter apathy. This time she was released after a short stay and resigned herself to her fate (Jung, 1961, p. 130).

Eventually, she found a job as a nurse in an sanatorium, where a young doctor "made a somewhat rash approach to her." She responded by drawing a concealed revolver and shooting him—fortunately inflicting only a slight wound. The incident revealed to Jung that she had been armed all along, even in her meetings with *him*. He was astonished and demanded to know why she carried the gun. She answered, "I would have shot you down if you had failed me!" (Jung, 1961, p. 130).

When he told the story in his autobiography, Jung showed little interest in the detail of the gun, and even neglected to point out the obvious parallel that connected his own fleshly self with the intemperate intern who evidently made a pass at the Moon Maiden and with the more dangerous figure of the lunar vampire. Clearly, the young woman had carried with her to the Moon the seductive brother who had driven her underground emotionally. There he was transformed into the kidnapping demon lover of the entire lunar world—the very picture of evil as sexual allure and spiritual promise. She was transfixed, sent into catatonia by the *imaginal* vision of her incestuous partner—no longer a naughty boy but an evil god.

She had slipped into the world of soul, where dreary fleshly realities faded into cosmic dreams, and demons of light soared much more compellingly than any mortal man can ever tread. Her fleshly eyes were glazed over, and she *saw* through the archetypal lens of *imagination*. She broke her silence in the only way she could. Not by talking about what her sensory eyes could not take in, but by speaking the myth she had been living. It was her sole reality, the only thing she had to talk about.

The concealed revolver suggests that, while she sat with Jung in his office, she was, in her own mind, talking to the vampire—or at least a suspected vampire, someone who might force her to accept his reality in place of her own, someone who might try to overpower her. Furthermore, she was curious to know more about this powerful masculine figure who held her fate. If he made a wrong move, she had the weapon she needed to free a whole world of captive women. In this delusional sense, she was really living on the Moon. The insane asylum did not exist for her. Its shadowy figures were the lunar population in disguise who had locked her up underground.

No doubt Jung had not been the first to try to reach her. But the others had been Earthlings who had insisted that she, too, was a denizen of this dreary planet. They never learned how far away she was. Jung succeeded by allowing himself to be transported to her lunar soulscape, where he listened to her plight without judgment, admiring her heroism. Like the vicious watchdog who had been her only emotional contact before entering the hospital, Jung made no move to deny the reality of her life on the Moon.

She was mad not because she lived on the Moon, but because she refused to visit the Earth. This is the crucial difference between her and representatives of the New Age, like Monroe and Strieber, who also live elsewhere as beings of light or "part aliens." The Woman Who Lived on the Moon had relinquished her fleshly identity in favor of her extraterrestrial journeyer and fallen victim to the vampire Archon who ruled the lunar sphere. Monroe and Strieber struggle with conflict and dread because they are trying to live in both worlds. They are in search of a myth that will contain both their fleshly ego and their journeyer. The Moon Maiden was mad because her mythic world was too small. Its beauty and compelling meaningfulness were beyond denial. It just left no room for the public reality of space and time.

Those who had preceded Jung in trying to reach this woman had begun by denying the only thing she knew for certain. Jung took the opposite approach. He started from the assumption that, wherever she was, it must be more vivid in its reality than the world of space and time, for only a greater reality has the power to overwhelm and blot out this one. Until her third collapse into insanity, when he knew she was struggling with a monumental choice—either the Earth or the Moon—he sat at her feet and listened. He made no effort to instruct, cajole, or persuade. He allowed himself to be informed. He accompanied her on her *imaginal* journey to the Moon.

In doing so, he allowed her "left brain" to draw its own conclusions. As she compared the beauty and heroic destiny of her lunar existence with the dreary shades trudging about on this ugly planet in ignorance of a greater reality, she fell into the conflict that has tormented Monroe and

Strieber. She could hardly avoid noticing that she was telling this story to a man in a white coat, seated in an earthly chair, one who was familiar enough with the Earth, but eager to learn about the Moon. Telling the story brought her face to face with the duality of her life. What she had *lived* on the Moon could be recounted on Earth. In fact, telling the story and having it believed proved to be more important than living it. This constituted her betrayal.

Once she had acknowledged the unavoidable fact that she was sitting on the Earth telling her story to an earthly man, the Moon became a place she had to get *back* to. But a Moon that could be talked about on Earth no longer had an exclusive claim to reality. From that point on, it could only be *another* place. Furthermore, it was a place of emotional isolation—a beautiful captivity to be sure, but a captivity nonetheless. She received Jung's message, *you cannot return to the Moon*, in silence and apathy, because she had already recognized its truth. She knew her choice had already been made.

The shooting incident implies that vestiges of the lunar drama persisted even after "resigning herself" to her earthly fate. She still saw herself as vampire bait, ready with a concealed weapon to destroy any man who might threaten her with seduction and conquest. Pulling the trigger, however, brought the lunar myth into collision with public reality here on Earth. It evidently proved such an embarrassment that it finally ended the young woman's enchantment with the Moon. Jung says: "When the excitement over the shooting had subsided, she returned to her native town. She married, had several children, and survived two world wars in the East, without ever again suffering a relapse."

Like the folklore heroes who could not get back to the mermaid palace, she had to get on with her earthly life. Although rejoining the public world was preferable to insanity, something of destiny and cosmic significance had been irretrievably lost. The vampire faded out like the fairies, and her opponents became the dreary Nazis and communists of earthly history in the 20th century. She was no longer psychotic, but we might wonder whether the fleshly world of her sanity did not remain as flat and ugly for her as she had once described it to Jung.

In fact, within ten years of the Moon Maiden's return to Earth and before the outbreak of the First World War, Jung himself had already decided that the sane public world was a pretty dreary place. He had ended the first decade of his professional career by interpreting the dreams of another young woman he judged schizophrenic. Although he had consciously seen this work as defining his differences from Freud, it had a surprising emotional effect upon himself. Writing the book, *Symbols of Transformation* (1912), had convinced Jung that myth describes the deeper reality of every human life, that a meaningful and vital existence is impossible without it. It brought him face to face with the superficiality of his own life. In the introduction to the second edition of *Symbols*, he says:

> I . . . had to admit that I was not living with a myth, or even in a myth, but rather in an uncertain cloud of theoretical possibilities which I was beginning to regard with increasing distrust. . . . So, in the most natural way, I took it upon myself to get to know "my" myth, and I regarded this as the task of tasks. . . . Here I discovered, bit by bit, the connecting links that I should have known about before if I was to join up the fragments of my book (Jung, 1912, p. xxv).

Jung *took the task upon himself* by deliberately "letting himself drop." On December 12, 1913, he *imaginally* fell through the surface of the Earth and entered a realm where he encountered frightening and nauseating visions, dead bodies and rivers of blood, and sat for months at the feet of a winged god he called Philemon who instructed him in the realities of a cosmos greater than that of the public consensus, and greater as well than the psychoanalytic world he had shared with Freud (Jung, 1961, p. 179). He worked hard at painting his visions, questioning Philemon and the other figures he encountered, and studying the mythological parallels he found between his visions and the art and religion of humankind.

In this way, he strove to bring together the *imaginal* realities of his dreams and visions with the critical thinking of his left-brained ego. Like Monroe and Strieber, he sought to integrate both worlds and discover a fleshly existence that is deepened and given mythic significance by invisible realities. But the process was by no means a task designed and directed by his rational mind. His fleshly ego was not in control. Rather it struggled to keep up with an unconscious journey that took him where *it* wanted him to go and was so vivid that he stood in constant danger of losing his orientation in space and time. He says he had to remind himself daily of his name and address, the names of his wife and children, and his obligations to his patients (Jung, 1961, p. 189).

Like the Woman Who Lived on the Moon and Miss Frank Miller, whose dreams he had analyzed in *Symbols*, he found himself on the brink of psychosis, where *imaginal* realities threatened to overwhelm the more dreary facts of the fleshly world. He slept with a loaded gun in the drawer beside his bed and resolved to end his life if he could not succeed in his task. He withdrew from public life for the greater part of the second decade of the 20th century, published almost nothing, resigned from his teaching post, and restricted himself, in the words of his son Franz, to "painting pictures of circles all day long" (Donn, 1988, p. 174).

Jung emerged from his near-psychosis without having to choose between the world of the winged sage and the world of space and time. He had found a way to unite them, where Philemon's wisdom became the broader and deeper mythic dimension of his fleshly existence. In the end, therefore, he had learned more from the Woman Who Lived on the Moon than he had taught her. We might wonder, in fact, whether he did not tell her story with sadness and regret. Because she had not had the "ego strength" to integrate the mythic realm with the world of space and time, she had had to repudiate her winged god. A few years later, however, the very psychiatrist who had supported her choice had found a winged god of his own and built his life around what that god had taught him.

Thus, when Jung told the story of the Woman Who Lived on the Moon and insisted she had really *lived* on the moon and not just believed she had, we have to take this bold assertion in the context of Jung's own life. She really lived on the Moon in the sense that Jung lived the myth that Philemon had revealed to him. To live on the Moon, in this sense, is to live the timeless meaning that lurks behind the temporal events of everyday existence. It means to live one's "own" myth and to do so consciously.

Jung's discovery in the second decade of this century was a kind of New Age myth before New Agers had come up with a name for themselves. By using our *imaginal* faculties to explore the timeless soulscape through which our larger self sojourns, it is possible for us to bring our fleshly ego into harmony with that larger self. When we do so, life has a much more satisfying and comprehensive meaning. It does not save us from the world of space and time, as the Woman Who Lived on the Moon hoped it would. Rather, it revalues the fleshly world, places its anxieties in a larger context, and reveals a depth not available to those who are unfamiliar with the experience of cosmic consciousness.

ALIEN MESSAGES

"Channeling" is a new word for the age-old practice of entering trance in order to receive messages from disembodied intelligences. A century ago, when "spiritualism" was all the rage and people assembled in one another's parlors to contact the spirits of the dead and obtain information from beyond the grave, there was a "scientific" basis supporting their efforts to rediscover cosmic consciousness. In 1888, neurologist Jean-Martin Charcot had thrown his considerable reputation behind the method of hypnosis to uncover forgotten memories. Philosopher Pierre Janet earned a medical degree in order to devote his career to studying the dissociation of the human personality. What was most astonishing in these researches is that the unconscious mind proved to be comprised of several "alternate" personalities, some of which seemed capable of extraordinary knowledge that lay well beyond sensory experience.

This prompted the English classical scholar, F. W. H. Myers, to produce a huge two-volume work to prove that the human soul exists independently of the body, *Human Personality and Its Survival of Bodily Death* (1903). The first volume devoted almost 700 pages to a careful and intelligent summary of the dissociation studies published by Janet and other hypnotists. The second volume built on this foundation with accounts of encounters with ghosts and made several leaps of logic that most readers will find hard to follow. Nevertheless, Myers provided a theoretical foundation for the Victorian parlor games in which deceased relatives spoke through the entranced minds and mouths of mediums.

The whole structure was based on extraordinary findings derived through hypnosis, and it collapsed when it was discovered that Charcot's patients had been inadvertently "taught" the expected behaviors which he "demonstrated" in his famous lectures. Because hypnosis worked by suggestion and almost any word or gesture could be taken as a "suggestion" by the hypnotic subject, hypnosis itself fell under a cloud of suspicion which prompted Janet to write angrily in 1919, "Hypnotism is quite dead—until the day of its resurrection" (Janet, 1919, p. 203). It began coming back to life in the 1950's and has today recovered all the mystique it lost a century ago. The phenomena of multiple personality and traumatic stress syndrome have simultaneously been rehabilitated and cause as much excitement today as they did a hundred years ago.

The practice of entering trance to receive messages from disembodied intelligences, too, has been revived—although the souls of the dead have become less interesting than other disembodied entities. Probably the most influential figure in this movement has been Jane Roberts (1970), a journalist who tells us that she was in search of a topic for a best-selling book when she came across reports of occult messages gained by individuals in altered states of consciousness. Thinking that, if this were a universal human capability, she ought to be able to produce similar results herself, she rediscovered herself as the medium for an alter ego who called himself Seth. His message was not so much about the century-old concern with death and a life beyond the grave as about higher potentials of human consciousness in life.

More recently, a number of people, usually UFO sighters and abductees, have begun to use the technique to gather information about flying saucers and their inhabitants' intentions by going directly to the source, the higher-level aliens themselves. They are producing a body of writings and testimonies that appears quite absurd, being filled with popular misconceptions of scientific concepts and histories of the Earth that are highly improbable. Anyone who is patient enough to wade through this material, however, will be struck by its similarity with wisdom literature the world over and, indeed, with the New Age myth.

The stories told by these channelers agree in their basic structure. An ineffable creator, who is pure light, long ago dispatched lesser beings of light to execute the details of creation, right down to the physical nature of this planet and all the others in the universe. Humankind was created with what we, today, would call astounding capabilities— including cosmic consciousness. This is how they schematize our pre-Taurean ancestors.

But a great tragedy occurred hundreds of thousands of years ago, when a group of rebellious beings of light who had forgotten their origins in the One became obsessed with their own power. These modern Archons took over the Earth and caused us to forget our higher nature by robbing us of our natural twelve-stranded DNA helix, leaving only the double helix that biology knows. In doing so, they made us like themselves, obsessed with power and conquest and unaware of our higher nature. This corresponds to the "fall" from cosmic consciousness that occurred during the ages of Aries and Pisces.

Now, as the New Age is about to dawn, a benevolent universal council of extraterrestrial beings of light has come to set things right. They are "bombarding the planet" with rays of wisdom and light in order to restore the missing ten strands of DNA and help us remember who we are. The elite on Earth are assisting the benevolent aliens by remaining open to the beams of wisdom and increasing their familiarity with cosmic consciousness. Others are friendly nonparticipants, while a third group is still in thrall to the power-hungry enemies of the light. Earthly governments definitely belong to this last category.

Apart from its technology-inspired details, the structure of the New Age UFO myth is very similar to that of ancient Gnosticism. It provides the same sort of hierarchy under the pure spirituality of the One as origin and destiny of all that is. It interprets our bodily life in the sensory world as a misleading distraction that keeps the eyes of our souls blinded

to greater realities. Intermediate between humans and the One are beings of light, some of whom are demonic (Archons) and will lead us into
error. It also divides the population of the Earth into three groups: flesh
people, who know nothing of the light world; soul people who know
something about it, but have not taken it seriously enough; and spirit
people who live it fully.

These three groups also correspond to Castaneda's three relations to
"power": those who have merely heard about it, those who have experienced a bit of it, and those who know it lives within them. Abductees'
reports articulate this "living within" as "implants," high technology
computer chips embedded in their bodies by the aliens who have abducted them.

An old myth comes back in new guise to teach us our origins and
help us make a monumental leap forward. Coming at the end of the rational Age of Pisces, the UFO myth no longer speaks explicitly of spirits, but of physical aliens. The voice that speaks the language of cosmic
consciousness emanates from extraterrestrial masters of physics and en-
gineering. If it is the same voice that spoke to our ancestors in the Age of
Taurus, it has become garbled and trivial with its freight of techno-talk.
The wisdom is perennial, but whether it may be "downloaded" as simply as its enthusiasts believe remains to be seen.

North Carolinian, Barbara Marciniak (*Bringers of the Dawn,* 1992) is
a fairly well-known UFO channeler with an interested following. She
describes her life as filled with extraordinary opportunities that have
made her aware of a world of experience that lies beyond the public consensus. She grew up with a retarded older brother who had a special
glow around him that made her feel privileged to be closely associated
with him. Her Polish grandmother, Babci, lived in a magic domain and
radiated a dignity and pride that transcended earthly experience. Barbara
immersed herself in Jane Robert's "Seth Material" in the late 1970s,
which led her into association with various "metaphysical" groups
(Marciniak, 1992, pp. xxi–xxiii).

During the "Summer of Harmonic Convergence," in 1987, and
again the following March, she experienced several "brief reality collapses" in which she recalled having encountered three bright blue aliens
in her bedroom in the early 1980s (Marciniak, 1992, pp. xxiii–xxiv).
Now she knows that they were real and that they have been "hovering
over" her and calming her for years. During a trip with a "metaphysical"
society in May of 1988, she visited the Temple at Delphi, where thousands of years ago, Greek maidens channeled the wisdom of the gods.
There Marciniak had the sudden intuition that *she* was capable of this
kind of access to cosmic consciousness. She retired immediately to her

hotel room to try it out. Entering into a meditative state, she experienced an alien with a whispered voice quite different from her own, whom she questioned with her own rational voice (Marciniak, 1992, pp. xxiv–xxv).

Enlisting her sister Karen, whom she describes as more accepting than herself, as her amanuensis, Marciniak channeled and argued with her disembodied intelligences for two years. They described themselves as Pleiadians, extraterrestrials from that group of stars we see as the Pleiades, benevolent aliens who know our history and potential far better than we do. They are representatives of a Universal Council of Beings of Light who are bombarding this planet with rays of wisdom and light from "mother ships" circling the Earth. Between 1988 and 1990, Marciniak established a "deep bond" with these beings so that, "Today we live in fine accord, and truly, I feel more ET than human" (Marciniak, 1992, pp. xxv–xxvi).

The message the Pleiadians are transmitting through Marciniak is the twelve-stranded DNA doctrine just described. It agrees very well with the New Age myth described in chapter 6, that cosmic consciousness is, in each case, an individual discovery and achievement. The Pleiadians describe themselves as "triggers and catalysts" who are striving to help us, individually, to uncover the answers that are "buried deep inside." As we Earthlings raise our consciousness, the Pleiadians benefit, for their "system" needs transformation as well. Our earthly transformation will effect a beneficial change in the whole universe. To speed up this process, the Pleiadians are giving us "sensational" messages to "shake us up." We are to be jolted into discovering our own truth, not into taking their messages in a literal manner:

> Never stop where we define an idea, since we are simply here to open up your paradigms and rattle your cages so that you can begin to find the activation of the real knowledge, the true knowledge, that is stored up inside of you. That is where the data is, and we have come to awaken it in you (Marciniak, 1992, p. 9).

Unfortunately for the sympathetic reader of Marciniak's *Bringers of the Dawn*, the Pleiadian message is schematized with references to made-for-television movies, fabulous versions of biochemistry, and inaccurate accounts of contemporary technology. Human beings are compared to "library cards" which must be "sparked" by sexuality (Marciniak, 1992, pp. 69–70). Evil beings of light are called "Dark T-Shirts" and "Lizzies," "space beings who are part human and part reptilian." The universe has been behaving like a dysfunctional family, but the creator gods are trying to "learn how to be good parents" (Marciniak, 1992, p. 31).

Clearly the Bible is one of the main sources of Marciniak's schemata. In an oblique reference to the Book of Revelation, she channels that those who have been "implanted"

> are 144,000 members of the spiritual hierarchy who are infused in the gridwork of the planet at this time. Each master has its own seal that represents one portion of the Language of Light, and you have 144,000 seals of energy that will eventually be infused with your being (Marciniak, 1992, p. 181).

St. Paul's doctrine of the many gifts but one spirit is a recurring theme, and the Pleiadians sometimes sound like Jesus warning his disciples of his coming death: "At one time or another, you will come to doubt everything we have shared with you" (Marciniak, 1992, p. 125).

Parables abound. Life is like a restaurant, for instance, in which we order our food and trust the waiter and chef to get it right. "Don't keep calling up Spirit to see if they got the order or give advice on how to fill it. You ordered it. Trust that it will come." The call to assist the Family of Light will come when we least expect it. "You may be . . . chatting with friends or picking strawberries, and something strikes you—a sound. You excuse yourself and say, 'I am being called. I will return later.'" We must have the patience of turtles. "Don't deny the virtue of the turtle who moves very slowly, stops to go inside and contemplate, is close to the ground, and sees very well" (Marciniak, 1992, pp. 121, 83–84, 75).

There is a certain wisdom in this silliness. It is a Gnostic doctrine decked out in motley and bells. We are advised each to develop our own relationship to cosmic consciousness, to avoid comparing ourselves to one another, and to grapple with our own limitations so as to enter "the Merkabah structure" of the greater cosmos. Meanwhile, we must learn to let others dance the choreography of their own beings without judgment. At the same time, we are shamelessly flattered:

> If you were to have a business card, . . . it would say something like: "Renegade Member of Family of Light. Systems Buster. Available for altering systems of consciousness within the free-will universe. On Call." You go for it! This is what you do (Marciniak, 1992, p. 112).

Notwithstanding the Pleiadians' protest that their words are not to be taken literally, all the bunk that clutters Marciniak's message is precisely what has given the New Age its reputation as a haven for lunatics and the gullible. I had to place a firm rein on my initial reaction in order to wade through the apparent nonsense and discover that the central message is ultimately not so very different from the findings of Monroe, Strieber, and other intelligently critical discoverers of the New Age myth.

Furthermore, Marciniak's *Bringers of the Dawn* is by no means the most outrageous of the channelers' reports. Sheldon Nidle's message, *You Are Becoming a Galactic Human* (1994), co-written with a "Christ-channeler" answering to the improbable name of Virginia Essene, is even more difficult to struggle through. Nidle claims that the DNA "upgrade" from two strands to twelve will be accomplished by the Earth's passage through a "Photon Belt" between March, 1995, and December, 1996, that will plunge us into a darkness that will "blot out the sun and even the stars" (Nidle, 1994, pp. 35–37). But his primary interest seems to be with a fabulous history of the Earth, in which different strains of aliens occupied the continents of Atlantis and Lemuria 35 million years ago. It was the outcome of their battles that caused our "fall" from cosmic consciousness. Interestingly, in Nidle's account, it is the Pleiadians who are the bad guys, while the benevolent extraterrestrials hail from the star system Sirius.

What are we to make of this nonsense? It seems that the accounts of channelers have produced a genre that might be described as the "romance novel approach to the New Age." The human conduits of these intergalactic messages appear to be individuals who are so steeped in the flotsam and jetsam of pop culture that they cannot discern the difference between gold and dross. The only thing that gives us pause before we drop their books in the recycle bin is the fact that there are nuggets of wisdom buried in the overload of bunk.

Truth to tell, the Gnostic systems of 2000 years ago are also filled with fabulous histories and abstruse accounts of how the One emanated the greater cosmos and this material planet. A huge variety of systems was elaborated, often conflicting with one another in their details, but agreeing in their essence. It appears that the Gnostic impulse to find one's own version of truth by the earnest employment of our human *imaginal* faculties leaves us open to random schematizing.

Even though our *imaginal* faculties are shaped by the archetypal structure of our knowing apparatus—providing a common framework of wisdom—the way we put this information together for ourselves is vulnerable to corruption by fragments of our internal monolog. The gaps are automatically filled in with poorly remembered Bible passages, science fiction novels, sensational movies, and beer commercials. This is the way the human imagination works. Anthropologist Claude Lévi-Strauss calls the human faculty for myth-making "*bricolage*," an assembling of odds and ends (Lévi-Strauss, 1996, pp. 16–36). The *bricoleur* is a kind of Jack-of-all-trades who fashions useful, well-functioning devices out of whatever materials lie ready-to-hand.

We might imagine a spectrum of *bricolage*. At one end, eclectic geniuses like Leonardo and Wagner have constructed art works of universal enduring significance out of their wide-ranging interests. At the other end, inventive clowns like the fictional Rube Goldberg assemble devices of absurd intricacy to accomplish simple tasks. On a spectrum like this, myth-makers like John Climacus and Whitley Strieber would be located near the Leonardo end while Marciniak and company would be perched closer to Rube Goldberg.

As arbitrary and comical as their pop-culture analogies may be, however, we must not imagine that the Marciniaks and Nidles of the New Age are engaged in a trivial task. They have been confronted with something compelling that they cannot dismiss lightly. They have struggled with their doubts and have discovered a perspective on our fleshly existence that provides transcendent meaning. Their own lives have been changed by unthinkable forces. Although the absurdity of their imagery may leave us puzzled and disgusted, the deeper structure of what they report has a universal Gnostic character. If the channel mediums appear unduly gullible, we must recall that it requires a great deal of discipline to take a critical stance before winged beings who speak with uncontested authority.

Nevertheless, if the New Age is not to collapse under the weight of its bunk, we will have to retain something of what the human race has learned during the Age of Pisces. We cannot abandon our critical intellect without risking a fate that resembles that of the Woman Who Lived on the Moon. Seduced by the beauty and power of her extraterrestrial vampire, she became unfit for a fleshly existence outside the total care of a psychiatric ward. In contrast, Jung courted madness as he sat at the feet of his winged Philemon, but refused to relinquish his critical intellect. He picked through the dross, collected the gold, and put together a *bricolage* that made superior sense of his own life and provided an approach to the human psyche which is still producing valuable results.[1]

Intuition and imagination are valuable tools, but also dangerous. According to an apocryphal maxim of Jung's, *Intuition is 100 percent reliable, 50 percent of the time.* The difficulty resides in discerning to which

---

[1] I have developed the idea of Jung as a *bricoleur*, a "Jack-of-all-concepts," in my doctoral dissertation (1973), which may soon be published.

"50 percent" a given intuition belongs. This is the reason the great mystics like John Climacus and Ignatius of Loyola place "discernment" at the core of their approach to the life of the soul.

"OLD AGE" FERVOR

More disturbing than their low-brow *bricolage* is the tendency of alien channelers to work themselves up into emotional transports of revival meeting fervor. The benevolent aliens are promoters of a Divine Plan, emissaries of the Prime Creator, who has chosen the Earth, and more specifically the United States ("the land where you can make the most progress," Marciniak, 1992, p. 89), as the centerpiece of an operation that will transform the greater cosmos and vanquish the evil Archons. Television, computers, newspapers, urban violence, and public issues such as the pro-life/abortion debate: all these things are the means by which the evil forces control us through "factions in our governments." We are urged to wake up, repudiate the world around us, and "submit" to the intuitions spirit is sending us. We must choose whether we belong to the love-professing White T-Shirts or the power-mongering Dark T-Shirts. There is an ominous threat in all of this that resembles the fire and brimstone of rural preachers who move about the country with their tents folded up in battered vans.

> Because everyone is so frightened of giving up the system in the United States, they are going to be *forced* to give it up. The system is corrupt, it does not work, it does not honor life, and it does not honor Earth. That is the bottom line. If something does not honor life and does not honor Earth, you can bet it is going to fall, and it is going to fall big time (Marciniak, 1992, p. 89).

The Earth, this argument goes, is controlled by an intergalactic "holographic industry" that inserts deceptive models of the world "through portals into your reality" in order to manipulate and control the consciousness of the masses. "Many, though not all, UFO sightings have been holographic inserts." Even the crucifixion of Christ was a "holographic entertainment movie" (Marciniak, 1992, p. 101). The education system is a sham that "teaches malarkey" because it is based on these lies. The awakened individuals of the New Age "begin by saying, 'I believe that I formulate my world. I believe that I do not need these [academic] credentials to define my existence. I can be unique unto myself, sovereign unto myself'" (Marciniak, 1992, p. 93).

214 • *Perils of the Soul*

The big cities are "holes through which chaotic energy enters the entire North American continent, raping us of our life force." Violence and unrest in the cities are "vehicle[s] for manipulating the entire nation" (Marciniak, 1992, p. 94).

> The planet is headed for a major confrontation with certain entities. We are simply pointing this out; we are not here to promote fear. Fear is what the other team wants you to feel. We want you to understand that *you can change anything you want to change* (Marciniak, 1992, p. 226).

Those under the influence of the Archons and their earthly minions, the national governments, are likely to demonize New Agers, "the human members of the Family of Light" as "witches" or "devils." These power-hungry cabals are unaware that we are all beings of light. Even we well-intentioned and love-inspired citizens of the Earth are fleshly individuals who have forgotten our cosmic intentions upon becoming incarnate. The Pleiadians are helping us to remember what we have forgotten.

> It is your goal to ascend off this planet and to be taken, literally, up into the higher cosmology of mother ships. You will ascend into the cities of light and be able to dwell within the other realities that are all around you that you simply do not permit your third-dimensional eyes to see. . . . After a while, you will want to move on to new assignments to transform other worlds. Remember, you are renegades, and you like a very exciting time (Marciniak, 1992, p. 179).

To harmonize ourselves with this invisible reality, we are urged to cultivate our Native American heritage, to drum, rattle, and dance, and to use our sexuality inventively to open new frequencies of consciousness. Human orgasm is a preparation for the "cosmic orgasm" that results when we recognize the Earth as part of the greater cosmos (Marciniak, 1992, p. 211). We need to develop deep breathing programs and to start spinning while focusing our attention on our thumb: "If you are able to work up to thirty-three spins, three times a day, so that you are spinning ninety-nine times, well, we will see how long you stay on the planet—or at least in this dimension" (Marciniak, 1992, p. 226).

Like the Christian revivalists who have played an important role in American religious history, Marciniak's channeling preaches an ecstatic "born-again" experience in which one knows one is "saved" by attaining emotionally compelling altered states of consciousness. There is a kind of whipping up of immanent expectations according to which the world will be changed within our lifetime. Although the "cosmic orgasm" may be peculiar to Marciniak's message, the idea of immanent change through cosmic consciousness belongs to the New Age wherever it appears.

What distinguishes the Pleiadian doctrine from the New Age manifestations we have seen in previous chapters is the threat of a cosmic Armageddon, a final battle between the forces of darkness and the forces of light in which we are all being forced to take sides. Although the Pleiadians do not fail to assert our free will, they often seem to do so as a kind of after-thought. The main message is that we are occupying a planet that has become a prize for powerful beings who are engaged in a warfare not unlike the legendary battle in Christian lore between the angelic armies of Michael and Lucifer. To choose the right side is to be saved and "ascend to the mother ships," while to choose the wrong side is "to fall big time."

This heaven/hell opposition is foreign to the experience of the near-death journeyers. These people have been relieved of their guilt and fear of damnation. Surely, they have been encouraged to learn compassion, but even the assassin Brinkley was not subjected to punitive torment. He had his eyes opened to what he had been doing to others. He experienced the results of his own fleshly actions by way of opening his eyes to a compassionate way of life. He found the beings of light who were his mentors in the greater cosmos to have compassion for his own sinful self and to have taught it to him. No sin was final, every mistake was an opportunity to learn.

Marciniak's aliens preach a doctrine of winnowing, in which the grain will be taken up to "the higher cosmology" of the nested spheres of light, the "*merkabah* structure" of a heavenly cosmos, while the chaff will be cast out and destroyed. Behind a weak doctrine of love ("honoring life and Earth") lurks a doctrine of power, force, compulsion, and punishment that belongs more to the Age of Aries than to that of Aquarius.

There is a great deal of "shadow projection" in the Pleiadian doctrine: we are good, they are evil. In contrast to Monroe, Brinkley, and Strieber, who have found the biggest obstacle to cosmic consciousness within themselves, those who simply *listen* to Marciniak's message are already on the side of the White T-Shirts. "The mere fact that you are reading this book shows that you are Family of Light" (Marciniak, 1992,

p. 17). Everyone else is under suspicion, vulnerable to falling under the sway of the Dark T-Shirts. Despite the occasional pleas to avoid judging one another—or even ourselves—and to allow each person to dance to the choreography of his or her own being, lurks the implied threat that some dances serve the forces of evil and that this cannot be tolerated.

The true devils in this cosmic vision are the Archons, the power-hungry beings of light who cleverly confuse and mislead us. If our planet is strife-ridden and filled with fear and ignorance, it is not so much we who are at fault, but they. They have been in charge of the Earth for many thousands of years, and they are more clever and powerful than we are. The Pleiadians counsel us to pity the ignorance of humans who hold political power, for they serve the Dark T-Shirts *unconsciously*. Nevertheless, they are on the wrong side and have thrown their weight behind the forces of darkness. Evidence of their heinous manipulations is found everywhere. They are heading for a *fall*.

Although the Pleiadians assert, *We are not here to promote fear; fear is what the other team wants you to feel*, they are surely doing so as effectively as the Christian maxim, "He who is not with me is against me" (Matthew 12:30). The human minions of the Dark T-Shirts are doing evil. They will destroy us if they can. We are, in fact, surrounded by evil; we live in a world governed by evil intentions. Even though we are encouraged to confront the resistances in ourselves to the intergalactic doctrine of light and love, the real enemy is "out *there*." The human race is dividing itself between those who hear the Pleiadians and those who are opposed to the light.

In a world where we have to choose sides, there is little room for the New Age ethic of each individual's struggle to bring his fleshly ego into harmony with his journeyer through a learning process that will surely involve many lifetimes. Ultimately, the Pleiadians do not preach a gentle doctrine through the whispered voice of Barbara Marciniak. They promote a panic in the face of an immanent Armageddon in which right belief ultimately renders impotent a personal struggle to find one's own truth by experience and critical reflection. The Pleiadians are using the trappings of the New Age to take us back to the chaos and terror of an earlier age.

NEW AGE MYSTICISM, OLD AGE CHURCH

The "preacherly" form of what the channelers are telling us about the aliens distinguishes them in a radical way from the reports of people like Monroe and Strieber. Preachers tell us about what they want to be able to *hope* for. They couch their homilies in the style of, "This is the way things are," but they do not speak with the full authority of personal experience. They rhapsodize on a doctrine that has been handed to them. They always preach a "True Doctrine" (*vera doctrina* in the language of the Middle Ages). They deal in "faith," what St. Paul calls "the evidence of things not *seen*." They exhort us to conform ourselves to a transcendent reality that is not exactly *known* but only intimated. Reason, for them, *serves* faith; it does not criticize faith. The True Doctrine is absolute. The ultimate expression of faith is Tertullian's ancient formula, *Credo quia absurdum est* (I believe it *because* it is absurd).

For this reason, the channelers—whether they know it or not—aspire to become the founders of a church, to articulate a doctrine which will gather a community of believers, a society held together by a common faith. They are channeling for us all, teaching us what we *ought to believe*. The implied threats warn us of finding ourselves outside of the community of the elect on the last day, when there will be a New Heaven and a New Earth, when the grain will be gathered and the chaff cast out into the eternal fire. They give us norms for what among our many experiences are to be trusted and what discarded. They set out to define Truth in a final manner and exhort us to conform ourselves to it with the "carrot" of *ascending to the mother ships* and the "stick" of *falling big time.*

Churches belong to the style of human consciousness we have been familiar with throughout the Age of Pisces. They deal in a myth which is not perceived *as* a myth, that is used as a useful schema to make sense of what we vaguely glimpse but cannot know definitively. They present myth as if it were literal fact. They offer us the illusory comfort of believing that we know the unknowable. They set limits to our doubts. They make life safe. They build a floor beneath the tame lake of human conscious experience. They congratulate themselves for having set secure limits to the "real" and convict non-believers of living in chaos, terror, and the "unreal." They alone are conformed to the "good," while the rest of us are flirting with evil and running the risk of damnation. They have not departed from the ancient Christian formula, *extra ecclesiam nulla salus* (outside the church there is no salvation).

An attitude like this, which reserves the true, the good, and the real for a believing elect and projects the false, the evil, and the unreal upon those outside the "church," describes very well the symbol of Pisces—two fish, each swimming in a different direction. The New Age has made much of this image as describing a spirit of opposition that will be overcome during the 2200 years of Aquarius. There is surely truth in the claim that the Age of Pisces has been dominated by the notion of ab-

218 • *Perils of the Soul*

solute right versus wrong and the near-constant warfare that has divided us from one another. It has, indeed, reached an end-point in the specter of the nuclear destruction of the planet that has seemed quite immanent over the last half-century.

The two opposed fish of Pisces also symbolize the structure of "ego consciousness," the reality-testing that we have been using during the last several centuries to learn the laws of nature and come to a position of scientific excellence. Science works by proposing theories that can be "falsified." Every experiment has an expected outcome—either its hypothesis will be supported or it will be proven false. True versus false is the structure of ego consciousness.

Applied to the rather new "science" of psychology, this reality-testing venture has brought us to a new knowledge of ourselves. Its origins lie in Descartes' formula, *I think, therefore I am.* The "I" is placed over against the world at large and everyone else's "I." During the Age of Pisces, we have learned who we are in a new ego-centered manner. Now, at the end of the age, we are dissatisfied and restless with what we have found. We are at the limits of what reality-testing can teach us. We mourn the loss of myth, of God, and of transcendence. We are on the look-out for evidence that will lead us out of the broom-closet of our rational world construction.

Coming as a potential answer to our dilemma are the experiences of the out-of-body and near-death journeyers, the readers and manipulators of auras, and those who have encountered angels and aliens. They speak to us of new possibilities which are "unthinkable" in traditional Piscean consciousness. To turn these discoveries into articles of faith, into true doctrine, is to reduce them to our old Piscean categories. Churches maintain our true/false dichotomizing. They convert Aquarian mystery and novelty into that "old time religion" that was good enough for Abraham.

In contrast, Monroe and Strieber have modeled an approach to the experience of cosmic consciousness that in no way reeks of preaching or churchly dichotomizing. They have taken their experiences seriously, but critically, in a manner that has changed their own worldview without presenting it as a true doctrine that everyone must accept. They are not even sure that they have reached a final opinion for themselves. No doubt they believe their findings are in some sense factual, that they are earnest attempts to schematize their "unthinkable" experiences; and they believe that these experiences are not unique to themselves. They have published books in order to report the events that have impinged on their consciousness, as well as tentative hypotheses about their significance, so that anyone who is interested may also consider them. In short, they have tried to bring together their Piscean critical faculties with the cosmic consciousness that has dawned on them. In this sense, they stand closer to scientists than to theologians.

In another sense, they are mystics rather than theologians. Mystics have had direct personal experience of the holy, while theologians work in concepts *about* the holy. Surely these are not exclusive callings. Mystics have generally tried to conceptualize their experience, and some theologians have had close encounters with the holy. The great medieval theologian, Thomas Aquinas, was one of these, but he found the two sides of his spiritual life tended uneasily in separate directions—indeed, to such an extent that, on his death bed, he spoke of his *Summa Theologica* with great regret: "All is straw." Clearly, Aquinas had *seen* something unspeakable that rendered his theologizing foolish.

The great German scholar of comparative religion, Rudolf Otto, wrote *The Idea of the Holy* (1958) in 1923 to address this central, irrational dimension of religious experience. He invented the term *numinous* to describe the feeling of being "dust and ashes" before a reality that makes us feel overwhelmed by our own nothingness. The holy, itself, he described as the *mysterium tremendum et fascinans*, the uncanny mystery that makes us tremble and shudder, but also holds us with a fascination we cannot escape. Such religious awe makes us stand aghast in "daemonic dread" before a reality that is wholly other than anything that belongs to the world of space and time. It makes our "blood run cold" and our flesh "creep." "Something supra-rational throbs and gleams, palpable and visible in the 'wrath of God,' prompting to a sense of 'terror' that no 'natural' anger can arouse" (Otto, 1958, p. 19).

For Otto, the self is annihilated before an urgency that strikes us dumb. A tiny fragment of this shuddering stupor may be experienced upon encountering a ghost. We have a sense of the gruesome and dreadful, but cannot leave it alone. It entices, bewilders, and confounds us even as it strikes horror in our hearts. We feel we have been stripped of everything we have known of ourselves, down to the ground of our soul. Rapturous though it may be, there is nothing comforting about this experience. It brings us an exaltation that verges on the bizarre and abnormal. It thrills in the same moment that it nullifies.

At bottom, an encounter with the holy is an irrational experience for which we have no words or imagery. Nevertheless, as rational, thinking beings, we have no choice but to try to "schematize" (Otto's word) this dreadful reality that would do with us as It will. Theology has tried to do so, but badly misses its mark in calling God the Highest Good. Theology is not wrong in addressing God with the words, "Thou alone art Holy," and conceptualizing the Holy as supreme goodness. It is not wrong, but it badly underestimates the tortured outburst of feeling that moved the disciple Peter to say, "Depart from me for I am a *sinful* man, O Lord" (Otto, 1958, p. 50). It is not that Peter saw himself as having broken the rules of morality, but rather as incapable of standing before a remorseless reality that so nullified him. He felt his creatureliness, as "a numinous *disvalue* or unworth" (Otto, 1958, p. 51).

Everything Otto says about encounters with the holy is familiar to us, for we have seen it all in connection with alien visitations and abductions. Those who have had direct contact with aliens, and not just channeled them, have been nullified, moved to dread, and held in awful fascination. Their reality has been reduced to dust and ashes; they were made to feel "disvalued," tagged like wild animals, overwhelmed by beings of uncanny power that made their blood run cold. They were struck dumb, could hardly deny the reality they faced, but found it so bizarre and abnormal that they fumbled to find words and images to schematize what had happened to them. Although they spoke most prominently of an unfathomable mystery that terrified them and placed them in an "animal panic," those who bore with the experience went on to speak of fascination, a sense there was some transcendent promise in the experience. Many said that they had to revise their notion of who they were, placing their old fleshly identity within a larger spiritual context.

We may come away from their stories unclear as to what an alien might be, but we can hardly doubt they have encountered a *mysterium tremendum et fascinans*. Some even used religious language in their attempts to find schemata to make sense of what happened to them. They spoke of aliens as intermediaries between the human race and the One who is the origin and destiny of the greater cosmos. It is surely possible to read of their dreadful adventures and feel that these things have nothing to do with us. But it is not possible to doubt that something deeply unsettling has happened to them. Even if we dismiss their interlude of shuddering fascination as a momentary insanity, we remain certain that they have been disturbed somewhere near the root of their soul.

Theologians can speak rhapsodically, but they do not arrest us as the mystics do. Theologians speak of things that have happened to other people. Mystics speak of what has happened to themselves. Theologians threaten, cajole, and try to convince us. Mystics are simply shattered. St. John of the Cross says:

Therefore God destroys, crushes and overwhelms the soul in such a deep darkness, that it feels as though melted and in its misery destroyed by a cruel death of the spirit. Even as though it were to feel it had been swallowed by some savage beast and buried in the darkness of his belly (John of the Cross, 1979, p. 337).

As we stand at the gate of the New Age, studying those who pass in and out, we cannot but remark that some of the New Age monks have merely heard of wonders and very much hope some day to encounter them, while some speak glibly of what others have *seen*. A few have little language at all, but they move as though they have *seen* something they will never forget. They do not doubt that what has happened to them has relevance for us all, but they know we will not take it seriously until it happens to us. They do not preach, but they are so taken by what has happened to them that there is nothing they would rather talk about.

In the last analysis, this describes why the channelers leave us so unconvinced. They have discovered the myth of the New Age, but they have not been shattered by it. This is why their books sound so trashy. They are hauling in messages from mother ships and promising us that we will soon be downloading another ten strands of DNA. A largely passive and blissful transformation awaits us all. All we need do is fall in line and take orders from someone else's inner voice. The Pleiadians warn us of dangers. Demons abound. We may *fall* if we cannot distinguish the Dark T-Shirts from the White. But wisdom and light are beaming down upon us. Unless we are stiff-necked beyond all reason, some of this transforming energy is bound to get downloaded—if only while we sleep. And the more new strands of DNA we pick up, the more ready we become for more. The New Age is sweeping in like a cosmic breeze. Those who have *seen* the aliens are sure a rather more shattering experience awaits us.

Chapter

10

MUTTERINGS IN THE GLOBAL VILLAGE

In the enfolded order, space and time are no longer the dominant factors determining the relationships of dependence or independence of different elements. Rather, an entirely different sort of basic connection of elements is possible, from which our ordinary notions of space and time, along with those of separately existent material particles, are abstracted as forms derived from the deeper order. These ordinary notions in fact appear in what is called the explicate or unfolded order, which is a special and distinguished form contained within the general totality of all the implicate orders.

(BOHM, 1983, P. XV)

You must turn down the volume of the first channel while you learn to attune your attention to the second. This process you call dissociation.

(ROBERTS, 1970, P. 59)

We want you to realize that those space beings on and around this planet who you feel are "bad guys"—and with whom your government forces have made deals—are dealing with the same issues that you are. . . . They have been accused of heinous behavior, of performing mutilations and abductions upon the human species . . . yet, these beings act as a mirror to show you your own world . . . There is a complacency upon Earth. The consciousness on this planet is, "You do it for me. I don't want to be responsible. You become my government official. You become my teacher. You become my boss. Someone tell me what to do."

(MARCINIAK, 1992, P. 47)

Power remains today just as it always has, but not authority. Authority has all but vanished. Its disappearance from American life is just as significant an event, I believe, as the closing of the frontier.

(GELERNTER, 1995, P. 10)

When I arrived in Zurich in 1975, clad in Earth Shoes, Levis and battered sport coat, I thought I had been transported back in time to Lansing, Michigan in the 1940s. Not that the big square buildings and elaborate trolley network of Switzerland's largest city had anything in common with the small-town capitol of my home state, but rather that there was something in the spirit of the place that led me to expect to encounter the bald head of my squat little grandfather coming around every corner. My grandfather had died in 1949, but it seemed to me that the world he had inhabited had not disappeared from the Earth.

For all its cosmopolitanism, Zurich had the feel of a tradition unbroken and unchallenged since World War II. Young men in old-fashioned Army uniforms and olive-drab backpacks were boarding trains, rifles in hand, for weekend exercises. There was a slow-moving politeness and decorum on the streets. People were well dressed by American standards. The craziness of American cities was nowhere to be seen. As it rained almost every day, I bought the first umbrella I have ever owned and one day left it at a trolley stop at the edge of the city, not realizing it was missing until I had reached my destination miles away. Nonplussed, I rode the line back to my starting point and found the umbrella where I had left it. Such an incident might not have been unusual in Lansing in the 1940s, but it was unheard of in Boston, New York, or Chicago in 1975.

I felt the old-fashioned atmosphere as both charming and stifling. The old people let their wrinkles show. There was no shame in being over 60 in this tradition-bound society. It came as a breath of fresh air. Yet where were the "crazies"? How could a large city exist without bizarrely clad and obstreperous misfits or shabby "street people" slouching from doorway to doorway? I imagined doing a photo-essay on "The Dachshunds of Zurich," for people were walking everywhere with the short-legged canines on leashes. I wondered whether I would stay in Zurich long enough to witness the Swiss version of the American 60s, when conventions were thrown to the winds and a new spirit of freedom emerged.

As it happens, I missed the 60s by a year. They came in like a storm in 1981, when the Zurich Opera House underwent remodeling and tried to take over the "Red Factory" that had been serving as a youth center. In 1982, when I returned to the city to give a series of lectures on the French influences on Jung's psychology, I found the trolley center and kiosk at Bellevue Platz festooned with candles, flowers, and wreaths, protesting repressive police attacks on demonstrating youths.

In one sense, Zurich has gone downhill since then. By 1990, heroin addicts were shooting up in full public view on the lake shore. I was almost run over by an ambulance rushing to get to a young man who had overdosed behind a public toilet. Protest signs were spray-painted on the sides of buildings. The craziness whose absence I had puzzled over had arrived. Neighborhoods that had been sleepy residential areas had been taken over by prostitutes and drug-pushers. People my wife had met pushing their baby carriages in the late 70s, confident of their safety, were now afraid to leave their homes at night.

The last fifteen years in Zurich represent a pale microcosm of what has happened to the United States over the last fifty years. David Galernter, a computer scientist at Yale, has written a very touching book on the unsettling transformation our society has undergone in the second half of the 20th century, *1939: The Lost World of the Fair* (1995).

Galernter has found brochures, statistics, speeches, and photographs and has interviewed people who visited the 1939 New York World's Fair as often as twenty times. The theme of the fair was "The World of Tomorrow." It was a paean to progress, a utopian vision of how technology would transform our lives. It was all there like a glorious dream: refrigerators, televisions, motor cars, super highways, suburbs. People were delighted to pay an exorbitant dime for a hot dog and spend a whole day touring the exhibits in their suits, ties, hats, and Sunday dresses (Galernter, 1995, p. 92). People fell in love, declared engagements, and celebrated weddings on the grounds of the fair. They lived in a world of hope and "concrete confidence," although the majority feared the Axis Powers would win the war in Europe and that America had better "arm to the teeth, despite the cost." Hitler had destroyed Czechoslovakia before its pavilion was completed. Three-quarters of Americans favored immediate imposition of a military draft, yet 43 percent (to 36 percent) were optimistic about "the future of civilization" (Galernter, 1995, p. 27).

New York was a different place in 1939. Dynamite could be stored at building sites without lock and key. Forty people died of gunshot wounds in the course of a year, while today that many are shot to death in ten days. Full-time secretarial employment left a young woman with enough money for a cup of coffee each morning for breakfast, a fifteen-cent lunch, and four sixty-cent dinners per week (Galernter, 1995, p. 52). The working poor were considerably less well off than they are today, but they were not discouraged. They lived in a world of propriety, politeness, and proper dress. They placed their hopes in a glowing future designed by a technology that was still wedded to art. The *Guidebook* to the fair gushed: "The true poets of the twentieth century are the designers, the architects and the engineers who glimpse some inner vision, create some beautiful figment of the imagination and then translate it into valid actuality for the world to enjoy" (Galernter, 1995, p. 169).

By 1975, everything that had been predicted at the 1939 World's Fair had been accomplished, and more. But hope was gone. "Democracity's utopian World of Tomorrow amounts, in essence, to the modern suburbs" (Galernter, 1995, p. 67). We have the superhighways, and they are crowded. Our automobiles and appliances are more efficient and accomplish greater marvels than 1939 was able to imagine. Our poor are materially better off. But we have lost heart; our society is filled with conflicts unthinkable fifty years ago. We are disillusioned. Galernter observes, "When you live in utopia, you can't yearn for utopia any more, and the community of faith is dead" (Galernter, 1995, p. 72).

In my first month in Zurich, I lived in a commune with several Swiss 20-somethings who described themselves as communists. They all had motorcycles, but could not afford the insurance required to ride them. Communism was hardly a possibility in Switzerland, but they were very earnest, filled with theories and statistics, and scornful of me for what they perceived to be bourgeois sensibilities. I felt misunderstood. It was not that I preferred my capitalist comforts to their communist struggle, I just could not accept their idealistic certainty. In my American world of the 1970s, things were not as simple as these counter-culturalists seemed to believe.

In retrospect, I can see that their earnest simplicity belonged more to the Lansing or even Detroit of 1947 than it did to Boston two American decades later. My culture shock resulted, not so much from the language spoken, as from the public consensus. There was a unanimity among the Swiss—including even the communists—that seemed childishly naive to me. They did not seem to realize that the world is not run by ideas, but by something much more primitive.

Apparently, New Yorkers in 1939 also did not realize this. Galernter describes it as an "ought" culture. Americans lived by the rules for no other reason than that they were *the rules*. They dressed for every occasion, spoke in polite formalisms ("How do you do?"), and would never think of going near the dynamite stored behind the warning sign. They were polite, not because they were sissies, but because they did not want to make fools of themselves. They did not want to be boorish, as they would no doubt judge we have become. People knew where they stood in society and how they were expected to act. They gained a security from this and a sense of community that we have lost. Galernter calls it a "religious community," the American civil religion (Galernter, 1995, p. 49).

He also calls it respect for "authority." The recordings that informed people of the exhibits at the fair were spoken with authority. The future was described with an indubitable certainty that we would call "camp." Strangely enough, the world of authority worked a half-century ago. New York City itself had been fashioned by three ruthless men of vision and authority, FDR, Fiorello LaGuardia, and designer Robert Moses, who more than tripled the number of city playgrounds, built fifty miles of arterial urban highway, as well as three major bridges and 110 smaller ones (Galernter, 1995, pp. 78–80). In a world like this, it paid to go along and formally comply without questioning one's obligations.

What Galernter calls "authority" does not reside merely in the resonant tones of a leader's voice, or even in the seeming certainty of his personal convictions. It resides, rather, in the public consensus. Leaders speak with authority only when they are articulating what everyone already believes. The "authority world" of the 1930s was a realm in which Americans agreed upon certain standards and ideals, took them for granted as simply the ways things are. World War II and our role in it seemed made for that moral confidence. We might have lost, but we knew we were right; those who doubted that fascism was wrong were clearly a small minority. The mainstream of the public consensus was not substantially challenged.

The Korean War was another matter. There was serious doubt—even among those who agreed that communism must be "contained"—that we had a role to play on that Asian peninsula. The most horrifying stories to come out of the war had to do with "communist brainwashing," the fact that captured American soldiers had an insufficient conviction about what they were doing in the war, that they could have their minds changed by psychological techniques, including torture, employed by their captors. In the 50s, communism became for us a sinister undermining force. We feared, not only that Russia could launch a war we might lose, but also that the communists among us (grossly overexaggerated by the mad figure of Joseph McCarthy) could sap our confidence and destroy our unanimity. We were already in a crisis regarding our belief in ourselves, even though we projected it upon "them," the demons behind the iron and bamboo curtains and their "fellow travelers" in our midst.

The crisis broke out in full force during the 60s, when the Vietnam War split us into hostile camps. The fact that we were losing the war exacerbated the crisis, but the tragedy lay with us and our failure to know who we were or what we were doing. We spoke of "falling dominoes," but the war was simply an *occasion* for our learning that our public consensus had dissolved. We had lost our taste for formal expressions of politeness. John Kennedy's famous bare-headed inaugural symbolized our impatience with the rules of the dress code simply because they were "the rules." The deepest crisis in our domestic identity was expressed in our distrust of our authority figures. Lyndon Johnson declined to run for a second elected term of office because he recognized he had become a symbol of our public dividedness. Richard Nixon demolished what was left of our hope to find a trustworthy spokesman for a public consensus that no longer existed. He proved that the appearance of consensus was a "cover up," behind which monumental deceptions lurked.

The New Age represents an attempt to build an alternate consensus to replace the one that no longer works. The hostility and Armageddon language of channeled messages from aliens reflects an awareness on the part of those who identify with the New Age that theirs is a minority consensus. The New Age appeal to beings of light who have a "bird's eye" view of our history and a radically new perspective on our psychic potential represents an attempt to find and establish a new source of authority. Because none of us fleshly beings has sufficient breadth of vision to create a new consensus, the wisdom needed for this new authority is placed in the skies, in mother ships piloted by beings whose technology is unthinkably greater than ours.

We no longer believe that General Motors or the National Aeronautics and Space Administration have our best interests at heart. We suspect them of narrow self-interest that may be doing us more harm than good. Our political leaders fall under the same suspicion. In an atmosphere like this, it is not at all surprising that the most attractive political leaders are the ones we know least about. Let them declare their candidacy for office, however, and we immediately dig up all the dirt on them that we can. Invariably, we find that they are flawed fleshly beings just like ourselves. They have no right to speak with authority.

Ronald Reagan succeeded in building a tenuous and flawed consensus by appealing, not to the future, but to a nostalgic, romanticized past. Jimmy Carter, George Bush, and Bill Clinton have been reviled for being "without principle" and of rushing to follow public opinion rather than to lead it. Pollsters tell us what we believe and advise our leaders as to what we want to hear. Public consensus has become evanescent. It changes faster than we can keep track of it. Our short-lived leaders have no ground to stand on, for we cannot agree among ourselves; and individually, we are changing our minds every day. Very likely, the 1939 World's Fair and World War II were the last manifestations of an American dream of unanimity and progress.

Galernter's book is held together by the story of a Jewish woman who accepted a marriage proposal from the love of her life on the grounds of the fair. Her diaries and interviews bring the fair to life, and we see it through her rose-colored glasses. We also become thoroughly involved in the tragic tale of her lost love. For, after having won her Jewish beloved from the rich *shiksa* who had enchanted him, she lost him to the war, whose shadow the fair barely kept at bay. This sorrowful end left the fair as the high point of her long life.

By the end of the book, rather more disturbing revelations are brought to light. It appears, in fact, that the wealthy Christian rival never relinquished her hold on the young man. She used her connections to further his career before his enlistment, organized regular trysts with him, even after the engagement, and managed to find a way to be with him in a European hospital just before he died of his wounds. The Bible he always carried with him was marked at his favorite passage with three strands of her hair (Galernter, 1995, pp. 323–331). It becomes clear that he had never lost his love for that wealthy beauty, that he had agreed to marry the central figure in Galernter's book in order to do what he "ought." He complied with his parents' demand that he marry within his Jewish faith. No doubt he loved his fiancée, but she never rose to first place in his affections.

Thus, by the end of the book, we realize that the whole phenomenon of the fair was an illusion. Not only was it a colossal money-loser for the City of New York, but it fostered an illusory American dream which subsequent history has uncovered as the false hope that it was. And the great love whose story unifies the book also falls apart when Galernter's leading figure makes her final confession. Ironically enough, the substance of that romantic deception rests upon the one factor Galernter praises about "the high Thirties" throughout the book: the religion of "ought." The young man did what he "ought" to have done, and this fostered an illusion that broke his fiancée's heart.

SHAMANS AND GHOSTS

Very likely, we face more than the end of a millennium, that symbolically loaded few years when an impending series of zeroes inspires us to rethink what we are about as human beings. If it is merely a matter of zeroes in our reckoning of the years, our crisis will pass once the naughts are covered with less formidable digits. Having considered Galernter's thesis, however, we might wonder if we are not facing the impotence of our public consensus. Perhaps we need a substantial revision of our worldview before the future again takes on the "glow" it still had in 1939. If our future is dead, uninteresting, or dreary, if we cannot imagine how to go on in a sufficiently meaningful way, we are facing the end of the world as we have known it.

A hundred years ago, the natives of our American plains faced the end of the life they had known. There was a great slaughter on December 29, 1890, at Wounded Knee in South Dakota. All accounts agree that a shot or other loud noise from an unknown source spooked inexperienced and frightened United States soldiers into a rampage in which men, women, and children died in enormous numbers. A factor that contributed substantially to the Indians' vulnerability and the soldiers' fright was a millennial movement among several nations of Plains Indians.

The Ghost Dance religion among Native Americans bears many similarities with what we now know as the New Age. The cultural crisis those essentially Stone Age people faced upon the encroachment of a civilization that had overwhelming numbers and unthinkably superior technology on its side, seemed to have found a solution in cosmic consciousness. The Ghost Dance was a peaceful movement that looked forward to the miraculous establishment of a New Heaven and a New Earth that would be danced into being. The buffalo would be restored, the dead would return to Earth, and all Native American nations would live in harmony. The proof for this was the sense of cosmic oneness experienced by those who danced. They had received a common vision of mythic proportions that gave them unrealistic hopes and inspired terror in Americans of European extraction.[1]

One of the Lakota who survived that massacre was a holy man who has enjoyed great renown in recent decades through the account he gave of his early life, published in 1932 by John Neihardt as *Black Elk Speaks*. Black Elk had been visited by Thunder Beings and voices from thunder clouds from the age of four. Not unlike those abducted by aliens, he knew they wanted something of him, but did not know what to do about it. At age 9 he fell seriously ill and experienced out-of-body journeys to an upper world where the gods or "Grandfathers," as he called them, granted him a great vision of the oneness of all humanity. He was given the mission of saving his people, and his great vision was to be the blueprint. He grasped the significance well enough, but had no notion of how to implement it (Neihardt, 1961, pp. 7–19).

---

[1] For detailed accounts of the Ghost Dance Religion, see Utley (1963) and La Barre (1972).

For the next eight years he found himself both blessed and cursed by repeated reminders of his vision and clairvoyant knowledge that enabled him to warn his people from time to time of coming dangers. Holy men *saw* that he glowed with a spiritual light. His wisdom was respected, but it offered him little consolation, for he was convinced he was not following his vision. Things were becoming urgent. The Thunder Beings were insisting, but still he did not know what to do. At age 17, his crisis had deepened to such an extent that everyone began to see that he was losing his sanity (Neihardt, 1961, pp. 20–47). He was induced to tell his story to an old medicine man named Black Road, who recognized that Black Elk's "sickness" was an incomplete shamanic initiation. Black Road's advice was that the entire community should dance Black Elk's vision, thus legitimating the young man's cosmic sojourns and spreading its message to the people for whom it was intended (Neihardt, 1961, pp. 160–165).

Dancing the great vision made the people feel good about themselves, and it freed Black Elk somewhat from his feeling of impotence. He became a shamanic healer of some effectiveness, but he healed individuals only and could find no way to translate what he knew and had *seen* into a program that would heal his people (Neihardt, 1961, pp. 198–207). He accepted an invitation to join Buffalo Bill's Wild West Show in the hopes of learning more about the wider world that was to be unified into a kind of Global Village, a planetary camp circle comprised of smaller camp circles, each representing a separate nation of the Earth (Neihardt, 1961, pp. 117–127).

An out-of-body journey in "Locale I" from Paris, where the Wild West Show was performing, back to South Dakota to *see* what was happening to his people convinced Black Elk that his show-business career amounted to an avoidance of his mission. He returned to Pine Ridge still not knowing what to do (Neihardt, 1961, pp. 228–232). In the late 1880s when the Ghost Dance was beginning, he recognized it had similarities with his own great vision. He had conscious doubts about the Ghost Dance, as it was much more ethnocentric than his vision, and the visionary experiences he had while dancing added to his doubts. But good men were involved in the movement, and he could not dismiss it (Neihardt, 1961, pp. 234–242).

The slaughter at Wounded Knee evidently was the last straw. We know little of what happened to Black Elk between 1890 and 1904. But it is fair to say that he suffered a crisis of major proportions, both in his own sense of mission and in the future of his people. In 1904, he converted to Christianity and spent the last forty-six years of his life as a cat-echist, teaching his people—particularly children—the doctrine of Christ on the model of the Good Red Road of his childhood vision. Michael Steltenkamp tells the story of his Christian years in *Black Elk: Holy Man of the Oglala* (1993).

Very likely, the event that ultimately guided him in his conversion occurred in the context of the Ghost Dance. He was on an out-of-body journey, carried by a great wind, when he looked down and saw his people trying to cross a dark and raging river. "Weeping, they looked up to me and cried: 'Help us!' But I could not stop gliding, for it was as though a great wind was under me" (Neihardt, 1961, p. 250). The vision took him to the teepee of the Sixth Grandfather, the Spirit of the Earth, and Black Elk apparently took this as a message to keep his feet on the ground, that vision-seeking was taking him away from the people he was trying to help (Neihardt, 1961, pp. 248–251). He resolved to find a much more practical means for giving his people a viable way to live on this Earth. Christianity, as poorly practiced as it may have been by people of European origin, must have seemed a more realistic doctrine to serve as a basis for implementing his great vision of world harmony.

The melancholy story of Black Elk suggests an uncomfortable future for the New Age. His great vision and the more unrealistic enthusiasms of the Ghost Dance aspired to monumental social change through *imaginal* experience. Cosmic visions sketched a paradisal future. The past was to be abandoned as a radically new day dawned. Similarly, the New Age urges us to leave space and time and shed our fleshly identity, even if only for moments at a time. For only the perspective of the greater cosmos reveals that we are, indeed, engaged in a common enterprise here on Earth. As long as we remain immersed in the day-to-day struggle, we are caught in our obsession with survival and cannot see the whole picture. The sensory form of knowledge we have honed and polished for the battle to survive must give way to cosmic consciousness. Whether we are forced out of our bodies by aliens or coaxed out by less shattering en-counters with "power," our horizons are re-arranged by a monumental shock. Only this can pry open the door of our broom-closet.

The New Age envisages a Global Village—very much like Black Elk's Hoop of the Nations—in which our defensive national, racial, and religious barriers dissolve, as we discover we are all human and we all live on this very limited Spaceship Earth. We are on the verge of experi-encing our oneness with the Earth and her inhabitants. We will love one another and our planet. We will stop our frantic plundering of nature and our fellows. Life will become more harmonious and meaningful than it has ever been. We are making a great leap forward. We will come to see things as they have never been seen before, and this will enable us to live as we have never lived before.

This is the ultimate utopia, the millennium without the second coming of Jesus Christ. A New Heaven and a New Earth. For us who stand at the gate of the New Age, wondering what brings people to pass in and out, these rhapsodic hopes have the ring of astonishing gullibility. Evidently, the New Agers are right about the power of cosmic consciousness to change people, for we have seen several instances of this. But do we dare to look forward to the day when such enlightenment will descend upon us all? We wonder how we can hope that those who are fighting for survival in political, religious, and economic wars will dare to drop their wary gaze to enter a meditative state. They would be quite realistic in fearing the loss of their bodily lives while their journeyer ascends into a greater cosmos.

Black Elk failed to convince his own community that a new way of being was required. They were impressed and uplifted by dancing his great vision, but it had little effect on their daily lives. Traditional everyday necessities such as food, shelter, and fending off their enemies held their attention too strongly. But even if his vision had inspired the entire Lakota Nation, how could he have convinced the white Americans and their armies? The entire world has never accepted a single vision. Even Christianity and Islam—each of which has deeply influenced large sections of the world's population with doctrines of love and compassion—have fallen into warfare with the partisans of other religions and undergone hostile divisions within themselves.

The New Age myth we have uncovered always manifests as an individual call to bring one's own fleshly existence into line with one's journeyer. The implementation of this personal vision is difficult enough. Monroe, Brinkley, Strieber, and Castaneda, indeed all of the New Age pathfinders we have investigated, have spent decades working on this individual moral task. Similarly, Black Elk's lifetime of visions changed *him*. He became a holy man who was able to heal and uplift those around him on a more-or-less individual basis. His struggle and tragedy resulted from his failed attempts to implement his great vision as a blueprint for world-wide transformation. New Age hopes seem reasonable and cogent when they concern individuals, one at a time. When the enthusiasm takes on global pretensions, the specter of the Ghost Dance inevitably comes to mind.

ᴀ HᴜNDᴙED MᴼNKEYᴊ

New Agers have frequently asked me if I have not noticed how much improvement the world has undergone since the meditative celebration of Harmonic Convergence in 1987. I am always astounded by the question. Do they not see the growing public fascination in America with "true crime" police stories and murder trials, the enthusiasm for the "death penalty," the repressiveness of "political correctness," the heinous public confessions proliferating on television talk shows, the growing polarization and rigidity of the political right and left, the inability of government to find solutions, as well as ethnic wars and genocide the world over?

The Harmonic Convergence enthusiasts seem nonplussed by the disturbing facts reported in our newspapers. Apparently these incidents and trends merely show that the Old Age is still with us. They know this well enough, but place their hopes in evidence of another sort, new converts to their way of thinking and new testimonies of rising consciousness gathered at workshops and other meetings of like-minded individuals. They are attending to a model of consciousness-changing that rarely finds its way into our newspapers—the so-called "Hundredth Monkey" phenomenon.

According to the legend of the Hundred Monkeys (sometimes reported as fact), a couple of remote islands belonging to Japan were inhabited by monkeys who had an insufficient food supply. To keep them alive, supplies of potatoes were dropped on the beaches from airplanes. The monkeys ate the sandy vegetables as expected, until one day, an enterprising female got the idea of carrying her potato to the sea to wash off the sand. Then gradually, over the course of weeks, other monkeys, females predominantly, began to follow her example. Once a significant number of monkeys (say a hundred) had accepted the new idea, suddenly the whole society of monkeys took up the washing practice.

This entire development might be understood as a case of "modeling" behavior, in which the monkeys learned from one another by observing, imitating, and appreciating the advantage of eating potatoes that were free of the grittiness of beach sand. But something even more remarkable is said to have occurred. As soon as the monkeys on the first island, where the inspired female lived, had all taken up the new practice of washing their potatoes, it was observed that monkeys on the other island—which was too distant from the first for direct communication to have been possible—also began to wash their potatoes in the sea.

The indirect access whereby distant monkeys were suddenly inspired to a beneficial new behavior is the heart of the "Hundredth Monkey" paradigm. It is believed that, when a significant number of individuals accepts a revolutionary new and useful idea, consciousness of this new idea spreads automatically by some sort of unconscious telepathy. The legend promotes a theory of cosmic consciousness. All monkeys have a sort of psychic radio band which gives them access to what other monkeys know. Generally, the signal in this band is too weak to have effect. But when it becomes strong enough (as by a "critical mass" of monkeys accepting a certain idea), this information becomes consciously available to all monkeys and the entire race has its consciousness raised.

The implications of this legend for the New Age are obvious. Like the inventive, intuitive female who first came up with the idea of potato-washing, New Agers live their lives outside the power-structure of their society. Their good ideas are ignored because the right people do not hold them. The New Age myth is already uppermost in the minds of a significant minority. It is expected to continue to expand its base among "disempowered" individuals until it reaches a "critical mass" of unspecified size, at which point the whole world will appreciate the wisdom and advantages of cosmic consciousness. The closed minds of those who presently adhere to an Old Age mode of thinking will be opened—as it were, from the inside—and everyone will see the light. Then we will truly enter the New Age, and the Earth will become a Global Village in fact. Even the most conservative of academics, business tycoons, and government officials will begin to think globally, ecologically, and spiritually.

The channelers are promoting a kind of "Hundredth Monkey" doctrine with their idea that some individuals have been "implanted" with alien computer chips in order to "download" the wisdom contained in those long-lost ten strands of DNA. They are the first human members of the Family of Light. They are "systems busters," because they are working to break up our old assumptions and spread cosmic consciousness, first by finding and developing it in themselves, and then by modeling it for others. They know that the vast majority of humans will be unable to accept such cosmic views until a "critical mass" prepares the way. Then the new worldview will spread suddenly and without resistance, just as the idea of potato-washing did among the monkeys. This, in fact, was the rationale behind the Harmonic Convergence of August, 1987. At a moment when the stars had moved into a particularly favorable configuration, groups of humans all over the Earth assembled in auditoriums, ashrams, and under the open sky to meditate upon harmony and cosmic oneness in order to produce a "critical mass" of human consciousness that would influence us all.

The "Hundredth Monkey" story is a legend and may therefore seem to be the flimsiest of foundations for a theory of consciousness-changing. Nevertheless, it belongs to a way of thinking which cannot be entirely dismissed. Biologist Rupert Sheldrake (*The Presence of the Past,* 1988) has assembled a great deal of evidence that bears a strong similarity to the New Age's favorite legend. For example, a small Northern European bird known as the blue tit learned in the 1920s to steal milk from bottles left on English porches in the early morning. Very possibly, this new source of nutrition was discovered by a single tit and, very likely, other tits learned by imitation. But a blue tit's range is only fifteen miles, making imitation an inadequate explanation for the fact that the milk-stealing activity appeared in tit populations hundreds of miles away from the region of its first appearance. These birds had to have learned the practice of milk-stealing in some way other than by observation and imitation. Indeed, Swedish, Danish, and Dutch tits picked up milk-stealing despite the seas that separated these populations from one another. Most remarkable of all, Dutch milk deliveries ceased during the years of World War II, depriving the blue tit of milk bottles for some eight or ten years. As a result, none of the milk-stealing birds lived long enough to model the behavior in the post-war period. Yet when milk bottles reappeared after the war, a new generation of tits again began stealing milk (Sheldrake, 1988, pp. 177–181).

Sheldrake postulates that such patterns of behavior are "remembered," not through some storage of images or ideas in the brain, but in what he calls "morphic fields." He bases his theory on the notion of "morphogenetic fields" well known in developmental biology as a means to explain how identical cells in an embryo take on different characters according to their location within the organism—becoming differentiated as muscle cells, bone cells, nerve cells, etc. The "memories" that guide this differentiation cannot be coded in the DNA, since bone, muscle, and nerve cells all have the same DNA. According to the well-established notion of morphogenetic ("form-generating") fields, the location of the cell within the energy-field of the embryo determines its destiny as a particular kind of tissue cell (Sheldrake, 1988, pp. 78–81).

Sheldrake has extended the notion of mophogenetic fields on the model of the several fields postulated in physics: the electron-positron field, the proton-antiproton field, the gravitational field, etc. Physics is the only science to have multiplied the number and types of fields present in nature to explain how the "building blocks" of matter and energy are related to one another. Sheldrake sees no reason why such fields need to be limited to subatomic particles and star clusters. It seems reasonable to him that everything in nature may be organized by fields—chemical bonds, crystals, proteins, cells, tissues, whole organisms, and even societies of individuals (Sheldrake, 1988, pp. 115–134).

In consciousness, for example, if the brain is thought of on analogy with the circuitry of a television receiver, the morphic fields would correspond to the programs it receives on its various channels. We "tune" ourselves to these fields and pick up organized patterns of thinking, imagining, and behavior. Morphic (i.e., "form-giving") fields have been established by the course of evolution in the universe. This includes everything from subatomic particles to the arrangement of the galaxies, although Sheldrake is most interested in the appearance and development of life forms in biological evolution, as well as guiding ideas in the evolution of consciousness.

> All organisms are structures of activity, and at every level of organization they undergo rhythmic oscillations, vibrations, periodic movements, or cycles. In atoms and molecules, the electrons are in ceaseless vibratory movement within their orbitals; large molecules such as proteins wobble and undulate with characteristic frequencies. Cells contain innumerable vibrating molecular structures, their biochemical and physiological activities exhibit patterns of oscillation, and the cells themselves go through cycles of division. Plants show daily and seasonal cycles of activity; animals wake and sleep, and within them hearts beat, lungs breathe, and intestines contract in rhythmic waves. The nervous system is rhythmic in its functioning, and the brain is swept by recurrent waves of electrical activity. When animals move, they do so by means of repetitive cycles of activity, as in the wriggling of a worm, the walking of a centipede, the swimming of a shark, the flying of a pigeon, the galloping of a horse. We ourselves go through many such cycles of activity, for example in our chewing, walking, cycling, swimming, and copulating (Sheldrake, 1988, pp. 108–109).

According to Sheldrake's theory of "formative causation," new structures and new individuals "resonate" in their multiple vibratory dimensions with long-established patterns "remembered" in the morphic fields. The past organizes the present, as a developing embryo is "tuned in" to the fields of its species. There are morphic fields that organize molecules, cells, tissues, organs, and entire organisms, as well as societies of individual organisms within a given species. Higher-order fields organize groups of lower-order fields in "nested hierarchies," so that the field for the entire body organizes the separate fields governing the organs, and so on down to the proteins and the subatomic particles. Occasionally a "leap" is made and a new form of organism or a new form of behavior appears. When the new form is better adapted to its environment than an old one, its probability of surviving to influence subsequent individuals is enhanced (Sheldrake, 1988, pp. 283–285).

Sheldrake's theory is not defended with mathematical proof. However, he does make a case that it accounts for an organizing aspect of reality that biologists, chemists, and students of behavior have been puzzling over for centuries. He gives a multitude of examples from various scientific disciplines that seem to support his theory, and he points out that his views are harmonious with David Bohm's physics-based theory of an "implicate" or "folded up" order of existence which becomes "unfolded" or "explicate" when it appears to the senses (Sheldrake, 1988, pp. 303–306). Bohm's theory (*Wholeness and the Implicate Order*, 1980) also lies outside the mainstream of scientific thinking, but incorporates what is known in physics and can even be defended with mathematical equations. Bohm, in fact, has accepted Sheldrake's claim that the two of them are working on a similar explanatory principle.

Thus, there may be some credible grounds for something like a "Hundredth Monkey" phenomenon. The New Age myth is surely a high-order morphic field that includes, "nested" within it, near-death journeys, shamanism, encounters with alien species from mermaids to angels and spacemen, aura reading, and channeling. Like all morphic fields, it has a history. We have noted the minor changes it has undergone from ancient Gnosticism through *merkabah* ascents to the Throne, the *mi'raj* of Muhammad, alchemy, and the Ghost Dance. Across many centuries and cultures, people have "tuned in" to the morphic field in which humans take on the appearance of a luminous egg and discover a journeyer who is their greater self and a compass which points the way to the One.

Following Sheldrake, we might say that the New Age is not the sudden appearance of a new activity, like potato-washing among the monkeys. New Agers are more like the blue tits of Holland in 1947 or 1948 when milk bottles reappeared on Dutch porches in the morning. They knew exactly what those bottles contained and how to open them, even though they had not been seen for generations. The tits did not know *how* they knew, they just knew. Involuntarily, they "tuned in" to the morphic field of milk-stealing, as though they had always done it.

The Ghost Dancers also must have been "tuned in" to an established morphic field—no doubt, the same one that swept Black Elk off his feet some two decades earlier. Indeed, because it was a vision of the end of time, the resurrection of the body, the coming of a New Heaven and New Earth, it may very well be that the Ghost Dance was a "tuning in" to a morphic field long-established in the invading culture of Europe. Perhaps the settlers and cavalry entered the West like aliens, bringing terror, destruction, and a new take on cosmic consciousness.

What Sheldrake has to say about morphic fields is very similar to what we have already concluded about the archetypal structure of the *imagining* psyche. Archetypes and morphic fields are *shared* forms. They manifest cultural and individual differences which we have ascribed to the differing schemata that derive from the conscious life experience unique to each society and individual.

What Sheldrake contributes to our view, in the first place, is that the human imagination is not unique in nature, but that everything, from subatomic particles to the human brain, is organized by structuring forms. To imagine is to "tune in" directly to these structuring fields. Moreover, as the blue tit example shows, even sensory experience has an imagining component. Those bottles of white liquid have to be *seen as* sources of nourishment that can be opened, somewhat as bark is stripped from trees to reveal the insects crawling underneath. When the bottles are no longer mysterious objects belonging to an alien species, they are *seen as* a vital part of the blue tit world.

In much the same way, for humans to enter the greater cosmos is to encounter the vital significance of the *imaginal*. The world of imagination is no longer merely the source of fanciful and trivial tales suitable for children's bedtime reading. To enter cosmic consciousness is to appropriate the *imaginal* world as a foundational reality in my own life. I *see* the *imaginal* as the greater field of my existence within which the sensory world is a much smaller domain.

In another sense, "tuning in" to the morphic field of the New Age is not at all like "tuning in" to potato-washing or milk-stealing. The skills the animals acquired only added another tool to their toolbox. The New Age asks us to abandon the toolbox and take up a whole new line of work. Out-of-body journeyers and alien abductees have not merely added an ingenious new behavior to their everyday lives. They have been shaken to their foundations. Reality has been called into question by unthinkable experiences. What these New Age pathfinders have *seen* has thrown them into an "animal panic." They worried they were going mad, risked having their souls devoured, faced immanent death, or at best were reduced to the status of polar bears in electronic collars. The New Age imagines not merely a few new practices that can be added to our everyday lives, but rather the outright destruction of our most cherished internal monologs.

MＯRPHIC FIELDJ AND THE NEW AGE MYTH

Sheldrake makes a second contribution to our understanding of human imagination. Although our public consensus over the last 400 years has seen imagination as a strictly personal and arbitrary dimension of psychic life, the concept of morphic fields reveals that the universal forms of imagination are *shared*. They do not belong to the "hard wiring" of our DNA or the neural circuits of our brain, but resemble more the "software" that "programs" our "hard wiring" (Sheldrake's analogy). We have to go to a computer store and buy the software programs that enable our computers to process words, organize our finances, or play video games. Furthermore, the word processing program that allows me to write this book is the same one that enables my neighbor to write advertising copy or business letters. There are only a few of these programs that we as a society own and can "tune in" to when we need to perform certain tasks.

Our public consensus, too, is a shared set of programs or imaginal fields. Although we generally assume that our society's "programs" are learned by conscious modeling and imitation, as they surely must be, Sheldrake's theory of morphic fields implies that it may also be the case that they are simply there and that we can "tune in" to them unconsciously without having first learned them in any conscious manner. To be born into a particular society would be like buying a computer that has already been programmed with word processing and gaming software. No doubt we have to learn how to use these programs by trial and error, reading our computer manuals, and calling the 800 number for "software support." "Software" like the American dream is held jointly by all who live in this society. We may use it differently than our neighbor does. We may be dissatisfied with it and on the look-out for a program that serves our needs better. But it is a social fact as inescapable as the Microsoft Works that Packard Bell programmed into the computer I purchased. I do not use it, because I found a better program, but it is there if I should ever decide I want it.

Many people who buy a preprogrammed computer never question the software with which they have been provided. Not knowing that more powerful programs are available, they stick with what they have. They may grumble sometimes, but it never occurs to them to seek out something better. In the same way, most members of any given society never seriously challenge the public consensus. They just live within this socially sanctioned worldview as though it is simply the way things are. Down through the ages, however, there have been individuals and counter-cultural communities that have "tuned in" to morphic fields that were unthinkable to their contemporaries.

Black Elk was evidently such an individual. In his grandparents' generation, it was possible for the Lakota to live their entire lives without ever encountering a white American. But by the time of his birth, the public consensus was in crisis. As a very young boy, Black Elk must have been semi-consciously aware that the Lakota lifestyle was in trouble. Some deeper source of meaning was required. He "tuned in" to this deeper, mythic field of the Lakota world unconsciously and, as a result, experienced unthinkable *imaginal* events, Thunder Beings in the form of luminous men descending from the clouds like arrows to tell him they had a mission for him.

His great vision, as compelling and transcendently meaningful as it evidently was, only increased his alienation from relatives and neighbors still stuck in the traditional Lakota consensus. He felt as much on the brink of madness as John Mack's patients or Whitley Strieber, and was able to rejoin his community only after the old shaman, Black Road, had identified what was "wrong" with him. He had "tuned in" to the morphic field of shamanism.

Once the nature of his experiences had been named and legitimated, he could begin to search for a way to employ them. Before that moment, it was as if he had tapped into an unknown and very powerful program in his computer and wondered why the screen changed so drastically at the touch of a single key. Black Road's understanding of these events alerted him to the presence of something like a graphics program that most people never find. Once it had been identified, he could begin to explore its rules and learn what capabilities it gave him.

The morphic field of shamanism is accessible to us all. It is a single field within the larger set of morphic fields we have been calling cosmic consciousness. They are the forms of *imaginal* experience, a set of "software programs," which remain unconscious to most people. The legend of the Hundred Monkeys implies that the New Age believes we can all learn to gain access to these fields and train ourselves to use them. If the

New Age is right about this, it envisages a radical change in our understanding of ourselves. Such a perspective has been unknown to the human race since our pre-Taurean ancestors. Over the course of Aries and
Pisces, cosmic consciousness and shamanism have become the province
of the few rather than the many.

In classical accounts of shamanism, such as Eliade's *Shamanism:
Archaic Techniques of Ecstasy* (1964), shamans are understood to constitute
an elite within their preliterate societies. Each community was limited to
one or two experts in the "techniques of ecstasy," individuals who had an
exceptional ability to leave their bodies and travel through the greater
cosmos in order to recover and restore the souls of those who had fallen
ill or to conduct the souls of the dead to the world of the after-life. These
few experts were not only favored by the spirits in undergoing a frightening "election" that subjected them to a dismemberment and restructuring that gave them the skill and power for out-of-body sojourns, but
they also underwent years of instruction and training which developed
and honed their new powers and provided them with an alternate explanation of the world. They left the everyday public consensus of the
hunters, gatherers, and planters of their community and learned to visit
the mythic world that gave their society its ultimate description and
deepest meaning. They became members of a very small elite who
learned how to find and use the pathways between the everyday fleshly
world and the greater cosmos.

If this classical view of shamanism is employed to understand what
is happening in the New Age, the myth we have uncovered will always
be the province of a very small elite. In fact, it appears that this elitism
describes our present situation very well. Aura manipulators like Barbara Brennan and the energy healers she has trained are specialists, experts in a technique that most of us have not developed and for which
we may have no special talent. Similarly, Michael Harner (*The Way of the
Shaman,* 1980) is training people in a kind of urban shamanism that is
again the province of an elite. Only those specially talented and trained
are able to restore lost souls or soul-fragments. Those of us who believe
we may profit from such alternate healing techniques are required to
seek out the experts and place ourselves in their hands.

Although these are surely manifestations of the New Age myth,
they seem to envision a hierarchical society, with a talented elite at the
top corresponding to the "spirit people" of ancient Gnosticism. Hopeful
believers who are less talented flock to workshops to learn more about
cosmic issues which they have merely "heard about" and not yet experi-

enced as incidents of "power" in their own lives. Perhaps they will be healed. Perhaps their consciousness will be raised. They are the "soul people" of the New Age. Inevitably, however, the vast majority remain ignorant of these things, going about their everyday lives as "flesh people," acting within morphic fields that belong more to the world of survival panic than to a myth founded on cosmic consciousness.

If we were to describe the very ancient morphic field that makes shamanism possible, we would have to include at least two factors. First would be a technique for entering an altered state of consciousness that is mythic. In this state, the shaman transcends the limitations of space, time, and our fleshly existence and gains access to a greater cosmos, generally stratified into one or a series of "upper worlds" located vaguely in the heavens and another one or more "lower worlds" sojourned *imaginally* beneath the surface of the Earth.

But a shaman is more than a sojourner. Shamanism requires a soul-to-soul connection between the expert practitioner and the sick or deceased individual who is being helped. The shaman has to be familiar with the soul of the patient, for, if the soul cannot be recognized, it cannot be found. Indeed the shaman's ability to *see* soul is essential at every stage of the process. The diagnosis that the soul is missing from a sick individual implies that the shaman be able to *see* the patient as suffering a grievous lack. Upon leaving her fleshly body, the shaman has to be able to "feel" the missing soul, to know which direction to take in order to find it, and to have some way of grasping it in order to bring it back. Pursuit of the missing soul requires some kind of connection between the empowered soul of the shaman and the lost or straying soul of the patient.

The morphic field of shamanism, therefore, involves at least these two factors: a familiarity with the greater cosmos and the techniques for negotiating it, and an ability to use his own soul to connect with the soul of the patient. Indeed, classic accounts of shamanic activities that have resulted in a failure to heal generally involve the shaman's inability to "find" or to "connect" with the patient's soul. A shaman who can *see* that the patient's soul is missing but cannot acquire a "feel" for where that soul may be will surely declare the patient's prognosis to be hopeless.

Having described the morphic field of shamanism in this manner, we might ask ourselves whether it is necessary also to assert that an ability to enter cosmic consciousness and connect with another individual's soul has to be limited to a very small elite. Surely, the Hundredth Monkey legend implies that the New Age does not believe the shamanic field is so limited. Moreover, there is anthropological evidence that gives some credence to this New Age hope. The !Kung[2] people of Africa, for example, employ the morphic field of shamanism in a more egalitarian manner. Marjorie Shostak (*Nisa: The Life and Words of a !Kung Woman*, 1981, pp. 291–292) tells a rather classical story of how a !Kung shaman restored the soul of a woman who was critically ill. The shaman traveled to the lower world and found the woman's soul cradled in the arms of her dead father. There, he persuaded the soul of the deceased man to allow his daughter's soul to return to her body so that she could live out her full life before joining him in the greater cosmos. The shaman brought back the soul, and the woman was restored to health. A people who tell a story of this kind have surely incorporated the morphic field of shamanism in their understanding of the world.

For the !Kung, however, this is a rather exceptional tale, for their healing ceremonies generally involve, not a single expert who sojourns out-of-body in search of a lost soul, but rather an entire community that enters cosmic consciousness. Although some individuals are recognized to be more gifted than others, everyone participates in healing ceremonies that involve singing, clapping, and dancing for hours on end; and everyone enters an altered state of consciousness. In fact, it may be precisely this communal aspect that gives their healing efforts effectiveness. The shamanic morphic field is "tuned in" collectively. Using Sheldrake's analogy of the television receiver, we may speculate that, when everyone in a community participates, the channel between the brains of the dancers and the shamanic morphic field is strengthened. The !Kung articulate what they are doing in these ceremonies by speaking of a natural but invisible soul energy they call *n/um*. They enter trance in order to gather *n/um* and impart it to those in the community who are sick.

According to Richard Katz's !Kung informants (*Boiling Energy: Community Healing Among the Kalahari Kung*, 1982), sickness results from soul-loss, when "arrows" of soul-energy "pop out of the body and go out into space." The healer (i.e., anyone in the community, but especially one who has a particular talent) accumulates *n/um* while dancing the trance dance. *N/um* becomes palpable in the sweat of entranced healers, and they rub the soul "arrows" back into the sick individual's body with hands moistened in their own sweat. "When we do that, your breath and soul return properly to your body. But if we

---

2   The unusual marks that appear in such words as *!Kung* and *n/um* refer to spoken "clicks" incorporated in the !Kung language.

don't do that, then you might die" (Katz, 1982, p. 214). The healer's state of being is also enhanced in the process. The enhancement comes at some risk, however; for their "souls leave their bodies," and they "may die and not come back" (Katz, 1982, pp. 160, 45). Kau Dwa, a blind man renowned for his healing talents, says that God keeps his eyeballs in a cloth bag. When he dances, God lowers the bag and, when the trance gets strong enough, God returns the eyeballs to his sockets (Katz, 1982, p. 216).

> "At a dance, when people sing and clap, I see everybody. When the women sing, I can see everything [the people who need healing and] even if there's a snake crawling through the bush out in the dark. I say to everybody, 'There's a snake crawling through the bush. Watch out for it.' . . . When I look out to the bush, I can see a lion making low growling sounds, far away. I can see his face very clearly. . . . And the lion sees me, it sees me too. When it sees my face, it lowers its head to the ground."

> [Katz]: "What if people say, 'Bullshit'?"

> "There are people who say that. Then later on they see the tracks of the animal and say, 'Kau Dwa was right'" (Katz, 1982, pp. 216–217).

Evidently, the !Kung healing trance represents a classic case of cosmic consciousness, for Kau Dwa not only *sees* and "feels" soul and its fragments (the "arrows") and knows how to manipulate them to restore the health of the patient, he also enjoys clairvoyant *sight*. He *sees* accurately in what Monroe calls "Locale I," the ordinary world of space and time. It is a "right-brain" mode of experience, for while consciousness is enhanced with *n/um*, "no thoughts are in your head" (Katz, 1982, p. 202). Kau Dwa *sees* what is invisible to the fleshly eyes he no longer has—a snake crawling through the bush in the dark and a lion that is apparently so far away that fleshly eyes would be unable to see it in daylight. He *sees* its face so clearly that he must have made an out-of-body journey. In trance, he *sees imaginally* what is inaccessible to the fleshly eyes he has lost.

If the morphic field of shamanism can be shared by an entire community of !Kung, New Age hopes for a monumental change in consciousness that will be shared by the whole world may not be impossible. That morphic field is there for anyone to "tune in" to. It must be noted, however, that the !Kung represent one of the best instances of a people that has preserved something very close to Taurean consciousness in an apparently unbroken line down to the 20th century. They are a relatively unstratified people and recognize very little specialization from individual to individual. The hierarchical arrangement of classes that has dominated the majority of humankind from the Age of Aries to the present is pretty much unknown among them. Thus they may represent an excellent model for the Global Village.

By contrast, however, they also reveal how far from that ideal of equality and oneness with the greater cosmos those of us in the industrial world presently are. For us to embrace the morphic fields that govern the public consensus of the !Kung would require vast disruptions in everything we have come to know about ourselves and about the world we have been inhabiting for millennia. Anyone of us who was thrust into the !Kung world without warning would surely undergo a monumental shock. No doubt, we would eventually learn there was a community of support for such a worldview, but in the meantime we would find ourselves as shattered by the experience as those who have encountered aliens or been thrust out of their bodies as Monroe was. We might find with time that our eyes were opened to cosmic realities that provide a sense of meaning that would render the industrial world as drab and meaningless by comparison as the Woman Who Lived on the Moon claimed it to be. But we would reach that stage only through a serious reality crisis that would involve everything we have taken for granted our whole life long.

PSYCHOTIC PROCESS

Clearly, there are two sorts of morphic fields that organize our social life. We might call them the "wild" and the "tame," as Sheldrake does. The disruptive and shattering experience that so many people report upon involuntary entry into cosmic consciousness reveals the wild field. The fright inspired by this reality crisis might be compared to what an unassuming computer programmer would surely feel if he were to step outside his office one day and find himself suddenly in the Amazon jungle. He would be confronted with new and dangerous forms of life and have no idea how to protect himself. Furthermore, he would be correct in guessing that the dangers he could see were trivial compared to those he could not. All the *imaginal* forms that lie outside the reality with which we have familiarized ourselves belong to the wild and dangerous morphic fields.

On the other hand, there is a set of *imaginal* forms that we have tamed. These are the morphic fields that comprise our public consensus. We incorporate them in our internal monologs, talk to ourselves about them constantly, and use them to maintain our everyday world. They are open to public debate. Even as we live within them, we can discuss with one another such social themes as the American dream, free trade, Social Security, or the drug problem. We may disagree on the details of these issues, but we have no doubt they describe aspects of the "real world." There are dangers like automobile accidents, being fired from our jobs, and even drive-by shootings; but they are as familiar to us as potholes in the spring and thunderstorms in summer.

The vast majority of us believe the tame realm of public consensus is the only world there is. We use our internal monologs defensively to maintain the barriers that keep out the wild dangers of the cosmic jungle and the enchanted lake. But evidence seems to be accumulating that our public consensus is in trouble. More and more people are falling outside the mainstream. Those on welfare are scorned and resented. Our homeless population has attained alarming numbers. A sizable "drug culture" fails to contribute to our common life and indeed supports itself with robbery and theft. More and more people have lost faith in the ability of government to find solutions, some going so far as to arm themselves for the civil anarchy they feel is immanent.

The New Age is not oblivious to such facts, but may be unrealistic about the solution. It imagines a Global Village of peace, harmony, and brotherhood that will be attained as soon as a "critical mass" of humanity has discovered and learned to utilize the wild morphic fields that belong to cosmic consciousness. Those of us who stand at the gate of the New Age may well be skeptical of such hopes. We know that the survival world is awfully compelling and not easily relinquished, and that those like Monroe and Strieber, who have begun to see it for what it is, have had to wrestle with themselves for decades. We may not doubt that the New Age issues a call to each individual to bring the fleshly ego into line with the journeyer. But we wonder whether the New Age can ever be a blueprint for social change.

When we consider the array of morphic fields available to us humans, the tame fields of the public consensus resemble society's ego and the wild fields its unconscious. The Industrial Revolution represented a disturbing change for society's "ego." On the one side, there were new jobs and new aspirations. On the other, there were overcrowding, poverty, pollution, tuberculosis, and lawlessness, to name but a few of the problems. The process of changing society's conscious attitude about itself (its "ego") was long and difficult. New notions of fairness had to be found—not just imposed, but discovered as morphic fields to which the majority could "tune" itself. We are still working on the problems of industrialism, as current wrangling over "protecting the environment" shows.

Western society has been struggling for more than 200 years to adapt its "ego-attitude" to tame a new set of morphic fields in response to the crisis caused by industrialization. Because this lengthy development is typical of a normal process of adapting our social "ego," the sudden transformation that enthusiastic New Agers expect seems unduly hopeful and naive. The process of social change, therefore, is not so different from the individual process of changing one's ego-attitude. It is normally slow and gradual. People enter therapy to hurry up the process and are often not disappointed, but it still may take an individual several years to revise a set of internal monologs to better meet social requirements on the one hand and internal pressures on the other.

The slowness of such changes reflects the degree of attachment we have to old monolog themes (morphic fields). Our habitual monologs were developed to solve problems in our past and cannot generally be abandoned or revised until we truly appreciate their implications and the fact that they are no longer serving us well. Society is in very much the same boat. The old themes of our public consensus are hard to relinquish, regardless of how poorly they have been serving us recently, simply because the devil we know is preferable to the devil we have not met. We cling to long-established morphic fields out of fear that, without them, we will not be able to handle the survival issues that they have been addressing for perhaps centuries.

We may occasionally hear stories of individuals who made an overnight transformation of some sort in their ego-attitude. But these incidents are very rare and, even when they happen, the individual generally requires years of adjustment until the new morphic fields are fully tamed and effective. Christianity and Islam represent movements of monumental social change based upon a new religious guiding idea—not so different, perhaps, from what the New Age imagines. But these transformations, too, required centuries to effect and, in the process, caused large-scale disruptions and dissent. Even after fifteen or twenty centuries, their original hopes have not been fully realized.

Psychiatrist John Weir Perry has discovered a typical sort of process in individual transformation that involves a radical change in ego-attitude over the course of months rather than years (*The Far Side of Madness*, 1974). This may be the best model to describe the kind of social change envisioned by the New Age, but it is not a comforting prospect. Perry calls it "psychotic process."

In Perry's view, schizophrenia is the psyche's natural response to a woefully inadequate ego whose internal monologs are failing in nearly every respect. Faced with repeated disasters and impotence in daily living, the schizophrenic abandons these tame morphic fields abruptly and enters a kaleidoscopic world governed by the unregulated and wild morphic fields of the archetypal imagination. Drastic disorientation and panic results—significantly more shattering than the encounters with aliens we have examined (Perry, 1974, pp. 5–11).

Perry's approach stands well outside the mainstream of psychiatric attitudes to schizophrenia. In his view, psychotic process is so frightening to those of us who are sane that we cannot bear to contemplate it. We want to shut it down as quickly as possible, generally by prescribing "anti-psychotic" medication to silence the voices schizophrenics hear and to halt the frightening flood of wild images. This shutting-down response teaches the psychotic individual to have as much distrust for his process as we have. The reorganizing process is halted, and the unfortunate individual is trapped in an impossible no-man's land between madness and sanity (Perry, 1974, pp. 1–4).

In an attempt to remedy this regrettable situation, Perry selected a group of young schizophrenics (around 20 years-old) who were experiencing their first encounter with psychosis and who had never been exposed to the repressive policies of the mainstream mental health community (Perry, 1974, p. 25). He trained his assistants to trust the psychotic process: to listen with empathy and support to what the schizophrenics had to say about what was happening to them and to maintain an attitude that the process was meaningful and would effect a beneficial outcome (Perry, 1974, pp. 154–157). What Perry and his team discovered was that, in each case, the schizophrenics "tuned in" to an ancient morphic field that derived from the Age of Aries. It is a process of deposing an old king and installing a new one. Perry has assembled an anthology of these ancient myths from several different cultures, all of them variations on the theme of renewing kingship (*Lord of the Four Quarters*, 1970). For the schizophrenic individual, the "old king" is the inadequate ego-attitude that has failed, and the "new king" represents a new ego-attitude that emerges from a sojourn in the wild morphic fields of the archetypal imagination.

There are typically several stages in "psychotic process": a return to the center which resembles the Gnostic's compass of *gnosis*; death by torture, dismemberment, or poisoning, which resembles the shaman's initiation; a return to the beginnings to witness the creation of the world or Garden of Eden, a theme that is similar to the experiences of Monroe and the messages of the channelers; cosmic conflict, an Armageddon-like battle between the forces of darkness and the forces of light which is also common to the channelers; a threat of opposites, generally a fear of the opposite sex, which suggests the experience of abductees who report a frightening but fascinating alien guide of the opposite sex; an apotheosis as royalty or divinity ("I'm Jesus Christ"), an experience New Agers report as discovering their identity as beings of light or "part alien"; a sacred marriage, the union of the opposites feared in stage five, which abductees report as having an alien lover; a new birth, the offspring of the divine marriage, a new savior of the world, corresponding to abductee reports that they are producing a race of hybrid children who will be the new inhabitants of the Earth; a new society, a utopian social order, the New Heaven and New Earth theme that predominates in New Age social aspirations; and a quadrated world, the goal of the process, an orderly worldview seen as a mandala that represents a tamed morphic field to govern the new ego-attitude (Perry, 1974, pp. 28–30).

The parallels between New Age experience and psychotic process are astounding. Perhaps we should have expected this, since the underlying structure is the same in both cases. Both the schizophrenic and the New Ager are dissatisfied with the tame morphic fields that organize our attitudes as individuals and as a society. Both have unconsciously hit upon the same radical solution, namely to abandon those tired and ineffectual fields and plunge into the shattering wilderness, where everything is topsy-turvy, where unthinkable beings confront us with overwhelming power. Both expose themselves to the dangers of a madness from which they may never return. Schizophrenics have had no choice in this matter. Their weak egos have simply suffered shipwreck. But something very similar has happened to the near-death journeyers, the alien abductees, and those the spirits have favored with a shamanic dismemberment.

The "spirit people" of the New Age, like the mystics, shamans, and schizophrenics, have been shattered. Those who have survived to tell their stories and serve us all as pathfinders have fared far better than the general run of schizophrenics. Despite advances in therapy and biochemistry, the dreary statistics on schizophrenia have not changed in a hundred years: a third recover after a single psychotic break, a third undergo repeated psychotic episodes with periods of sanity in between, and a third become chronic. New Age pathfinders are a sturdy lot. They have entered a greater cosmos, with its wild morphic fields, and tamed them sufficiently to become superior individuals. Many, like Monroe and Strieber, obviously possessed a relatively strong and flexible ego structure before their unthinkable experiences began. Betty Eadie has become a new woman. After some years of confusion, Dannion Brinkley has been able to relinquish his defensive posture as an assassin and learn compassion.

As long as we stick to the essential structure of the New Age myth— the fact that it is an individual call to bring one's fleshly ego into line with one's own journeyer—it describes a cogent and compelling way of life. The myth is remarkably realistic. It recognizes that not everyone is ready for such a call. It assumes that a fleshly life in the survival world of this planet is a kind of schooling in which many lifetimes may be required before one's journeyer has forgotten sufficiently and remembered enough that it may be encountered directly. According to the New Age myth, there is nothing shameful in requiring additional life-long visits to the world of space and time. Each being of light is on its own quest and must be allowed its own good time.

New Age enthusiasts who want to turn this individual calling into a requirement for everyone living on the planet, however, present us with a very frightening future. They imagine a "downloading of wisdom" into a magic number of "monkeys" that within the space of months or a very few years will result in a utopian Global Village. They imagine psychotic process on a global scale. No doubt this *would* occasion a kind of Armageddon battle. On the one side would stand, not so much the forces of evil and darkness, as a frightened and inexperienced cavalry, clinging in panic to tame but failing morphic fields, justifying them no doubt with fervent appeals to our traditional scriptures. They would be sure that God was on their side and that the New Agers were the minions of Satan. On the other side, the New Age Ghost Dancers, the self-described forces of light and love, might well be proud to call themselves "systems busters" and a "Universal Council of Light," but they would be betraying the myth of the New Age by the very fact of their joining battle.

When John Perry's schizophrenics describe their proud but trembling role as the vanguard in a world-wide battle against communism or Nazism, we have no difficulty in perceiving that they are suffering from delusions. No doubt they are meaningful delusions, for they are describing internal battles, part of the re-arrangement taking place between the wild morphic fields of their archetypal imagination as they search for a new "king" to govern their conscious attitudes. Taken as a description of what is going on "inside" of them, this Armageddon image is not a delusion at all, but a statement of fact. What is delusional about it is their conviction that the internal upheaval is taking place in the social world, the planet inhabited by Americans, Russians, and Germans. Their seeing it as an "outside" battle, we call "projection." They have taken their internal battle and "projected" it out upon the world of space and time. In this sense, they are as mad as the Woman Who Lived on the Moon—and just as in need of a sympathetic ear.

We can hardly avoid the suspicion that literal-minded New Age hopes for an overnight transformation of the Earth are also projections. They have mistaken what is no more—and no less—than a call to make peace with their own journeyers and to begin the work of taming the wild morphic fields of cosmic consciousness, for an interplanetary summons to the entire human race. In one sense, they are not wrong. For, according to the New Age myth, we are *all* called, even though some of us will require several more lifetimes before we are ready to hear the voice. The New Age myth is patient. The Age of Aquarius is some 2200 years long. Raising the consciousness of a "critical mass" is very likely to be a slow process. The Ghost Dance failed because it imagined too much and overwhelmed its patience with frenzy. The 1939 World's Fair failed because it imagined too little. The New Age had better avoid both suits and ties and Ghost Shirts[3] if it is to avoid the devils we know all too well.

---

[3] The Ghost Dancers wore animal-skin shirts decorated with paintings inspired by their visions.

Chapter

11

THE RAINBOW BRIDGE TO THE PROMISED AGE

On the fourth day after death the soul [of the Zoroastrian man] has to cross the bridge, called Chinvat, which connects this world with the unseen world. . . . It seems to [the righteous soul] as if his own conscience were advancing to him . . . in the shape of a maiden, fair, bright, of white arms, courageous, beautiful, tall, with prominent breasts, beautiful of body, noble, of glorious birth, of fifteen years, and of a form as fair as the fairest of creatures.

(MASANI, 1968, P. 73)

Man is a rope, tied between beast and overman—a rope over an abyss.

(NIETZSCHE, 1994, VOL II, P. 281)

I stared at the bridge of fog, dumbfounded. And then I either lifted myself to its level, or the bridge lowered itself to mine. Suddenly I was looking at a straight beam in front of me. It was an immensely long, solid beam, narrow and without railings, but wide enough to walk on.

• • •

"There are worlds upon worlds, right here in front of us. And they are nothing to laugh at. Last night if I hadn't grabbed your arm you would have walked on that bridge whether you wanted to or not."

(CASTANEDA, 1972, PP. 157, 166)

Anthropologist Hank Wesselman began having spontaneous out-of-body experiences in 1983. Like Monroe, Cayce, and most of the near-death journeyers, abductees, and aura readers, he had had a number of extraordinary psychic experiences earlier in his life, particularly while on a "dig" in the African Rift Valley (Wesselman, 1995, pp. 18–20). He had seen these earlier episodes as unexplainable exceptions to "real life" and paid them relatively little attention. Between 1983 and 1986, however, a series of powerful and related sojourns in what Monroe would call "Locale III" (this planet in an unfamiliar place or time, attained only by fusing with a specific individual in that foreign dreamscape) have led Wesselman into a process of spiritual growth that he sees as crucial to his understanding of himself and of human existence in general. He has written an account of this learning process in *Spiritwalker* (1995).

Just as Monroe entered the life of a specific individual (the failed architect-contractor) in Locale III, so Wesselman has been entering the life of an Hawaiian historian named Nainoa. Wesselman was living in Hawaii at the time of his first journeys and has since acquired a small coffee farm there. He has a strong affinity for Hawaii and its indigenous culture and has come to understand his experiences in Hawaiian terms. Hawaiian shamanism has a somewhat more elaborate psychology of altered states of consciousness than what we have considered in this book, but it agrees in all essential respects. The human being is seen as comprised of body, soul (Wesselman says "mind"), and spirit. He calls his journeyer *ku* and sees the goal of this mysticism as learning and becoming oriented through spirit (*aumakua*) in a greater cosmos. Whether or not there is a "One" at the center of this cosmos is unknown to Wesselman, Nainoa, and Nainoa's shaman/mentor, William (Wesselman, 1995, pp. 161–165; 171–176).

Spiritwalker is a vivid and intelligent account of shamanic journeying by an individual drawn into this path by forces greater than his own fleshly ego, but it so much agrees in its tentative conclusions with everything we have seen that it makes little sense to consider the book in detail. Except for one uncomfortable fact. Hank Wesselman believes he is *seeing* the future. Nainoa lives on the North American continent some 5000 years *after* us. Wesselman's sojourns take him to what New Agers might call a "simultaneous future life." Hank does not rule out the possibility that Nainoa may be a subsequent incarnation of his own journeyer, but he calls Nainoa his "descendant," and Nainoa refers to him as his "ancestor."

As a reader of this series of adventures in alternate reality, I cannot suppress the suspicion that the journeys might better be understood as *symbolic* events rather than a literal foray into the future of the planet. Understood symbolically, the truth of Wesselman's journeying lies in its being a vehicle for his own personal encounter with and development of cosmic consciousness. There are too many convenient parallels between these two lives separated by 5000 years—the fact, for example, that both Hank and Nainoa are impressed by the uncanny physical and psychological resemblances between their respective wives, or the fact that Nainoa is exploring an area of present day Nevada where Hank grew up (Wesselman, 1995, pp. 231–233, 220). This latter detail resembles a suspicious element in my own shamanic journeying, the fact that I am always taken to a long, curved, mountain-lined lake that resembles the Lake of Zurich, sometime in prehistory when its environs were inhabited by animals and not people. Such parallels remind me of Monroe's architect-contractor and how easy it is to see that social misfit as personifying Monroe's unresolved issues. I cannot rule out a similar factor in Wesselman's adventures, or indeed my own.

Nevertheless, the "future" hypothesis is worth considering, if only because it diverges so radically from what New Agers would like us to believe. Wesselman agrees with the near-death experiencers and abductees that the Earth stands now, at the end of the second millennium of Pisces, on the brink of catastrophe. However, he makes no appeals to his readers to mend their ways. He does not believe Nainoa has been called out of the future to warn us of what we are doing to our planet. He is much more fatalistic than that. He has *seen* five millennia into the future of the Earth and encountered a new Stone Age!

By reading Nainoa's mind and participating in his descendant's life through his own *ku*, or journeyer, Wesselman has learned that Nainoa is probably a bastard son of the Hawaiian king of a colony in seventh-millennium California, which is separated from the mainland of North America by a great inland sea (Wesselman, 1995, p. 27). A warrior people is threatening the Hawaiians and Nainoa has been sent by his king to explore the other side of the Rocky Mountains to discover arable land and look for the Americans of legend, as well as their horses (Wesselman, 1995, pp. 104–105), which have become fabulous animals for the Hawaiian settlers in the first quarter of the Age of Sagittarius (A.D. 6600–8800).

On his lonely six-week journey through the mountains, Nainoa is favored by a number of mystical experiences as he "tunes in" to the morphic field of shamanism and learns that he has an ally in the form of a leopard-man and an "ancestor" shaman in the form of Hank. Meanwhile, Wesselman has also been having visionary encounters with a leopard-man and recalls his boyhood affinity for the leopards he saw in zoos (Wesselman, 1995, p. 108).

Upon reaching what is now known as the Washoe Valley in western Nevada, Nainoa's leg is broken by a charging longhorn bull and he is rescued by a nomadic hunter-gatherer people who call themselves the Ennu. Apart from dogs, the Ennu have no domestic animals. They wear ornaments hammered from the soft metal they find in the ruins of our twentieth-century cities (Wesselman, 1995, pp. 201–209). Iron and steel are completely unknown. Even the great I-beams of our superhighways have been reduced to rust streaks in the soil. The great American deserts have become tropical grasslands populated with the animals of present day North America, South America, Africa, and Asia, including great herds of horses, longhorn cattle and elephants, as well as lions and other large cats.[1] The Ennu speak a language closely related to Eskimo tongues and use a large number of words evidently of French derivation (Wesselman, 1995, pp. 255–266).

Wesselman concludes that our Western Machine Age culture has been brought to an end by global warming, the worst-case scenario of our contemporary climatologists. The sea level had risen perhaps 300 feet as the polar ice caps and mountain glaciers melted. Once this process begins (and it may have already begun), the sea level could rise far enough in less than a decade to destroy coastal cities, render ports useless, and end the world-wide distribution of petroleum. Without the fuel to run them, machines would be rendered useless and begin to rust (Wesselman, 1995, pp. 212–219). The only survivors would be those who could work out a subsistence lifestyle. Within a few generations, most of these people would die out due to in-breeding. Hawaiians would have a genetic advantage, given the racial diversity of their island group. Evidently the few nomads living in the great plains in the middle of the continent, the Ennu, represent a sturdy hybrid of Eskimos and French Canadians (Wesselman, 1995, pp. 187–190).

This construction of our future is as plausible as it is alarming. Wesselman goes so far as to speculate that, once the Machine Age is dead, a new Iron Age may be impossible to attain. The Iron Age of our pre-

---

[1] Wesselman speculates that the Asian and African animals have descended from the prisoners of our 20th-century zoos.

history was made possible by ore that was easy to find, but we have used all of that. We have reached the point in the 20th century where we need high-technology machines to *find* hard metals buried deep in the Earth's crust. Thus, iron and steel are necessary to locate and unearth the ore that makes our machines possible. Without machines capable of discovering and mining iron ore, human beings may never again be able to devise the technology we now take for granted. The Machine Age may be a one-time, short-lived occurrence, some two or three hundred years of Golden Age before an irreversible return to our pre-Taurean past.

If Wesselman is indeed *seeing* the future and not just a symbolic representation of the tenuousness of human existence on Spaceship Earth, the Age of Aquarius will have a far different meaning from what New Agers presently suppose. The global-warming scenario lends new significance to the image of the Water Bearer of Aquarius, that man pouring an endless supply of water onto the Earth from a stone jar carried on his shoulder. The much ballyhooed great leap forward may in fact turn out to be a tragic Fall of monumental proportions.

Perhaps the day will never come when cosmic consciousness is integrated with the critical conceptual thinking we have been developing throughout the Age of Pisces. If so, the smug certainty with which Carl Sagan and his like debunk the right-brain irrationality of the New Age may be the ultimate expression of our culture's arrogance (Sagan, 1997). Sagan's search for extraterrestrial radio signals, ostensibly the most "rational" approach to verifying the existence of intelligent life outside our solar system, is predicated upon our culture's assumption that technological progress—implying a Machine Age—is an inherent characteristic of intelligent consciousness. Wesselman's "future," however, questions this myth of progress in a radical manner. For the progress we have known may be the merest flash in a planet's pan.

The future inhabited by the Ennu represents a new beginning for the human race, a new Paleolithic Era, where even the wheel has not yet been rediscovered. Cultural progress for them is not unthinkable. Indeed, the Hawaiian culture from which Nainoa has come represents a "later" development, where society is stratified and writing has been preserved. High cultures like those of ancient Egypt and the Incas would again be possible. But a world driven by electronics and producing radio waves might be impossible. Although the wheel, agriculture, and the domestication of animals, as well as the disciplines of reading, writing, and arithmetic, might easily disseminate from the Hawaiians to the Ennu, the iron and steel necessary for sharp spear points were already rusting relics among the seventh-millennium Hawaiians. Perhaps flaked stone tools will be the best our descendants in the Ages of Capricorn and Sagittarius will be able to produce.

If Wesselman's sojourns into the future of this planet are substantially correct—and we have no stronger grounds for rejecting them than we do for Sagan's more optimistic views—the New Age may have a significance entirely different from what its enthusiastic partisans now imagine. Those of us who have looked into the history of the human psyche are aware that cosmic consciousness is not the evolutionary new development many believe it to be. It is rather a rediscovery, a "tuning in" to what our ancestors took for granted.

We would like to believe that we are "tuning in" to cosmic consciousness because we have finally reached a point where conceptual knowledge based on our five senses has become insufficient for us. Our optimism lays out a future in which we can recover the morphic fields of cosmic consciousness without relinquishing history, philosophy, and science. We hope that mysticism and science can finally be reconciled. For a future like this, the New Age is teaching us what we need to know for the next stage in the progress of human consciousness.

But if Wesselman's vision is not wrong, we are in for a "monumental shock" of an entirely different order. Our New Age flirtation with "non-ordinary" morphic fields could well represent an unconscious attempt to prepare ourselves for a future of unthinkable primitivity. Perhaps we are aware of the immanent deluge much the way dogs and cats are supposed to be alerted to impending earthquakes. If so, there is no escape from the disaster. In such a future Dark Age, human survival may be impossible without the dream-like cosmic consciousness of our distant ancestors. Possibly this is the future for which our New Age workshops are preparing us.

TOMORROW AND THE DAY AFTER

If we are neither on the brink of a new Stone Age nor poised for an evolutionary leap forward, perhaps life will go on as it always has. This would seem to be the most likely hypothesis. Revolutions, wars, new trends in thought, new forms of religion, new styles in art, rediscoveries of forgotten truths and styles of the past: all these things belong to life as we have always known it. When we look at things this way, the New Age loses its millenarian éclat and may be set alongside some of the other enthusiasms of the day.

For example, in recent decades the fastest growing form of religion in the world has been fundamentalist Christianity. At first glance, this may seem to be a massive throw-back to a past we thought we had out-grown. But so is the New Age. Indeed, the New Age takes us further back than Jesus or even Abraham. Although fundamentalist Christians may be as preoccupied with rules as the Aries-conscious priests of the Old Testament, cosmic consciousness is not missing from their experience. The gifted among them heal others by calling down the Holy Spirit while entranced with religious fervor. Others heal by "laying on" their hands, evidently convinced that something invisible, but more powerful than flesh, is being transmitted through those palms and digits. The best of them take no credit for what is accomplished through their efforts, but ascribe the agency to God whose divine Grace simply flows through them like a conduit. Still others are "overtaken by the Spirit" and "speak in tongues." For all these people, Christianity is not a set of propositions to accept the way we agree on the Pythagorean Theorem. Rather, it is something to *experience*. They feel they have begun to shed their flesh and realize the nature of their soul.

Not unrelated to fundamentalist Christianity are the mediumistic religions now growing rapidly in Latin America, the largest among them being Santería. These are all relatives of Haitian Voodoo, that is an amal-gam of Christianity, African tribal religions, and American Indian reli-gions. The central ritual involves the entire worshipping community attaining a trance state, very much like that of the !Kung. Those most talented at "tuning in" to the appropriate morphic field become pos-sessed by one of several spirits described in the theology of the religion. They then take on the distinct and well-codified mannerisms and fig-ures of speech of that spirit to convey a message to the assembled faith-ful. Even those who do not function as mediums experience cosmic consciousness and participate in healings by collectively opening a chan-nel between the worlds of flesh and spirit.

Cosmic consciousness is by no means the exclusive preserve of the New Age. There is a variety of morphic fields "nested" within it. Per-haps the most enthusiastic New Agers will say that fundamentalist Christians and the followers of Santería also belong to the New Age, even if they do not know it. They are preparing the way, adding to the "critical mass" needed to transform us all—the eightieth and ninetieth "monkeys." When enough of us "get it," the Christians and followers of Santería will be able to drop their limiting theologies and sojourn freely through the nested spheres of the greater cosmos. Perhaps they are right. The New Age myth does eschew formulating its own dogmas. It allows a great number of alternate schemata to stand uneasily side-by-side. The issue is not what we believe, but what we have *seen*. On the other hand, the Christians will make a similar claim: if New Agers have really *seen* the Spirit, they will inevitably be led to Christ.

If we are inclined to believe that neither fundamentalist Christianity nor a religion like Santería is apt to convince us all, we might reserve the same doubts for the New Age. After all, movements inspired by cosmic consciousness are very much a part of life as we have always known it. The spiritualism craze of a hundred years ago was one manifestation, the Ghost Dance another, Christian revivalism a third. Two millennia ago Christianity and Gnosticism convinced large numbers of people of the soul as a greater reality than the flesh, and yet the Christianity which became the dominant religio-cultural force in the West has been guided less by cosmic consciousness than by rationally structured theologies and rules of conduct. Very likely, one or more movements inspired by cosmic consciousness has occurred in every century during the much maligned Age of Pisces.

A realistic historical context raises the suspicion that what we now know as the New Age could turn out to be just another fad. It seems that enthusiasms for one or another of the morphic fields "nested" in cosmic consciousness may arise in any generation when an overly rational public consensus has become boring, flat, or too widely questioned. The 50s, for example, was a period of relative security and apathy to which large numbers, especially the youth, reacted radically in the sixties, courting cosmic consciousness by ingesting psychedelic drugs, experimenting with sexuality, and questioning authority. Those least invested in the public consensus of the fifties responded to reports of the "Doors of Perception" being opened with a kind of "Oh, Wow!" Unthinkable possibilities fell within the reach of anyone who could lay hands on a tab of LSD or secure peyote buttons. The heedless among them dreamed of speeding up the "revolution" and "turning on" whole cities by adding large quantities of LSD to the water supplies—evidently a crude, earlier manifestation of the Hundredth Monkey notion.

The excesses, the "bad trips," the deaths from overdoses, the social chaos, and the emergence of AIDS all scared us into the social conservatism of the eighties. Access to cosmic consciousness shifted to group meditations, the rituals of the "New Paganism," workshops designed to foster intuition and healing techniques, and the growth of Christian fundamentalism. These things, too, have inspired an "Oh Wow!" response among the newly converted. A new fad has replaced an old one, and again the future is anticipated with visions of peace, love, and harmony. The Global Village is just around the corner. Cosmic consciousness is available for immediate "downloading" by anyone who cares to participate.

Surely the New Age is not wrong about some of these things. If the history of social movements inclines us to soberly doubt that our earthly societies will all be changed in the twinkling of an eye, the history of human consciousness affirms that cosmic awareness is indeed a universal human capability. Even if it cannot be "downloaded" as easily as we add new texts and graphics to our computers, it can be experienced, explored, and developed. The wild morphic fields *can* be somewhat tamed. They can provide the data that forces us to revise our internal monologs. Direct meetings with our journeyer soul can profoundly influence our lifeworld. It certainly lies within our capability to work with our fleshly ego and to bring it into better harmony with our journeyer. The more we succeed in this endeavor, the more likely it is that our lives will become more meaningful and satisfying. But this requires discipline. We have to pass beyond the "Oh Wow!" and get down to work.

Thirty years ago, R. E. L. Masters and Jean Houston published a sober but encouraging account of the effects of LSD upon the human personality (*The Varieties of Psychedelic Experience,* 1966). A study published ten years later by Stanislav Grof (*Realms of the Human Unconscious*, 1976), substantially supports the conclusions of Masters and Houston, while pursuing some of the issues in greater depth. These investigations have taken an approach similar to Kenneth Ring's recent studies of near-death and UFO experiences, *The Omega Project* (1992). They have asked what happens *after* the "Oh Wow!" experience. What may the lasting effects of these brushes with cosmic consciousness be in people who have taken them seriously and made them part of their lives?

The initial encounter with LSD-enhanced perception might be described as the "Oh Wow!" stage, where flowers, rocks, grains of sand, and other people appear to the subject as amazing visions that reveal beauties and hint at meanings never before guessed (Masters and Houston, 1966, pp. 11–12). Most individuals do not advance beyond this first glimpse through the open "Doors of Perception," for the next stage is rather less gratifying. Masters and Houston describe the second level of psychedelic experience as the "recollective-analytic" stage (Masters and Houston, 1966, pp. 144–147). Here, the wonders of heightened sensory awareness lose importance and individuals begin to explore some crucial episodes in their own lives. Neurotic and unresolved issues are encountered, usually in the form of vivid, emotionally charged memories. If these painful dramatic scenes are consciously "lived through" in a visionary manner while the subject remains open to and explores the emotional values that accompany them, there occurs a kind of life-review in which one gains real insight into the meaning and consequences of one's former actions.

As an example of this second-level experience, the authors present the case of a 40-year-old philosophy professor troubled by depression and "a sense of maladaptation to self and world." When he entered the recollective-analytic phase, he suddenly realized, "It's Granny death! I must examine Granny's death!" He then dashed to the bathroom to vomit. Upon his return to the session room, he recalled that, as a young boy he had "killed his grandmother by a magical act—by smashing the head of a doll he had identified with her." He also realized he had identified himself with the doll and that smashing its head actually had caused "the destruction of my world, the concrete world of affection and real persons." He relived the smashing of the doll with powerful emotions and more vomiting and spent a long time examining the guilt he had never allowed himself to feel (Masters and Houston, 1966, pp. 203–212). He later wrote:

> In the state of deep relatedness of the psychedelic experience, I was able to experience these negative emotions in a way I had never been able to before. There was a sense of totality in the experience, as if I had actually entered into the mythic framework of the world I had destroyed by my magical act (Masters and Houston, 1966, p. 208).

Although we are not told what prompted the rage this man must have felt toward his grandmother when he was a little boy, it is clear he must have "tuned in" to the morphic field of "black magic." No doubt he is as skeptical today as we are that this magical act of smashing the doll's head actually brought about his grandmother's death. But that is not the point. What is important is how the ritually enacted rage became a repressed secret. His aggressive and murderous feelings were revealed to his childhood consciousness as disturbingly powerful, and he surely recoiled from them in horror. Evidently, he constructed internal monologs designed to restrain his self-assertion and represent the world as a place where he could avoid disaster and guilt only by assuming a passive, "feminized" stance. Masters and Houston describe him as uncomfortable with his masculinity, timid in his dealings with his peers, and unable to relate effectively with his wife (Masters and Houston, 1966, pp. 203–204).

Following the encounter with a childhood action that had constricted and limited his subsequent life up to the age of forty, his psychedelic "journey" took him through a series of rituals. He did not consciously design these rites, but found himself subjected to them in his psychedelically enhanced state. Evidently he "tuned in" to wild morphic fields designed to revivify the deadened aspects of his personality and recover his masculinity. In one, he was deeply involved emotionally and through his bodily sense in a rite designed "to bring something to life." In another, he participated in a puberty initiation and "vomited up the whole of his feminine identification." There was a warrior initiation that involved "killing the father" and another rite that initiated him into Christianity. Subsequent to his psychedelic experience he was more confident, able to stand up for himself more effectively, enjoyed a more satisfying relationship with his wife, and was able to find deeper meaning in the philosophy he was teaching (Masters and Houston, 1966, pp. 208–212).

Only those subjects who have dealt with their limiting personal issues go on to what Masters and Houston call the "symbolic level" of psychedelic experience. Those who have "recollected" and "analyzed" their neurotic issues take with them what they have learned about themselves and the changes they have made in their lifeworld as they proceed to the third stage. "Now, on the level of the symbolic, these memories and psychodynamic materials may emerge restructured in a purposive pattern of undisguised symbols cast in a glowing dramatic form that illuminates the subject's life and may even transform it" (Masters and Houston, 1966, pp. 147–148, 214). Here, we may recall how long it took Monroe to obtain his myth of the demiurge who lives on death and his vision of the luminous dome.

At the symbolic level, the subject enters into mythic dramas. Masters and Houston provide a partial list of these mythic themes which closely resembles what Perry has discovered about "psychotic process." It seems that only when people have dealt with their personal limitations—what we have been calling the defensive internal monologs that maintain our habitual lifeworld—are they able to "tune in" to the wild morphic fields of the archetypal *imagination.* Some of these individuals go so far as to have mystical experiences. Formerly agnostic and atheistic subjects find themselves embarrassed to admit that only "God language" is adequate to what they have experienced.

Even at this point, however, all is not joyful and glorious. For those who have come near to what they name as the Divine find themselves faced with a reality so big and powerful that it threatens to shatter them.

Some wrestle with forces they call demonic or satanic. In short, they are encountering the deeply disturbing and ineffable reality that Rudolf Otto called the *mysterium tremendum et fascinans*. It appears that psychedelic experience, when conscientiously pursued, leads to results very similar to near-death experiences and encounters with aliens. It questions our personal identity and public consensus in an ultimate way. If anything is "downloaded," it requires substantial effort, discipline, and persistence. Masters and Houston's final word on such mystical transformations does not at all support the naive enthusiasms of the more starry-eyed New Agers. They conclude, in effect: "You have to be there to get there."

> Those few subjects who are sufficiently prepared for and able to attain to introvertive mystical states are already persons of exceptional mental and emotional maturity and stability. The present potential of the person already has been in large measure realized. It is also possible, however, that the aforementioned tendency of these subjects to avoid or minimize work with psychodynamic materials [the "recollective-analytic" stage] may preclude the possibility of transforming the experience (Masters and Houston, 1966, pp. 311–312).

Thus does life go on pretty much as it always has. The availability of cosmic consciousness does not relieve us of the struggle with ourselves. It represents no effortless overnight transformation. Rather it provides the occasion and impetus which may prompt us to deal with the personal issues we have been avoiding in a systematic way. Cosmic consciousness enables us to confront the defensiveness of our internal monologs—an encounter which challenges the reality we have constructed and come to accept as simply "the way things are." In each case, cosmic consciousness is an individual challenge that will disrupt the course of our lives if we take it seriously. It is not so much a glorious transformation of the Earth as an invitation to hard work. If we succeed, it is not the planet that is changed, but the way we live on it.

Still, there is a social dimension to the New Age that we cannot overlook. The wide-spread enthusiasm it has spawned offers an immense opportunity to those who take the challenge seriously. For it has stirred up, if not a "critical mass," at least a supporting subculture. Those who wish to or find themselves obliged to go beyond the "Oh Wow!" stage and begin to work on their internal monologs can do so in a social environment that is no longer so ready to brand altered states of consciousness as the exclusive province of the insane. Such people will surely find others on the lookout for similar pathways into cosmic consciousness. We live in a time when cosmic journeys are sometimes discussed with sympathy and understanding. Unfortunately, however, they are all too often greeted with naive amazement. Glazed eyes and boundless hopes are the stuff of which fads are made. When the novelty wears off, the merely gullible move on.

If, like John Climacus, the Ladder Man, we place "discernment" at the center of our soul-work, we will not limit our attention to the mere fact that cosmic visions are possible. We will want to know: What good are they? What can people do with them? We will go beyond idle amazement and look to the moral exhortation of the New Age myth: Work to bring your fleshly ego into line with your own journeyer. Those who take up this "recollective-analytic" challenge are the real New Agers. Those who have enjoyed the tacit support of the New Age to enter the world of soul generally have to stand at the gate and occupy their minds with the limitations of their internal monologs in order to find the gaps. They are no longer interested in what strikes such amazement in the people around them. Tomorrow and the day after they will still be standing there. They are not apt to notice when the starry-eyed chase off after some new enthusiasm. The New Age does not need a hundred monkeys. It needs a hundred monks.

CRᴏSSING THE GREAT RIVER

The rainbow is probably the most wide-spread image of the New Age. Its seven colors refer to the layers of the human aura, as well as to the chakras. It also stands for the multiplicity of a world full of races, religions, and languages living in peace and harmony. It evokes the well-known biblical image of Yahweh's promise never again to destroy the world with a flood. It is the path to a fabled pot of gold—here understood as a *spiritual* goal. In Norse mythology, the rainbow is the bridge to Valhalla. It has been the road to transformation for prophets from Zoroaster to Nietzsche. As the bridge to the New Age, it bespeaks the sublime world of peace and love we are believed to be entering as soon as we can overcome Arien and Piscean opposition, war, and prejudice.

The rainbow bridge in all these traditions implies a moral task. We can only attempt that crossing when we have "overcome" ourselves, conquered our instinctual impulsivity, and faced the "animal fear" that keeps us trapped in our habitual limitations. This involves an inward journey and a wrestling with ourselves. Only warriors, heroes, and saints have crossed that bridge.

"Crossing the Great Water" is a central image in the ancient Chinese classic, the *I Ching*. In the most recent translation, the image is rendered as "Wading the Great River." It means to "consciously move into the flow of time, to enter the stream of life with a goal or purpose, to embark on a significant enterprise" (Ritsema and Karcher, 1994, p. 796). The *I Ching* names the One as Tao, the ever-changing principle of harmony and wholeness. To have wisdom is to have a feel for the Tao and to know when the time is right for making the great crossing. It is not a matter of merely wanting to succeed, but rather of knowing oneself and one's limitations and strengths. The *I Ching* counsels waiting on this nearer bank until the time is right, when the forces of one's own personality as well as those of the greater cosmos are favorable. Entering the flow of time unconsciously or for a trivial purpose will lead to disaster.

In Buddhism, which influenced the most recent contributions to the *I Ching*, the great river is the central obstacle and mystery of human life. The Nearer Bank of that river is the world of fleshly egos and the public consensus. Buddhism calls it the realm of *samsara*, the eternal round of birth and death. Those who remain on this side of the river and never dream of crossing it are fated to one fleshly life after another. It never dawns on them that a life is possible outside the struggle for survival. In the language of the New Age, these are the people who have not yet discovered their journeyer and have no means for attaining a cosmic perspective.

Those who have heard about the Buddha and his monumental achievement, however, know that it is possible to cross the great river. For the Buddha demonstrated that the farther bank is attainable, the realm of *nirvana*, where one's spiritual eyes are opened. Only from the viewpoint of *nirvana* can we appreciate that the fleshly world of everyday existence is a faulty construction based on ignorance and obsession with everything that belongs to "me." The practice of Buddhism amounts to a "deconstruction" of our fleshly ego and the social assumptions which support it. Alternatively, Buddhist practice is described as building a raft in order to make that passage. The boards and twine of the raft consist of all the little hints that occur in the gaps of our internal monolog. One who builds such a raft has to attend to those absurd events that break in upon our habitual assumptions. The vast majority of the human race discards these moments as meaningless interruptions in "real life." Some notice them with momentary amazement, exclaiming, "Oh Wow!" but never allow them to change their lives.

Buddhism knows two rafts. In its earliest form, Buddhism understood itself as a path of enlightenment and transformation designed for an elite, the monks and nuns who devoted their lives exclusively to the pursuit of *nirvana*. They relinquished all earthly possessions apart from the robes on their backs and the begging bowls which left their daily nourishment up to the charity of their contemporaries. Like Climacus' monks in the Sinai Desert, they regarded their fleshly survival as a low priority. Because of its elitism, this tradition has become known as that of the "Smaller Raft," *Hinayana*.

Buddhism as a path for all of humanity, monks and lay people alike, calls itself the "Greater Raft," *Mahayana*. According to this tradition, each individual is uniquely conditioned by his past, his character, and his temperament and must use the means best suited to his own make-up to reach enlightenment. It is an ideal valid for all human beings, regardless of their station in life. Early Mahayana teachers reviled the Hinayana for its apparent selfishness in seeking *nirvana* as a personal goal. The "Smaller Raft" seemed to deny the central Buddhist doctrine of compassion for all living beings. For, if a monk does not work for the enlightenment of all, he lacks the most essential form of compassion. True compassion does not merely wish for the temporal comfort of one's fellow beings. It strives for their ultimate freedom from the fleshly ignorance of *samsara*.

"Greater Raft" Buddhism therefore found itself 2000 years ago in much the same place the New Age finds itself today. The great river can be crossed only by those who deconstruct their egos, undermine their internal monologs, and encounter cosmic consciousness as a personal reality; and yet the Mahayana appeals to everyone to construct a Global Village on the farther bank, as well as a raft to transport us all. A monk's compassion for all of humanity is surely a laudable thing. But those who have attained the farther shore have all been exceptional individuals. The task of overcoming an internal monolog is always a personal struggle. How can the great mass of humankind engaged in the *samsaric* struggle to survive ever be expected to make that crossing?

Around A.D. 800, about a century after the death of Climacus, the New Wisdom school of Buddhism tried to address this contradiction with its central paradox: "*Nirvana* and *samsara* are the same" (Conze, 1959, p. 134). There is no alternate world, no crossing to make. We are there already, we just do not realize it. While living in this fleshly world of ego-centered ignorance and not seeking to escape it, the enlightened one is already beyond it. Such a one lives on both banks at the same time, participating in the world of space and time and yet *seeing* through it to the greater reality that gives it meaning.

The New Wisdom School represents both an optimistic and a pessimistic understanding of human existence. Optimistically, it supports the hope that, even while living in this fleshly world of space and time, we can exist beyond it, *seeing* it with eyes informed by the cosmic consciousness Buddhism calls *nirvana*. On the other hand, it is pessimistic, for, even while living the reality of *nirvana,* we are still denizens of the fleshly world. We are still human. We still retain our fleshly ego. As long as we live, we cannot slip the confines of our sensory existence.

The New Wisdom School hit upon the central paradox of human life. We are body, soul, and spirit. Our journeying soul, therefore, lives simultaneously in two worlds. On the one hand, it animates the flesh and, on that account, has chosen to conform itself to a temporal existence, limited to the world of birth, growth, and death. It schools itself in time and matter in order to discover itself as a distinct ego, a single one within the greater One. But in doing so, it forgets its journeying nature. It loses its grasp on spirit. As it takes up sensory knowledge and nourishes itself at the flesh-pots of Egypt, it loses *gnosis*, the nonsensory knowledge of the spirit.

Those who, against all odds, have begun to recover a feel for *gnosis* have had to do so by leaving their fleshly egos behind—at least occasionally, at least momentarily. They have sojourned in the greater cosmos, crossed the great river. Some have nearly died. Others have faced madness, death, and the devouring of their souls by the Archons. But it is never a final achievement to make such a sojourn. Their journeyer always returns to their body. Mostly, they are relieved that it does so. They have not died. They have survived the ultimate danger. But now they face the paradox. How can they live these two realities simultaneously? How can they be soul people who are alive to the greater cosmos while they still tread this fleshly planet? They find themselves on the rainbow bridge.

The rainbow bridge is not built of lumber and steel. It is a very fine mist refracting the sunlight of consciousness into bands of insubstantial color. To stand on that bridge is to see right through it into the raging river of chaos and meaninglessness. Like Jesus and the Buddha, both of whom walked on water, denizens of the New Age have to make an "impossible" crossing. The substance of the bridge is the mythic story that gives living meaning to our hope for transformation. As all humans, from the Age of Taurus to the present, we cannot live without a myth to give our lives meaning. But as ego-centered beings living at the end of the Age of Pisces, we cannot live a myth without knowing it *as* a myth, i.e., as a story that "makes sense" of the unknowable. The New Age myth provides the footway. Our knowing it *as a myth* makes it transparent.

At the dawning of the Age of Aquarius, we finally know what myth is. It is a sacred story that provides an ultimate sense of meaning to human existence, a description of human life that tells us how things really are, that explains the visible, tactile, and auditory world in terms of a greater cosmos within which space and time are the broom-closet. In earlier centuries, people lived within their myths without recognizing them *as* myths. As extra-sensory as mythic claims have always been, they were taken as literal facts of life. They were the unquestionable foundation of a culture's daily activities. Myth was that which was always and everywhere true. People might dispute what happened yesterday or a generation ago, but the myth was never questioned. It was the ultimate explanation. It was assumed in every moment, retold with wonder and satisfaction, ritually enacted to lend cosmic power to hunting, planting, marrying, and dying.

Today we can no longer speak of myth as though it were a single, undisputed thing. We know there are Buddhist myths, Hindu myths, Greek myths, Gnostic myths, a Christian myth and a New Age myth. The !Kung of Africa's Kalahari Desert have their myth; the Yanomamo of the Upper Amazon have another. History and anthropology have buried us in myths. Every one of them is a sacred story. Every one of them tells us how things really are, and yet they disagree among themselves. Every one of them is right insofar as it provides an ultimately satisfying meaning for the community or culture that remembers it and recounts its incidents in hushed tones. And every one of them is wrong insofar as it is only one sacred story among many.

The same critical intellect that has made our history, philosophy, and technology possible has jaded us with regard to myth. Myth may never again be ultimate and final for a people who can say, "I think, therefore I am," or "Human existence is Being-toward-death." Yet the wild morphic fields that myths were designed to account for remain as human possibilities. People are leaving their bodies, encountering beings of light, discovering their journeyer as their greater self. The morphic fields we have tamed as our public consensus leave us dissatisfied and disgruntled. We long for something more; and if we find it, we have to resort to mythic language to describe it.

We are in an awful pickle. To live life meaningfully and with deep satisfaction, we have no choice but to live a myth. But knowing what we know, we are condemned to recognize it *as* a myth. The myth of the New Age describes a sacred and thrilling destiny, but it is still one story among many that we might tell ourselves. It is a fiction. No doubt it is a powerful fiction, one that accounts for the wild morphic fields we have the ability to "tune in" to, and gives us some idea what to do with them.

Perhaps we cannot come up with a better one. But still it is no more than a set of schemata, a story we tell ourselves to make sense of what is ultimately unknowable.

Some of us have no choice but to set out across those colored bands of mist. Our journeyer insists. Monroe is out on that bridge, saving souls lost in the "M-Band noise" of the Lower Spheres. Strieber is there, struggling with his "visitors." Wesselman is enmeshed in the seventh millennium. When we keep our gaze fixed in the direction of the farther shore, a road of seven colors stretches out before us as far as we can see. We are on a journey from which we fully expect to return. But there is no getting off the rainbow bridge. The world of everyday existence will never again be solid enough to support us. One moment it will glow with a thousand colors, and then we will see right through it to the black river below.

In the last analysis, this is what it means to say that *nirvana* and *samsara* are the same. This is how life goes on as it always has—even when we recover cosmic consciousness as a universal human capability.

BIBLIOGRAPHY

al-'Arabi, Ibn. *The Bezels of Wisdom*. Translation and Introduction by R. W. J. Austin. Preface by Titus Burckhardt. New York: Paulist Press, 1980.

Amis, Robin. *A Different Christianity: Early Christian Esotericism and Modern Thought*. Albany: SUNY, 1995.

Bellah, Robert Noah. "Religious Evolution" in William A. Lessa and Evon Z. Vogt (eds.). *Reader in Comparative Religion: An Anthropolgical Approach*. New York: Harper & Row, 1965.

Bohm, David. *Wholeness and the Implicate Order*. New York: Ark, 1983.

Bowie, David. "Starman" in *Bowie: The Singles, 1969-1993*. Salem, MA: Ryko Disks, 1993.

Brennan, Barbara Ann. *Hands of Light: A Guide to Healing Through the Human Energy Field*. New York: Bantam, 1988.

Brinkley, Dannion with Paul Perry. *Saved by the Light: The True Story of a Man Who Died Twice and the Profound Revelations He Received*. New York: HarperCollins, 1994.

Bryan, C. D. B. *Close Encounters of the Fourth Kind: Alien Abduction, UFOs, and The Conference at M.I.T.* New York: Knopf, 1995.

Bucke, Richard Maurice. *Cosmic Consciousness: A Study in the Evolution of the Human Mind*. Secaucus, NJ: Citadel, 1977.

Burckhardt, Jacob. *The Civilization of the Renaissance in Italy*. New York: Phaidon, 1944.

Burnham, Sophy. *A Book of Angels: Reflections on Angels Past and Present and True Stories of How They Touch Our Lives*. New York: Walker, 1990.

Castaneda, Carlos. *The Teachings of Don Juan: A Yaqui Way of Knowledge*. New York: Ballantine, 1968.

———. *A Separate Reality: Further Conversations with Don Juan*. New York: Simon and Schuster, 1971.

———. *Journey to Ixtlan: The Lessons of Don Juan*. New York: Simon and Schuster, 1972.

———. *Tales of Power*. New York: Simon and Schuster, 1974.

———. *The Second Ring of Power*. New York: Simon and Schuster, 1977.

Climacus, John. *The Ladder of Divine Ascent*. Translation by Colm Luibheid and Norman Russell. New York: Paulist Press, 1982.

Cole, Joanna. *Best-Loved Folktales of the World*. Garden City, NY: Doubleday, 1982.

Conze, Edward. *Buddhism: Its Essence and Development*. New York: Harper, 1959.

Corbin, Henry. *Creative Imagination in the Sufism of Ibn 'Arabi*. Princeton: Princeton University Press, 1969.

———. *The Man of Light in Iranian Sufism*. Boston: Shambhala, 1978.

Crichton, Michael. *Travels*. New York: Ballantine, 1988.

Donn, Linda. *Freud and Jung, Years of Loss*. New York: Scribners, 1988.

Eadie, Betty J. with Curtis Taylor. *Embraced by the Light*. New York: Bantam, 1994.

Eliade, Mircea. *Shamanism: Archaic Techniques of Ecstasy*. Translation by Willard R. Trask. New York: Pantheon, 1964.

———. *Yoga: Immortality, and Freedom*. Translation by Willard R. Trask. Princeton: Princeton University Press, 1969.

Elkin, A. P. *Aboriginal Men of High Degree: Initiation and Sorcery in the World's Oldest Tradition*. Rochester, VT: Inner Traditions, 1994.

Essene, Virginia and Sheldon Nidle. *You Are Becoming a Galactic Human*. Santa Clara: S.E.E., 1994.

Ferguson, Marilyn. *The Aquarian Conspiracy: Personal and Social Transformation in the 1980's*. New York: G. P. Putnam's Sons, 1987.

Flournoy, Theodore. *From India to the Planet Mars: A Study of a Case of Somnambulism with Glossolalia*. New Hyde Park, NY: University Books, 1963.

Freeman, Eileen Elias. *Touched by Angels*. New York: Warner. 1993.

Galernter, David. *1939: The Lost World of the Fair*. New York: The Free Press, 1995.

Garrett, Eileen. "Notes on New Insights in Psychic Research." Manuscript, Parapsychological Foundation. November 9, 1967.

Gersi, Douchan. *Faces in the Smoke: An Eyewitness Experience of Voodoo, Shamanism, Psychic Healing, and Other Amazing Human Powers*. Los Angeles: J. P. Tarcher, 1991.

Green, Celia. *Out-of-the-Body-Experiences*. New York: Ballantine, 1968.

Grof, Stanislav. *Realms of the Human Unconscious: Observations from LSD Research*. New York: Dutton, 1976.

Haley, Jay. *Uncommon Therapy: The Psychiatric Techniques of Milton H. Erickson, M.D.* New York: Norton, 1973.

Happold, F. C. *Mysticism: A Study and an Anthology*. London: Penguin, 1970.

Harner, Michael. *The Way of the Shaman: A Guide to Power and Healing*. San Francisco: Harper & Row, 1980.

Haule, John R. *Divine Madness: Archetypes of Romantic Love*. Boston: Shambhala, 1990. Reprinted as *Pilgrimage of the Heart: The Path of Romantic Love*. 1992.

———. *Imagination and Myth: A Heideggerian Interpretation of C. G. Jung.* Doctoral Dissertation, Temple University, 1973.

James, Grace. *Japanese Fairy Tales.* London: Macmillan, 1979.

Janet, Pierre. *L'Automatisme psychologique.* Paris: Société Pierre Janet, 1973.

———. *Psychological Healing* (1919). In two volumes. Translated by Eden and Cedar Paul. Reprinted, New York: Arno, 1976.

Jaynes, Julian. *The Origins of Consciousness in the Breakdown of the Bicameral Mind.* Boston: Houghton Mifflin, 1976.

John of the Cross. *The Collected Works of St. John of the Cross.* Translated by Kieran Kavanaugh and Otilio Rodriguez. Washington, DC: Institute of Carmelite Studies, 1979.

Jonas, Hans. *The Gnostic Religion: The Message of the Alien God and the Beginnings of Christianity.* Boston: Beacon, 1963.

Jung, C. G. *Symbols of Transformation* (1912). *Collected Works, 5.* Translated by R. F. C. Hull. Princeton: Princeton University Press, 1967.

———. *Psychology and Alchemy* (1944). *Collected Works, 12.* Translated by R. F. C. Hull. Princeton: Princeton University Press, 1968.

———. *Memories, Dreams, Reflections.* Recorded and edited by Aniela Jaffé. Translated by Richard and Clara Winston. New York: Pantheon, 1961.

———. *Mysterium Coniunctionis. Collected Works, 14.* Translated by R. F. C. Hull. Princeton: Princeton University Press, 1963.

———. *Flying Saucers: A Modern Myth of Things Seen in the Skies.* Translated by R. F. C. Hull. *Collected Works, 10.* New York: Pantheon, 1964.

———. *Two Essays on Analytical Psychology. Collected Works, 7.* Translated by R. F. C. Hull. New York: Pantheon, 1966.

———. *Alchemical Studies. Collected Works, 13.* Translated by R. F. C. Hull. Princeton: Princeton University Press, 1967.

Katz, Richard. *Boiling Energy: Community Healing Among the Kalahari !Kung.* Cambridge, MA: Harvard, 1982.

Kiefer, Gene. "UFOs and Kundalini," in John White (ed.), *Kundalini: Evolution and Enlightenment.* New York: Paragon, 1990.

König, Reinhard. *New Age geheime Gehirnwäsche: Wie man uns Heute für Morgan programmiert.* Neuhausen-Stuttgart: Hänssler, 1988.

Kübler-Ross, Elisabeth. *On Death and Dying.* New York: Macmillan, 1969.

La Barre, Weston. *The Ghost Dance: The Origins of Religion.* New York: Delta, 1972.

Leach, Maria and Jerome Fried (eds.). *Funk and Wagnalls Standard Dictionary of Folklore, Mythology, and Legend*. San Francisco: HarperSanFrancisco, 1984.

Lévi-Strauss, Claude. *The Savage Mind*. [Translator not named.] Chicago: University of Chicago Press, 1966.

LeShan, Lawrence. *The Medium, the Mystic, and the Physicist: Toward a General Theory of the Paranormal*. New York: Ballantine, 1975.

McGuire, William (ed.). *The Freud/Jung Letters*. Translated by Ralph Manheim and R. F. C. Hull. Princeton: Princeton University Press, 1974.

Mack, John E. *Abduction: Human Encounters with Aliens*. New York: Charles Scribner's Sons, 1994.

Marciniak, Barbara. *Bringers of the Dawn: Teachings from the Pleiadians*. Santa Fe: Bear, 1992.

Masani, Rustom. *Zoroastrianism: The Religion of the Good Life*. New York: Macmillan, 1968.

Masters, R. E. L. and Jean Houston. *The Varieties of Psychedelic Experience*. New York: Dell, 1966.

Merkur, Dan. *Gnosis: An Esoteric Tradition of Mystical Visions and Unions*. Albany, NY: SUNY, 1993.

Monroe, Robert A. *Journeys Out of the Body*. Garden City, NY: Anchor, 1977.

———. *Far Journeys*. New York: Doubleday, 1985.

———. *Ultimate Journey*. New York: Doubleday, 1994.

Moody, Raymond A. Jr. *Life After Life*. New York: Bantam, 1975.

Myers, Frederic W. H. *Human Personality and Its Survival of Bodily Death*. 2 vols. New York: Arno, 1975.

Nathan, Debbie and Michael Snedeker. *Satan's Silence: Ritual Abuse and the Making of a Modern Witch Hunt*. New York: HarperCollins, 1995.

Neihardt, John G. *Black Elk Speaks: Being the Life Story of a Holy Man of the Oglala Sioux*. Lincoln, NE: University of Nebraska Press, 1961.

Nietzsche, Friedrich. *Werke in Drei Bänden*. Darmstadt: Wissenschaftliche Buchgesellschaft, 1994.

Otto, Rudolf. *The Idea of the Holy*. Translated by John W. Harvey. New York: Oxford University Press, 1958.

Pagels, Elaine. *The Gnostic Gospels*. New York: Vintage, 1981.

Perry, John Weir. *Lord of the Four Quarters: Myths of the Royal Father*. New York: Collier, 1970.

———. *The Far Side of Madness*. Englewood Cliffs, NJ: Prentice-Hall, 1974.

Plato. *The Collected Dialogues*. Edith Hamilton and Huntington Cairns (eds.). Princeton: Princeton University Press, 1961.

Popescu, Petru. *Amazonian Beaming*. New York: Viking, 1991.

Redfield, James. *The Celestine Conspiracy*. New York: Warner, 1993.

Ring, Kenneth. *Life at Death: A Scientific Investigation of the Near-Death Experience*. New York: Quill, 1980.

———. *Heading Toward Omega: In Search of the Meaning of the Near-Death Experience*. New York: Quill, 1985.

———. *The Omega Project: Near-Death Experiences, UFO Encounters, and Mind at Large*. New York: Quill, 1992.

Ritsema, Rudolf and Stephen Karcher (translators). *I Ching: The Classic Chinese Oracle of Change*. Rockport, MA: Element, 1994.

Roberts, Jane. *The Seth Material*. New York: Bantam, 1970.

Robinson, James M. (ed.). *The Nag Hammadi Library in English*. San Francisco: Harper & Row, 1977.

Sagan, Carl. *The Demon-Haunted World: Science as a Candle in the Dark*. New York: Ballantine, 1997.

Schimmel, Annemarie. *And Muhammad Is His Messenger: The Veneration of the Prophet in Islamic Piety*. Chapel Hill: University of North Carolina, 1985.

Sheldrake, Rupert. *The Presence of the Past: Morphic Resonance and the Habits of Nature*. Rochester, VT: Park Street Press, 1995.

Shostak, Marjorie. *Nisa: The Life and Words of a !Kung Woman*. Cambridge, MA: Harvard University Press, 1981.

Spangler, David and William Irwin Thompson. *Reimagination of the World: A Critique of the New Age, Science, and Popular Culture*. Santa Fe: Bear, 1991.

Stamer, Barbara. *Märchen von Nixen und Wasserfrauen*. Frankfurt am Main: Fischer Taschenbuch, 1987.

Steltenkamp, Michael F. *Black Elk: Holy Man of the Oglala*. Norman, OK: University of Oklahoma Press, 1993.

Strieber, Whitley. *Communion: A True Story*. New York: Avon, 1987.

———. *Transformation: The Breakthrough*. New York: Avon, 1988.

———. *Breakthrough: The Next Step*. New York: HarperCollins, 1995.

Sugrue, Thomas. *There Is a River: The Story of Edgar Cayce*. Virginia Beach: A.R.E. Press, 1994.

Talbot, Michael. *The Holographic Universe*. New York: HarperCollins, 1991.

Tansley, David. *The Raiment of Light: A Study of the Human Aura*. London and Boston: Routledge & Kegan Paul, 1984.

Time-Life Books. *The Enchanted World: The Lore of Love*. Alexandria, VA: Time-Life [n.d.].

Tompkins, Peter and Christopher Bird. *The Secret Life of Plants*. London: Penguin. 1974.

Tylor, Edward. *Primitive Culture*. New York: Gordon Press, 1974, 2 vols.

Utley, Robert M. *The Last Days of the Sioux Nation*. New Haven, CT: Yale University Press, 1963.

Vallee, Jacques. *Dimensions: A Casebook of Alien Contact*. New York: Ballantine, 1988.

———. *Revelations: Alien Contact and Human Deception*. New York: Ballantine, 1991.

Victor, Jeffrey S. *Satanic Panic: The Creation of a Contemporary Legend*. Chicago: Open Court, 1993.

Watts, Alan W. *The Way of Zen*. New York: Vintage, 1957.

Weinberg, Steven: *Dreams of a Final Theory*. New York: Vintage, 1993.

Wesselman, Hank. *Spiritwalker: My Journeys Through the Visionary Gateway*. New York: Bantam, 1995.

Wilhelm, Richard and Cary F. Baynes (translators). *The I Ching or Book of Changes*. Princeton: Princeton University Press, 1967.

Wolf, Fred Alan. *Taking the Quantum Leap: The New Physics for Nonscientists*. New York: HarperCollins, 1989.

———. *The Eagle's Quest: A Physicist's Search for the Truth in the Heart of the Shamanic World*. New York: Simon and Schuster, 1991.

———. *The Dreaming Universe*. New York: Simon and Schuster, 1994.

Zukav, Gary. *The Dancing Wu Li Masters: An Overview of the New Physics*. New York: Bantam, 1980.

INDEX

John Ryan Haule was born in 1942 and graduated from the University of Detroit in 1963 with a BS in Chemistry. A series of mystical experiences during his college years led him to enter a religious order after graduation, but he left after five years in response to persistent messages appearing in his dreams. He taught high school mathematics and chemistry and worked as a research editor for the Encyclopaedia Britannica in Chicago before entering the graduate program at Temple University, where he earned his Ph.D. in Religious Studies in 1973. He was an Assistant Professor of Religion and Culture at Northeastern University in Boston, 1973–1976, before leaving to train as a Jungian Analyst in Zurich. He returned to Boston in 1980 to establish the analytic practice which continues today. He has been President of the New England Society of Jungian Analysts, President of the C. G. Jung Institute-Boston, and Convener of the American Council of Jungian Analysts, as well as a member of the Executive Committee of the International Association of Analytical Psychology, based in Zurich. He is the author of *Divine Madness: The Archetypes of Romantic Love* (Shambhala, 1990) and *The Love Cure* (Spring, 1996). The theme of his professional work has been the generally overlooked spiritual and emotional dimensions of everyday life. His present project, *Perils of the Soul,* applies this theme to the region of popular culture that has been called the New Age.